New Jersey
Spotlight on Government

New Jersey

Spotlight on Government

Fifth Edition

League of Women Voters of New Jersey Education Fund

Compiled and Edited by Karen A. West

 RUTGERS UNIVERSITY PRESS
New Brunswick, New Jersey

The League of Women Voters of New Jersey Education Fund is indebted to the many state government officials and league advisers who so generously provided information and comments on the manuscript for this book. *New Jersey: Spotlight on Government* could not have been written without their kind cooperation and assistance.

The editorial committee wishes to thank Elizabeth Brody, editor of the first and second editions of this book and Helen M Kushner, editor of the third and fourth editions, together with the scores of volunteer league members who produced the original book as a public service. Because of the variety of their special knowledge and abilities, it was possible to prepare a book encompassing a wide range of subjects. This latest revision builds upon their initial contribution and includes information on legislation signed by January 1, 1985.

Editor: Karen A. West; *Editorial consultants*: Marie Curtis, Gloria Jones, Susan Lederman, Ruth Harrison, Roberta Francis, Linda Howe, Margaret Haskin, Kathleen Rae.

Publication of this book was funded by grants from the Beneficial Management Corporation, Johnson & Johnson, and the League of Women Voters of New Jersey Education Fund.

Library of Congress Cataloging in Publication Data
Main entry under title:

New Jersey spotlight on government.

  Bibliography: p.
  Includes index.
  1. New Jersey—Politics and government—1951—
I. West., Karen A., 1942-   II. League of Women
Voters of New Jersey.
JK3516.N48   1985   320.4749   84-27648
ISBN 0-8135-1110-0
ISBN 0-8135-1111-9 (pbk.)

Published and distributed
for the League of Women Voters of New Jersey
by Rutgers University Press

Contents

Figures

New Jersey's Counties and County Seats

Preface

This fifth edition of *New Jersey: Spotlight on Government* was made necessary by the many changes in state government that have come about since the last major revision in 1978. New Jersey's government is an institution created by people and responsive to them. To become acquainted with this unique entity, one must look at it as a dynamic, growing creation. The skeletal system is provided by the 1947 constitution; time-honored tradition fleshes it out. But one must also look at other forces shaping New Jersey government which are as broad in scope as international trade and as small as the determination of a single individual bent on making the government better serve the people. Between lie influences ranging from decisions of the New Jersey Supreme Court to the home rule tradition tenaciously adhered to by municipalities.

A recession in the United States and Europe in the mid-1970s and the early 1980s left its mark on New Jersey government. Hard times made old and inefficient manufacturing plants vulnerable. Jobs were lost to competition both from abroad and from the Sun Belt, with its newer plants and lower labor costs. Tax revenues dropped, while demands for government services increased. State government was caught in the middle.

A shift in emphasis resulted. New Jersey's government moved away from expansion of social services; the new theme was promotion of an economic climate conducive to the creation of jobs. A cabinet-level Department of Commerce and Economic Development was created in 1981, separating some functions from the old Department of Labor and Industry and changing the emphasis to active courting of new jobs. In support of this effort was renewed attention to education and to rebuilding the infrastructure in order to provide the trained work force, the utilities, and the transportation system necessary to keep and attract business.

The recession changed other perceptions of the role of state government. After several decades of rising expenditures for expanding services, a more conservative attitude prevailed. Social scientists have noted a corresponding attitude among the voters, an interest in preserving the status quo instead of seeking new initiatives in governmental activity.

At the same time New Jersey is striving to preserve and expand its economic base to provide employment opportunities for its citizens, the state is faced with pollution problems that have reached crisis proportions in the affected areas. One of the great political challenges for New Jersey politicians in the 1980s is to arrive at wise compromises when the needs of a healthy economy and a healthy environment are in conflict. Obviously New Jersey citizens need jobs *and* clean air and water.

The federal Budget Reconciliation Act of 1981 marked a turning point for the relationship between federal and state governments. The "new federalism" articulated by President Ronald Reagan acknowledged the need to sort out appropriate levels of decision-making and funding of government services. While the nationwide percentage of state and local governmental expenditures funded by federal grants-in-aid dropped from a high of almost 27 percent in 1978 to around 22 percent in 1982 and 1983, at the same time more open-ended block grants replaced narrow categorical grants and fewer specific program mandates were tied to the acceptance of federal funds. Thus, states regained power in setting priorities but lost a measure of federal largess.

The degree of control exerted by federally funded programs during the 1960s and 1970s (and to some extent in the 1980s) was especially apparent in the departments of

Transportation, Community Affairs, Health, and Human Services. As a result of federal funding incentives New Jersey has, for example, an interstate highway system, a wide range of housing and community action programs, preventive health programs, and intermediate care facilities for the mentally retarded as well as community based care for increasing numbers of previously institutionalized mentally ill and mentally retarded.

Perhaps a sign of the maturity of New Jersey governmental agencies in dealing with the interplay between state and federal programs is the creative manner in which a number of them have utilized federal funds. The waivers obtained by the departments of Health and Human Services to provide home health care services to some elderly and disabled, the Diagnostic Related Groups (DRG) cost-accounting program developed by the New Jersey Department of Health (and later adopted by the federal government for national implementation), the creative use of federal jobs training dollars to redirect youthful offenders—all come to mind as examples of New Jersey government officials taking charge of program design and maximizing the results.

Maximizing capital investment dollars is another area in which New Jersey leaders are showing creativity. Governor Thomas Kean attracted national attention when he proposed an infrastructure bank for New Jersey (one has subsequently been proposed for the nation as a whole). While the legislature did not fund the act establishing such a bank, the concept is beginning to take hold as various programs are funded. The Transportation Trust Fund is one example; the revolving funds established to provide low interest loans for purchase of green acres land and for improving water supply facilities are others. Much of the industrial development financing arranged by the state is based on low interest loans which, as repaid, generate funds for additional development. A major boost to the capital financing picture came when the Port Authority of New York and New Jersey gained new mandates allowing that bi-state agency to help purchase buses for the New Jersey Transit Corporation and private bus lines affiliated with it, to develop industrial parks such as the one in Elizabeth adjoining the port area, and to prepare Hudson River waterfront in Hoboken for development. In addition, Port Authority money and leadership are active partners in the construction plans for the Essex County resource recovery facility.

Along with these developments in the economic climate of New Jersey have been changes in the areas of law enforcement and the courts. The alterations made in the late 1960s and the early 1970s to strengthen law enforcement machinery in the state (creation of the State Commission of Investigation, statewide grand juries, and the Division of Criminal Justice) are bearing fruit. While crime and corruption still occur in New Jersey, both the machinery for fighting it and the population's acceptance of the inevitability of criminal activity have changed.

This difference in public attitude toward corruption in government has had some concrete expressions. A number of urban counties (Essex, for example), on citizen insistence, changed their charters to utilize professional managers instead of traditional political bosses. The citizens of Newark also voted to alter their school district's governing board from an appointed to an elected form. Around the state citizens' groups, aided by sunshine laws, have acted as watchdogs to see that laws were upheld. More often honesty was expected and demanded as the norm for politicians.

Into this climate of anti-corruption came an important new dynamic in New Jersey life and government. The approval of casino gambling in Atlantic City has brought new challenges to New Jersey's law enforcement agencies. Other effects of the decision to allow casino gambling have been varied—revenue from the tax on casinos has added to the state's ability to purchase goods and services, yet the hoped-for redevelopment of Atlantic City for the indigenous population has not yet occurred.

Nineteen eighty-four marked an important year for change in the judicial system as the district courts were absorbed into the superior court system, and a family part of the superior court was established. The unification of the court system is essentially complete. Yet the major problem now faced by the courts is the sheer volume of cases entering the system each year. Innovative procedures in case management, use of alternatives to court action, and the development of computer systems to assist in handling the paper work are part of the solution. The Speedy Trial program to deal more quickly with criminal cases was another attempt to deal with the volume of cases.

However, the successes of the Speedy Trial program merely compounded the problems of the corrections system. Due to revision of the criminal code in 1979 and more recent amendments, close to half of the state prison inmates are serving mandatory minimum sentences. Prison overcrowding reached crisis proportions in the early 1980s and prompted a major expansion of correctional facilities. In the interim, county facilities have been used to house state prisoners.

While many problems facing the state have been addressed by the government, not all have been resolved. Among the most pressing problems facing the state in the mid-1980s are cleanup of hazardous waste sites; siting and construction of facilities for the disposal of solid, hazardous, and low-level radioactive wastes; siting and financing housing for low and moderate income New Jersey citizens as mandated by the New Jersey Supreme Court in the Mount Laurel decisions; achieving meaningful reform in automobile insurance laws; relieving traffic congestion on New Jersey roads and highways; solving the myriad of other problems resulting from the rapid and haphazard development of suburban New Jersey; and revitalizing our cities.

It is too early to predict the solutions to these problems, but New Jersey government has some of the needed machinery in place to deal with the challenges. It has a sound structural base provided by the 1947 constitution, an increasingly better educated citizenry, and a highly sophisticated industrial and commercial complex led by businessmen who have shown commitment to the state's improvement. Surely this means that New Jersey will successfully resolve the problems it faces.

About This Book

New Jersey: Spotlight on Government is a citizens' book about the government of New Jersey, what it does, and who is in charge. It seeks to introduce and illuminate the departments, services, costs, organization, and development of the state government.

How much and what kind of information to include has been a constant concern. Our readers will probably be a special lot: interested and active citizens and students wishing to learn enough to judge their government's present course of action and to participate more intelligently in its future direction.

Because we believe informed citizens can make a difference in the decisions made by our government, opportunities for citizen involvement are included in the descriptions of departments and agencies. To place the present in better perspective, the book takes occasional glances at New Jersey's past and indicates the sometimes difficult choices that will face New Jersey in the near future.

Little attempt has been made to indicate the adequacy or efficiency of the government's operations. This evaluative task we entrust to the readers of the book. A caveat for readers: do not assume that because some legislation and governmental machinery are in place to address a problem, the problem will be solved. Often it takes the concerted effort of concerned citizens, acting individually or in groups, to energize the system and effect needed change.

New Jersey
Spotlight on Government

PART I

THE GOVERNMENT
AND ITS OPERATION

1.

The New Jersey Constitution

A constitution is a contract between the people and the government: the people grant governing powers to a government, and the government is bound by the stated restrictions. It is the fundamental law by which a nation or a state is governed. This fundamental law is different from legislation. Since a constitution is a product of a vote by the people (whereas legislation results from the votes of their elected representatives), making and changing constitutions must involve the people directly.

Theoretically, the states have a unique inherent power in our federal system. Under the United States Constitution, the federal government has only those powers granted to it by that document. Local governments have only those powers granted to them by the states. State governments have the residual powers—all those not bestowed on the federal or local governments or expressly prohibited by the federal Constitution. Therefore, to define and limit the powers of state governments, state constitutions can merely enumerate the powers that the government may not exercise, rather than those that it may. A state constitution also divides those powers within the government, and between the government and the people.

Though overshadowed in the public's mind by the United States Constitution, the fifty state constitutions nonetheless have a significant influence on the processes of government. They materially affect the functions of state and local government.

3

Constitutional Issues   Too often the citizenry believes itself to be far removed from its governing instrument, the state constitution, regarding it as a distant document long ago written, filed, and forgotten. In New Jersey nothing could be farther from the truth. This state has a modern constitution drafted by the people in a constitutional convention in 1947. Since the constitution was adopted in 1948, the citizens have been involved in fine-tuning and updating it through the amendment process. Indeed, New Jersey's constitution is a dynamic document responsive to the needs of the citizenry.

Just as the early proponents of constitutional revision sought reform and equity through an enlightened constitution, so do the modern proponents of egalitarianism. The constitution, with its definition of our rights and privileges, is constantly being questioned, challenged, construed, and amended in an effort to rearrange our very concepts of living. In the past two decades, constitutional issues have been much in the limelight.

Equal Rights
Both the New Jersey and the United States constitutions have been the object of a campaign for a guarantee of equal rights without regard to gender. The drive for an equal rights amendment (ERA) represents an attempt to make sex discrimination unconstitutional, as discrimination on the basis of race, religion, and national origin now is.

In 1975 the New Jersey legislature passed a constitutional amendment, subject to referendum, which read: "Equality of rights under the law shall not be denied or abridged on account of sex. The Legislature shall by law provide for the enforcement of the provisions of this paragraph." As a result of an anti-ERA campaign, however, voters defeated this proposed amendment in the November ballot referendum.

Land Use
During recent years state courts have shown considerable interest in conflicts arising from zoning procedures and standards as defined in the New Jersey Constitution.

The Legislature may enact general laws under which municipalities, other than counties, may adopt zoning ordinances limiting and restricting to specified districts and regulating therein . . . and the nature and extent of the uses of land. (Article IV, Section VI)

The Mount Laurel and Mount Laurel II New Jersey Supreme Court rulings found unconstitutional the long accepted suburban zoning laws that created bastions for upper- and middle-class homes. Law suits to secure housing for low- and moderate-income people in these areas have brought home rule proponents into direct conflict with the court's interpretation of the state constitution.

Apportionment

Not only the New Jersey Constitution but also the United States Constitution came under duress to provide equal representation. Legislative apportionment to insure fair and effective representation became the subject of a series of long debates and constitutional revision that brought the state constitution directly into the voting booth.

> The Senate shall be composed of forty senators apportioned among Senate districts as nearly as may be according to the number of their inhabitants as reported in the last preceding decennial census of the United States and according to the method of equal proportions. (Article IV, Section II)

In 1960 the New Jersey Supreme Court ruled that the legislature was required to fulfill its obligation to reapportion on the basis of current census data; it set a date for legislative action, posing the threat of the imposition of a court-devised plan if the legislature did not act. In light of the United States Supreme Court's ruling in 1964 that representation must be solely on the basis of population and that any other means of representation would be a violation of the equal protection clause of the Fourteenth Amendment, the New Jersey Supreme Court suggested a state constitutional convention to restructure the section of the New Jersey Constitution dealing with the apportionment procedures. As a result, in 1966 a constitutional convention set forth a new design for the legislature, abolishing the system of one senator for each county regardless of its population and establishing a bipartisan apportionment commission. (While this system for apportioning state legislative districts has worked well, the reapportionment of congressional districts which is done by the legislature itself has been the subject of repeated litigation. At issue have been criteria for drawing congressional districts that reflect the one person, one vote concept rather than the creative gerrymandering of political boundaries by politicians.)

Collective Bargaining

The right of public employees to resolve work issues by means of collective bargaining was also granted by the state constitution.

> Persons in public employment shall have the right to organize, present to and make known to the State, or any of its political subdivisions or agencies, their grievances and proposals through representatives of their own choosing. (Article I, paragraph 19)

In 1968 the legislature passed implementing legislation that established the Public Employment Relations Commission (PERC) and that defined appropriate negotiating procedures. The courts, in cases involving collective bargaining for public employees, generally chose a narrow statutory construction.

Education and Taxes

Educational issues in New Jersey also have a strong constitutional basis. In the now famous case *Robinson v. Cahill* (William T. Cahill, governor 1970–1974) the New Jersey Supreme Court unanimously interpreted the constitutional guarantee of "a thorough and efficient system of free public schools" (Article VIII, Section IV) to mean that equal educational opportunity was to be provided for all children; for want of a more usable standard, equality was to be measured in terms of dollars spent per student. Until this 1973 ruling, public schools were supported by local property taxes, with only minimal state financial help; but wide variations in place of residence, combined with differences in the availability of property tax monies, resulted in unequal expenditures per pupil throughout the state. In light of this substantial disparity in local per pupil expenditures, the court ruled that the state must develop a plan of financing that avoided heavy reliance on local property taxes. The legislature responded in 1975 by passing the state income tax.

The Drive for Revision

New Jersey's present state constitution is considered one of the country's most enlightened. Even today its judicial and executive articles are cited as models for students of government. The constitution of Alaska, for example, is largely patterned after that of New Jersey.

First adopted in 1776, the state constitution has attained its status through two hard-fought constitutional revisions, in 1844 and again in 1947. Although sporadic agitation for revision of the 1844 constitution began in the last century, pressures for reform reached a new intensity in the 1930s. Frustrated by their inability to influence legislation, groups dedicated to governmental improvement began working for constitutional revision. They hoped to use this route to change the partisan policy-making machinery that was then dominated by rural interests and by certain political leaders, most notably Frank Hague, mayor of Jersey City from 1917 to 1947.

Among the reformers' grievances were the constitution's complex court system, its cumbersome amending procedures, and the one-year assembly term that, combined with low pay, forced most members of the assembly to depend on county political organizations for their reelection campaign funds. The basis of representation in the state senate—one senator per county—led to rural domination and was another basic complaint of those seeking constitutional revision.

While the reformers charged that the constitution fostered a wasteful, complicated, inefficient, and irresponsible government, constitutional change could be initiated only by the legislature. The price of obtaining senatorial consent for a constitutional convention was protection of their power base. The senate required a stipulation in the con-

CONSTITUTION

OF

NEW-JERSEY.

WHEREAS all the constitutional Authority, ever possessed by the Kings of *Great-Britain* over these Colonies, or their other Dominions, was, by Compact, derived from the People, and held of them for the common Interest of the whole Society; Allegiance and Protection are, in the Nature of Things, reciprocal Ties, each equally depending upon the other, and liable to be dissolved by the other's being refused or withdrawn. And whereas *George* the Third, King of *Great-Britain*, has refused Protection to the good People of these Colonies; and, by assenting to sundry Acts of the *British* Parliament, attempted to subject them to the absolute Dominion of that Body; and has also made War upon them in the most cruel and unnatural Manner, for no other Cause than asserting their just Rights, all civil Authority under him is necessarily at an End, and a Dissolution of Government in each Colony has consequently taken Place.

AND

The opening portion of
the Constitution of 1776,
from a contemporary
copy. New Jersey
Historical Society.

vention's mandate that precluded any change of county territorial integrity or the existing system of defining legislative districts (each county, regardless of population, had to have one senator).

In 1940 both gubernatorial candidates came out in favor of basic constitutional reform. Soon thereafter, the League of Women Voters of New Jersey spearheaded the formation of a broad-based coalition of civic groups and individuals interested in constitutional revision. Its vigorous campaign sustained the momentum while Charles Edison (governor 1941–1944), Walter E. Edge (governor 1944–1947), and Alfred E. Driscoll (governor 1947–1950) provided political leadership. Despite a setback in 1944, when a proposed revision was rejected by the voters after a bitter campaign, the movement for revision culminated in a new state constitution approved by the voters in 1947.

Unlike most states, New Jersey can no longer attribute its problems to defects in its constitution.

As is customary, New Jersey's present constitution enumerates the rights and privileges retained by the people.

Rights Reserved by the People

Bill of Rights

It is of interest that the drafters of the New Jersey Constitution of 1776, which was hastily written during a forty-eight-hour period while the British fleet was anchored off Sandy Hook, did not feel the need to include in that document a list of traditional individual rights. A bill of rights, patterned after the United States Bill of Rights, was adopted as part of a major revision of the New Jersey Constitution in 1844. The 1947 constitution largely retained and expanded this statement of individual rights.

Among the personal and political rights guaranteed are freedom of religion, speech, press, assembly, and petition. Unreasonable search and seizure are banned. Accused persons are protected by guarantees of trial by jury and by prohibitions against double jeopardy, excessive bail, cruel and unusual punishments, and the suspension of habeas corpus except in cases of rebellion or invasion. Private property may not be taken for public use (eminent domain) without just compensation.

Two significant clauses were new to the constitution of 1947. Discrimination because of religious principles, race, color, ancestry, or national origin was prohibited. Also, persons in private employment were specifically permitted to organize and bargain collectively while those in public employment might organize and present grievances. Neither the state nor any local governmental unit may infringe on these rights.

Although a proposed equal rights amendment was defeated at the polls in 1975, some legal scholars believe that the New Jersey Constitution inherently contains a guarantee of equal rights to both sexes. Largely through the efforts of Mary Philbrook, New Jersey's first woman attorney, the constitution of 1947 changed the language in Article I on rights and privileges from "all men" to "all persons." A 1978 New Jersey Supreme Court decision in *Peper v. Princeton* affirmed that the phrase "all persons" signified equal employment and property rights for women. However, an unequivocal legal articulation of whether or not the New Jersey Constitution contains an unrestricted equal rights guarantee has yet to be made.

Suffrage

The right to vote for elected officials and on public questions is essential for citizen control of government. The New Jersey Constitution protects this right by specifying who is entitled to vote by setting citizenship, age, residency, and mental competency qualifications. The constitution authorizes the legislature to enact laws providing for absentee ballots for both military and civilian residents. The legislature is also empowered to deprive those committing certain kinds of crimes from the privilege of voting.

The earliest electorate in New Jersey included men and women who owned a specified amount of property. An act of the state legislature in the early 1800s removed this voting privilege from previously eligible women.

Whereas payment of county or state taxes was a qualification for voters until 1844, proof of literacy has never been required of New Jersey voters. Amendment attempts to lower the voting age from twenty-one to eighteen or nineteen failed until 1974, when an amendment to the United States Constitution lowered the voting age in the United States to eighteen.

Like the United States Constitution, the New Jersey Constitution establishes a framework of government, dividing powers and duties among the legislative, executive, and judicial branches. It names certain offices and specifies how the holders of those offices are to be elected or appointed and under what conditions they may be removed. The manner of creating and filling other top posts is outlined. One section describes the structure and composition of the two-house legislature and the standards for determining the districts from which the members are to be elected. Another section vests judicial power in a court system and specifies the number of members, length of terms, method of appointment, and compensation.

The Strengthened Executive

New Jersey's government has gradually shifted from a system of legislative dominance to one of separation of powers among the three branches, with a much-strengthened executive. The state constitution of 1947 clearly defines the separation of powers, providing that persons in one branch may not serve in another without constitutional authority.

The first constitution, adopted in 1776, did not separate the powers of government as did the subsequent United States Constitution. In reaction to the autocratic powers of their royal governors during the colonial period, the framers of the state constitution created an all-powerful legislature. This branch alone elected the governor annually and appointed all state and most county officials, including all judges. One of its two houses served as the highest court. Under this all-powerful legislature, the governor was limited to a few paltry judicial powers.

Under the constitution of 1844, the governor acquired somewhat more, albeit fairly inconsequential, power. From then on, the people, instead of the legislature, elected the governor, and the term was increased from one to three

The Framework of Government

years with the provision that the governor could not succeed himself in office. The governor's appointments of state
court judges and certain other officials always required the
senate's consent. The legislature retained the exclusive
power to appoint some judges and officials, including the
keeper of the state prison, who was head of one of the few
significant state agencies then in existence. A separate judicial system was created to assume all judicial power.

Through constitutional amendments adopted in 1875,
the governor's power to share in making appointments was
extended to include the prison keeper and certain lower
court judges. But by the early 1940s the legislature had created over one hundred independent or semi-independent
agencies, and the governor lacked the authority to administer them. Where the legislature did grant the governor the
right to appoint top officials, subject to senate confirmation,
their terms of office did not coincide with that of the governor. Thus, governors could only fill vacancies that occurred
during their tenure, and they could only remove officeholders under specific laws.

In the decade before the adoption of the constitution of
1947, the executive authority of the governor was strengthened by a number of reorganizational laws. Yet it was the
new constitution that considerably enhanced the powers of
governors and reduced their dependence on legislative lar-
gesse. The gubernatorial term was increased to four years,
and governors could succeed themselves in office once.
Although all agencies continued to be created by the legislature, that body had to group them into "not more than
twenty principal departments" under the governor's supervision. The governor was given the power to appoint the
heads of all deparments—whether single executives or
boards—subject to the consent of the senate. The legislature was prohibited from exclusively appointing any executive or judicial officers, except the state auditor. The terms
of the secretary of state and the attorney general—the only
department heads specified in the constitution—were ad-
justed to coincide with the governor's. Gubernatorial influence over legislation was increased by raising the legislative
vote necessary to override the governor's veto from a simple
majority to a two-thirds majority of each house and by giv-

ing the governor the power to veto line items in the annual appropriations bill.

Characteristics of the New Jersey Constitution

The New Jersey Constitution has earned accolades as a model chiefly for the brief, clear, and flexible way in which it provides for a more efficient government with relatively clear lines of responsibility drawn for each branch. The document places the governor in charge of the administrative structure and the chief justice of the supreme court in charge of a simplified and more unified court system; it leaves to the legislature the power to establish the administrative and lower judicial structures.

Like the United States Constitution, the New Jersey Constitution is limited, in the main, to a statement of basic principles. The legislature is left relatively free, not only to fill in the executive framework (as they did in 1948, reorganizing the various administrative agencies into the twenty or fewer departments required by the newly adopted constitution), but also to pass legislation for meeting the changing day-to-day needs of the state. Since the constitution does not provide for government at the local level, it is within the power of the New Jersey Legislature to create or to abolish all forms of local government. It must, however, comply with constitutional restrictions when using this power.

By contrast, in most states a cumbersome executive structure and specific curbs on the legislature's law-making powers are built into the constitution. Changes must be made by amendment. For example, in Georgia, an admittedly extreme case, voters were asked to approve 859 amendments in one twenty-five-year period. In New Jersey, on the other hand, only 42 amendments have been submitted to the voters between 1947 and 1983.

In the areas of taxation and finance, the constitution does place a number of significant limitations on the power of the legislature. Unlike the United States Congress, for example, the New Jersey Legislature must obtain voter approval before creating a debt beyond one percent of its total yearly appropriation. Thus, the state must submit bond referendums to the voters for most capital expenditures.

The 1947 constitution eliminated dedicated taxes and was touted as a standard for fiscal responsibility. According to that document all revenue, with a few exceptions, was put into the treasury general fund to be drawn upon by all governmental agencies. In recent years, however, the voters have approved constitutional amendments reintroducing dedicated taxes. In 1969 voters approved a state lottery with revenues restricted to financing state institutions. In 1976 popular approval of the personal income tax was linked to dedication of revenues to a property tax relief fund separate from the general fund. In the same year casino gambling in Atlantic City was approved, with the tax on revenues dedicated to tax rebates and other financial aid for senior and handicapped citizens. Currently a number of proposals for dedicating taxes are being discussed in the legislature.

Because constitutional provisions are difficult to dislodge, special interest groups have sometimes tried to place prohibitions of a particular activity within the shelter of the constitution. For example, what had originally been a statutory prohibition of gambling was converted into a constitutional prohibition in 1897. This was modified by an amendment in 1939 to permit betting at racetracks, then revised in the 1947 constitution to allow other kinds of gambling when approved by the voters. Since 1947 a number of amendments have been approved by the voters permitting various kinds of gambling, including approval of the state lottery in 1969 and casino gambling in Atlantic City in 1976.

Procedures for Amendment and Revision

To become part of the constitution, an amendment must be (a) initiated by the legislature, (b) presented at a public hearing, (c) passed by a three-fifths vote of all members of each house or by a majority of all members of each house in two successive years, and (d) approved by a majority of those voting on the amendment at a general election. Amendments must be submitted so that the public can vote separately on each one. If an amendment fails to win voter approval, it cannot be resubmitted for three years. There is no limit on the number of amendments that may be submitted

to the voters in an election. Gubernatorial approval plays
no part in the amendment process.

The New Jersey Constitution has been criticized for
omitting popular initiative and periodic review. The citizens of the state, acting on their own initiative, may not
place proposed amendments to the constitution on the ballot. Nor are voters asked, at stated intervals, whether or not
to call a constitutional convention. Many of the other states
do have such a review process.

In New Jersey only the legislature may call for a constitutional convention. The delegates to this bipartisan
convention are then elected by the voters. New Jersey's constitutional revisions as well as the 1966 revisions which
were limited to reapportionment of the legislature were
drafted by such conventions and submitted to the people
for ratification.

2.
The Executive
Branch

The executive branch is composed of the governor, the governor's staff, and the executive departments responsible for implementing the programs undertaken by the government. Together they are an important source of policy-making and administration. This chapter also discusses those departments and agencies that provide services to the executive branch as a whole: the Office of Administrative Law, the Division of Law, the Executive Commission on Ethical Standards, the General Services Administration, the Civil Service Department, and the Department of State.

THE GOVERNOR

From 1776 to 1985, New Jersey has had forty-nine governors. Most of them were lawyers or former legislators—one, Woodrow Wilson (governor 1911–1913) was a college president; one was a general, two were physicians; one a farmer; one a varnish manufacturer. A few, regrettably, could be labeled scoundrels. Some made indifferent chief executives; others performed well and provided effective leadership.

Until 1844, the governor was not elected directly by the people but indirectly by the legislature and served for only one year at a time—a policy that reflected the Founding Fathers' distrust of executive authority. After the constitution was revised in 1844, the governor was elected by the people and allowed a single three-year term.

By 1875, governors were complaining that the constitution had made their job impossible because it gave them administrative responsibilities without the powers needed for enforcement. Although governors could appoint agency heads, they could do so only when the appointee's term happened to end during their own term. Governors could compel agency heads neither to meet with them nor to submit reports. The governor's veto power over legislation was of little import, since only a simple majority was needed to override it. In short, according to Charles Edison (governor 1941–1944) "[the governor] is only a gentleman who happens to walk through without disturbing anybody." The 1947 constitution changed much of this.

Conditions of the Office

A governor must be at least thirty years old, a citizen of the United States for twenty years, and a resident of New Jersey for seven years. A gubernatorial term lasts four years. The governor may serve no more than two successive terms, but after a term out of office is again eligible to run for election.

Method of Election

The governor is the only state official elected in statewide elections. (Two United States senators are also elected statewide.) The gubernatorial election, both primary and general, is financed with public funds. (See chapter 5, Campaign Financing.)

Gubernatorial candidates from each party are chosen by the voters in a June primary election, sometimes in lively primary fights when political leaders cannot unite behind one nominee or when personally ambitious candidates challenge the parties' choices. The New Jersey gubernatorial election takes place in November of the year following a presidential election, a timing designed to insulate New Jersey elections from the enthusiasms of national contests. The governor-elect assumes office on the third Tuesday of the following January.

Salary and Residences

The salary paid to a governor may not be changed during an incumbent's term. In addition to the salary (eighty-five thousand dollars in 1984), the governor receives an allowance (fifty-five thousand dollars in 1984) for entertaining and other expenses for which no accounting is required.

The governor has the use of both Drumthwacket, the executive mansion in Princeton, and a summer home at Island Beach State Park. The former official residence Morven has become a state historical site.

Executive Succession
New Jersey is one of eleven states having no lieutenant governor. If a vacancy should occur because of the governor's death, resignation, or removal by impeachment or disability, the powers and duties of the office fall temporarily on the president of the senate until a new governor is elected. The speaker of the general assembly is next in line.

Procedures for Removal and Replacement
The governor, like all state officers, may be impeached for misdemeanors committed during a term of office. The general assembly has the sole power to impeach, by a majority vote. The senate, sitting as a jury, may then by a two-thirds vote find the governor guilty of the charge.

The governor may also be removed on the grounds of disability. Determining the disability of the chief executive is a thorny problem. First, the governor must have been continuously absent from the state or have been continuously unable to discharge the duties of the office by reason of mental or physical disability. Then, under the procedures established in the state constitution, the legislature first must adopt, by a two-thirds vote of all the members of each house, a resolution declaring a vacancy. Following this, the New Jersey Supreme Court holds a hearing to determine whether or not such a vacancy exists.

If a vacancy occurs in the office of governor, an election to fill the unexpired term is held at the next general election and the winner takes office immediately. However, if the vacancy occurs within the sixty-day period preceding a general election, the successor is elected at the second general election.

Staff

It has been said that the governor's staff serves as "an extension of the eyes and ears of the governor." This staff, which has more than doubled in size during the last decade (from twenty-four in 1976 to sixty-four in 1984), assists the governor in making policy as well as in overseeing the executive branch. Members of the staff are called upon to carry out varied and often demanding and delicate assignments. It is they who deal with the news media, handle mail, and schedule interviews and personal appearances of the governor. They conduct research, write speeches, and help determine and execute policy decisions; and they maintain liaisons with department heads, legislative leaders, and party leaders.

The two principal members are the chief of staff and the chief counsel to the governor. The chief of staff's major duties include overseeing the professional and clerical staff and acting as a buffer between the governor and the many claims made on his or her attention. The chief counsel to the governor is the legal advisor on legislative proposals. This staff member also investigates clemency requests, reviews sales of riparian rights, and handles extradition proceedings.

Executive Powers

The oath of office sets forth the responsibilities of the governor in general terms. "I, (———) (repeating his or her name), do solemnly swear that I will support the Constitution of the United States and the Constitution of the State of New Jersey and that I will faithfully, impartially, and justly perform the duties of the governor of the State of New Jersey to the best of my ability, so help me God." To carry out this mandate, the constitution gives the governor the power to go to court or to take other appropriate action to "enforce compliance with any constitutional or legislative mandate, or to restrain violation of any constitutional or legislative power or duty, by any officer, department, or agency of the State" (Article V, Section I)—except the legislature.

Power of Appointment

Since the adoption of the 1947 constitution, the governor has derived much strength from the power of appointment, a power that gives the governor considerable leverage to force passage of programs. The legislature may not appoint any executive or judicial officer except the state auditor. The governor alone has the power to nominate all other appointees. However, since most nominations require confirmation by the senate, there is considerable room for negotiating.

The senate confirmation of appointments is not just a formality. Not infrequently gubernatorial recommendations have been turned down. Most often this is done under the principle of senatorial courtesy, which requires that the nominee be acceptable to the senator from the nominee's home county. Political horsetrading is common, especially when the governor and the senate majority are of different parties.

Adding to the political importance of the power of appointment (and of senate confirmation) is the number of gubernatorial appointments, which average over five hundred per year. Posts filled by the governor with senate consent include all department heads (whether single executives or boards), many division heads, all judgeships, all county prosecutors, county boards of election and taxation, and the numerous policy-making and advisory boards and commissions of executive departments, authorities, and interstate agencies.

Power of Dismissal
Prior to 1947 the governor could remove state officers only through the cumbersome process of impeachment. Thus, the governor was virtually powerless to discipline corrupt or incompetent subordinates. With the adoption of the 1947 constitution, gubernatorial control became greater. The governor may remove department heads who serve at the governor's pleasure, and after a hearing, may remove the principal executive officers of departments headed by boards. The governor may remove "for cause" the secretary of state, the attorney general, and all other paid executive officers and employees. (A removal "for cause" must be preceded by a public hearing if the accused so requests and may ultimately have to withstand a court test.) The governor may conduct an investigation with subpoena powers into the official conduct of any such officer or employee.

The attorney general and the secretary of state serve

four-year terms by constitutional mandate, unlike the other heads of executive departments who serve at the governor's pleasure. This special status has, at times, caused governors embarrassment. Scandals involving these cabinent positions in the late 1960s led to a call to have the status of the attorney general and the secretary of state changed so that they too would serve at the pleasure of the governor. The voters rejected this proposed constitutional amendment. Later governors have chosen to place their closest political advisors not in the offices of secretary of state and attorney general but on their personal staffs, where they serve only at the governor's pleasure.

Legislative Powers

The governor can exert power over legislation by sending messages to the legislature and approving or vetoing bills. When the administration's party enjoys a majority in the legislature, the governor may also play an influential leadership role in the caucuses preceeding legislative sessions.

In actuality, the initiation and development of new policies and programs are more likely to come from the executive branch than from the legislature. The latter functions only part-time, and its action requires negotiations and consensus among 120 separate individuals. The governor, however, has executive departments that give full time to governmental problems and often shape proposals for new programs.

Communications with the Legislature

Beyond the mandatory annual message at the opening of each regular legislative session, the governor is allowed considerable latitude in communicating with the legislature. The types of messages and their frequency vary with each governor. The messages may be simple reports, recommendations for specific legislation, reports from study commissions, messages accompanying a veto, or the annual budget. Although not required, it has become customary for the governor to deliver in person both the annual State of the State and budget messages, and sometimes other messages, to joint sessions of the legislature.

Some governors set up regular communication patterns

with their legislatures using numerous conferences with party leaders to advance their legislative proposals. When held on a regular basis, such conferences furnish governors the opportunity to state their preferences and to determine the mood of the legislature; the conferences also permit both sides to devise strategies and tactics for dealing with new programs.

Veto Power

The power to veto or conditionally veto a bill is an important weapon in the governor's arsenal. (See figure 3.5.) A governor in complete opposition to a bill may veto it outright in the hope that its supporters lack the two-thirds majority required to override the veto. If the governor supports the bill in part, or thinks an override is likely, the conditional veto may be used and specific amendments proposed in the hope that a simple majority will adopt them and send the amended bill back for the governor's signature. Sometimes the mere threat of a veto, made while a bill is still before the legislature, can cause it to be amended to meet the governor's objections before its final passage. As with any use of power, much depends on the people involved, the strength of the political opposition, and public opinion. It appears that, when there is controversy between the governor and the legislature resulting in use of the veto, the governor usually wins.

The governor also has considerable power over the budget, which is presented to the legislature for consideration and over which the governor may exercise a line-item veto. (See chapter 6, The Annual Budget.)

The Power of Influence

The governor may evoke powers beyond those provided by the constitution. Many factors—qualities of leadership, personal popularity, desire to shape the policies of the state, and role as head of the administration's political party —contribute to the stature of the office of governor. The use of these personal attributes, which vary from governor to governor, significantly influences the control the chief executive can exercise over governmental policies and programs.

Gubernatorial influence can be exerted through many channels. Access to the mass media provides an avenue of appeal for support of administration policies. The governor or executive department heads can make speeches to influential groups. Special commissions or conferences set up by the governor can run interference in specific areas of concern.

It is significant that the governor is the only state official elected by the voters at large, a provision peculiar to New Jersey and Maine. Thus, the chief executive never has to compete for voter appeal with other officials who might wish to advance their own prestige by diminishing the governor's.

Other Powers

Only the governor may grant pardons and reprieves (in cases other than impeachment or treason), commute prison sentences, and cancel unpaid fines. The chief executive is also commander-in-chief of the militia and the only person with authority to call up the National Guard. As chairman of the Board of State Canvassers, the governor has power, pending an election, to fill any vacancy from New Jersey that occurs in the United States Senate. The governor also has limited control over certain semi-autonomous agencies, such as the Port Authority of New York and New Jersey and the New Jersey Turnpike Authority through veto power over the minutes of their meetings.

THE EXECUTIVE ADMINISTRATIVE DEPARTMENTS

The governor and the administrative departments that compose the bureaucracy together share executive responsibilities; they are separate but interdependent institutions. Whereas the governor sets policies, the executive departments implement them. The departments also have the primary responsibility for writing the rules and regulations and administering laws passed by the legislature.

In compliance with the guidelines of the 1947 constitution, a major reorganization of the executive branch was achieved in 1948 by the legislature which consolidated more than seventy agencies into fourteen departments. Since that time, six more departments have been created, bringing the total to twenty, the maximum number permitted by the constitution. (See figure 2.1.) Any new agency, except a temporary commission created for a special purpose, is assigned to a specific department. Some of these assignments create very loose ties between the department and the agency. Then the phrase describing the agency as "technically in, but effectively not of" a certain department applies; this is often shortened to "in but not of."

Department Leadership

New Jersey's governors are perceived to be strong executives, in comparison with the other forty-nine governors, where the power to appoint major executive officers is involved. Although it is the legislature's prerogative to decide whether a department is to be headed by a single executive or by a board (and there are some departments with each kind of leadership), once the decision is made, the governor's constitutional powers of appointment and removal apply.

A policy-making board heads the departments of Agriculture and Higher Education and a commission heads the Department of Civil Service. Vacant board and commission posts are filled by the governor with the consent of the senate; these appointees may be removed by the governor as provided by law. A chief executive officer is appointed by the boards or commission, with the governor's consent. The governor may remove the chief executive officer following a hearing.

The Department of Education is a hybrid—having some characteristics of departments headed by a board and some of departments headed by a single executive. The department is headed by a policy-making Board of Education, but the commissioner of education is appointed by the governor with senate consent.

The departments of State and of Law and Public Safety are each headed by a single executive who, as noted earlier, is appointed by the governor with senate approval, and who serves a term concurrent with that of the governor. Either of these, the secretary of state or the attorney general, may be removed by the governor for cause only.

The final fourteen departments—Banking, Commerce

The New Jersey Administrative Departments (listed in descending order by size of budget recommended for 1984–1985)

Figure 2.1

Education

Human Services

Treasury

Higher Education

Transportation

Corrections

Law and Public Safety

Community Affairs

Environmental Protection

Health

Labor

Public Advocate

Commerce and Economic Development

State

Energy

Civil Service

Defense

Agriculture

Insurance

Banking

and Economic Development, Corrections, Community Affairs, Defense, Energy, Environmental Protection, Health, Human Services, Insurance, Labor, Public Advocate, Transportation, and Treasury—are each headed by a single executive, who, upon appointment by the governor with the consent of the senate, serves at the pleasure of the governor. That is, the executive may be removed at the governor's will.

Department Structure

Varied approaches are used to structure each department. In some cases, the legislature has granted the department head the authority to organize the department and name the department directors; in others, the departmental structure is designated by law, and division directors are appointed by the governor with senate consent. The twenty single executives and principal executive officers collectively constitute the governor's cabinet. The extent to which the full cabinet is used as a policy-making or coordinating body depends upon each individual governor.

Under a law that went into effect in 1970, the governor may reorganize the executive branch below the departmental level unless the legislature objects to such a plan within sixty days of notification. Specific legislative approval, however, is required to create or abolish departments or to alter the functions assigned to them. Thus, the legislature was involved in the transfer of the Council on the Arts from the Department of Education to the Department of State, but much of the reorganization that occurred in the early 1980s as a result of the Governor's Management Improvement Plan did not require legislative approval.

Agencies and Departments with General Executive Responsibilities

The majority of executive departments and agencies are focused on a particular clientele—the banking industry, agriculture, or labor, for example. (These departments will be discussed in depth in the second part of this book.) Other departments and agencies serve the state government as a whole and are included in this chapter discussing the executive branch of New Jersey government.

Serving all the administrative agencies and departments, the Office of Administrative Law provides an impartial forum for hearing disputes involving these agencies and departments. The Division of Law and the Executive Commission on Ethical Standards, both attached to the Department of Law and Public Safety, work with all administrative agencies and departments. Purchasing goods and services for the executive branch is the responsibility of the General Services Administration in the Department of Treasury. The Civil Service Department provides personnel services for all administrative departments. Finally, the Department of State has several functions serving the other departments, in addition to providing services to the population as a whole.

The Office of Administrative Law

The Office of Administrative Law (OAL) is an agency of the executive branch, located technically in, but effectively not of, the Department of State. A director, who is also the Chief Administrative Law Judge, presides over the office and reports directly to the governor. The agency has two functions: first, to conduct administrative hearings, and second, to supervise the process of rule making by executive branch departments and agencies.

Prior to the OAL's existence, hearing officers were employed by most state agencies to hear contested cases. Because the hearing officer frequently presided over cases in which the hearing officer's employer was an interested party, there were some apparent conflicts of interest. In response to this problem, a centralized, independent agency staffed by professional administrative judges (the OAL) was created, with its sole function being to conduct administrative hearings. The judges, numbering about fifty, are full-time officers of the OAL, appointed by the governor and confirmed by the senate for a five-year term. The judges undergo a system of judicial evaluation and receive on-going legal education.

The OAL hearings are less formal than court proceedings. After evidence is presented by both parties, often including a state agency, the judge has forty-five days to make a decision and submit it to the head of the state agency involved. If that initial decision is not rejected or modified within another forty-five days by the head of the agency involved, the initial decision becomes final. While the agency head makes the final determination, if the recommendation of the OAL judge is rejected or modified, the agency head must explain the reasons.

The OAL also oversees executive implementation of legislation. Such implementation occurs through the appropriate executive department developing and enforcing rules that add particulars to the legislative intent spelled out in the statutes. These rules then make up an important body of law. Since legislative oversight committees have no power to veto or change administration rules (although a constitutional amendment has been suggested to give them that power), the legislature has charged the OAL with the task of ensuring that the intent of the law is not changed when the rules are written. This is accomplished by monitoring the drafting of rules so that the language is understandable and ensuring that interested and affected persons have a chance to comment on the proposed rules before they are adopted. In this capacity, the OAL is responsible for publishing the *New Jersey Register* (containing both proposed and promulgated rules) and the *New Jersey Administrative Code* (containing all promulgated rules arranged by subject matter). Those interested in commenting on proposed rules watch for their publication in the *New Jersey Register* and submit their comments during the designated thirty-day comment period.

The OAL is also involved in review of many existing rules. Since 1978 reviews of all new rules promulgated or sections of rules amended have been subject to an executive order requiring that they be given an expiration date of no more than five years from the date the rules take effect. At the end of this period each rule must be reviewed by the appropriate department to determine whether it is adequate, reasonable, and necessary for the original purpose intended. If it is not, the rule is allowed to lapse. If the rule passes the department review, it must go through an administrative procedure for re-adoption monitored by the OAL.

This procedure includes not only an economic and social impact statement, but also a thirty-day period for public comment. As a result, this body of law—including rules for the Department of Motor Vehicles and tax rules, among others—which directly affects every citizen of New Jersey, is being opened up periodically for public scrutiny. Rules proposed for re-adoption are also published in the *New Jersey Register*, and interested citizens may submit their written comments during the designated thirty-day comment period.

The Division of Law

The legal consultant for the state government is the Division of Law in the Department of Law and Public Safety. Assistant and deputy attorneys general staff this division under the supervision of the state attorney general. Some departments such as Banking are assigned a deputy attorney general on a full-time basis to provide legal assistance and to examine contracts and other legal documents. These services, including representation in court, are provided not only to the administrative departments but also to other state agencies, to county boards of taxation and elections, and to sheriffs.

The Division of Law drafts or reviews proposed legislation for all departments and prepares memoranda for the governor on the legality of proposed bills. This legal information supplements the advice rendered by the chief counsel to the governor.

At the request of agencies seeking formal legal guidance, the Division of Law issues the attorney general's formal opinions, which are binding upon the agencies. It also represents state administrative agencies in court in the enforcement of state laws and represents them before the Office of Administrative Law in the enforcement of administrative regulations.

The Division of Law recovers both abandoned property, typically comprising the estates of those who die without heirs, and unclaimed bank accounts, which escheat (revert) to the state. The division also defends state laws and administrative regulations when they are challenged in court.

These cases sometimes go before the New Jersey Supreme Court and can result in judgments that set precedents for later legislation and regulations.

To implement the New Jersey Conflicts of Interest Law the Executive Commission on Ethical Standards was established. The goal of the legislation and the agency is to ensure propriety and preserve public confidence in public officials. The commission, which is technically in, but effectively not of, the Department of Law and Public Safety, has jurisdiction over state officers and employees in the executive branch. It is also responsible for approving codes of ethics for the principal administrative departments. The seven members of the commission are appointed by the governor from among state officers and employees serving in the executive branch.

The commission has the power to initiate, receive, hear, and review complaints regarding violations of the law. It also has the power to conduct investigations and compel attendance of witnesses and production of relevant documents. Commission hearings are conducted by the Office of Administrative Law, which hears the evidence and makes a recommendation to the commission.

Those found guilty of violating the Conflicts of Interest Law may be fined from one hundred to five hundred dollars. Officers and employees may be suspended from office or employment for up to one year and, for willful and continued disregard of the law, may be removed from office or employment and from holding public office or employment for up to five years.

The commission may also render advisory opinions as to whether, in its opinion, a given set of facts, circumstances, or proposed activity would constitute a violation of the law.

Following voter approval of casino gambling in Atlantic City, the commission was vested with responsibility for enforcing sections of the Casino Control Act, i.e., of watching for any conflict of interest by members and employees of the Casino Control Commission and the Division of Gaming Enforcement. (See Chapter 14, Regulation of Gambling and Gaming Activities.)

The Executive Commission on Ethical Standards

The General Services Administration

The General Services Administration (GSA), in the Department of the Treasury, is reponsible for purchasing goods and services for the state, managing government property, and processing information about those transactions.

The bulk of state purchasing is currently done through a central purchasing office in the Department of the Treasury, both to save money through bulk purchasing and to enforce procedures that discourage corruption. The purchasing process is complex. In general, the purchase of goods and services costing more than twenty-five hundred dollars (a higher threshold has been recommended) must be handled through a bid system. Setting specifications, qualifying vendors (people who sell to the government), handling the bidding, ensuring that the agreed-upon goods and services are delivered at the agreed-upon time, and handling the paper work are all important parts of the process.

The GSA also maintains state-owned and leased buildings in the Trenton area, assigns office space, and purchases both real property for the state and insurance for state property.

The Department of Civil Service

Reacting to the corruption and inefficiency of the "spoils system," which placed political supporters in federal posts regardless of competence, reformers of the 1870s and 1880s successfully waged a campaign to replace it with a merit system. Over the years many states adopted similar systems for state employees. New Jersey adopted a civil service merit system for state employees in 1908.

This sytem has remained largely unchanged since its inception, despite calls for reform heard in each state administration since the 1940s. Reformers seek to have the responsibility for basic personnel services—recruitment, testing, and hiring—delegated to each administrative department. The Department of Civil Service would simply supervise these functions, monitor their procedures, and set basic policies. Such a reform, however, has not yet been adopted by the legislature.

Civil service is also an option for local governments, which may adopt the state civil service system by referendum. Once they do so, their employment practices are regulated by the New Jersey Department of Civil Service.

This department is headed by a salaried five-member commission appointed by the governor with the consent of the senate for staggered five-year terms. It has been customary to have at least token representation of both major political parties on the commission. The governor designates one commissioner "president" to serve as the department head.

Personnel Practices

The department is the central personnel office for the state government. Charged with administering the provisions of the civil service laws, it adopts rules and develops enforcement machinery to carry out its purpose. Major activities of the department include:

- classification of jobs to ensure uniform treatment,
- conducting reclassification and salary surveys,
- recruitment and approval (certification) of prospective employees,
- maintenance of an equal opportunity and affirmative action program,
- creating training and career development opportunities for employees,
- and resolution of employee appeals.

Unclassified jobs. Classified jobs are subject to civil service regulations and protection so that an employee cannot be discharged for political reasons. Certain policy-making posts, however, are generally exempt from classification on the theory that elected and appointed officials or boards responsible for the operation of their agencies should be free to select their own personal assistants. Also in the unclassified state service are such officials as deputy attorneys general and other legal assistants and investigators, superintendents of state institutions, licensed doctors and dentists, and a few support personnel for judges, department heads, and boards. Approximately 15 percent of state jobs are not classified. A number of tenure-of-office acts have given protection to various employees, such as deputy attorneys general. Another law also gives tenure to veterans appointed to those offices with no fixed term.

Recruitment and certification. Recruitment for entrance and promotion to civil service positions is carried out through written advertisments and visits by recruiters to educational institutions.

Testing is open, competitive, and job-related. When merit or fitness cannot be determined or when there are not enough eligible competitors, tests are not administered. Following a number of court cases, job requirements that needlessly bar applicants have been eliminated.

After scoring the tests, the department prepares employment lists of the top three persons qualifying. From these, an agency requesting an employee chooses one who, if he or she performs satisfactorily during a four-month probationary period, is then permanently appointed. Each state agency may prepare their own lists for the promotion of employees.

Veterans' preference in hiring. Laws giving preference to war veterans can materially alter an agency's choice. Eligible persons scoring seventy or better are ranked accordingly on an employment list. But placed at the top of the list is the group designated DV—all disabled veterans, wives, and widows of disabled veterans, and widows of servicemen who died while in service. Following the DV group is the group designated V—all veterans, widows of veterans, and mothers of servicemen who died while in service. If a DV or V is at the top of the list, he or she must be chosen. Furthermore, if the appointment is for a promotion and a veteran is first on the promotion list prepared by the agency, the person chosen from among the three individuals certified must be the veteran.

Equal opportunity and affirmative action. Statewide programs are focused on recruiting minorities, women, and the physically handicapped. A recent initiative has been the creation of a task force to address the issue of equitable compensation in state salary policies. The goal is to ensure a fair evaluation for dissimilar types of work so that services of equal value are recompensed equally, regardless of the gender of the persons performing the work.

Training and career development. The Certified Public Manager Program was initiated in 1983 to provide a degree patterned on the CPA for accountants. The program is geared to imparting a practical and common-sense knowledge of supervision and management: it uses the case study and other "hands-on" methods of instruction. New Jersey is one of six states to offer this program.

Through another innovative program, senior civil service executives with classified job status will be allowed to move into policy-making levels usually held by nonclassified employees. The department will gain from their expertise, and the employees will not lose their classified job status.

The Rights of Public Employees
Permanent employees under civil service may be removed for budgetary reasons and for causes such as neglect of duty, incompetence, inefficiency, insubordination, use of authority for political influence, and political activity during office hours. Unlike federal employees, however, public employees in New Jersey not working in federally aided programs may engage in political activities in their free time. The procedure for removal is not easy due to many safeguards against arbitrary dismissal.

In addition to social security coverage, state employees are covered by a number of retirement plans, chief among which are the Public Employees' Retirement System, the Teachers' Pension and Annuity Fund, and the State Police Retirement System. Each fund has its own board of trustees and receives contributions from both the employees and the state. The legislature sets the benefits and policies by law; the Department of the Treasury administers the pensions and invests the pension funds.

Whether or not they are covered by civil service, all locally-paid police and firefighters participate in a state-aided and state-administered retirement plan. Other local government employees may participate in a similar but non-state supported plan if the voters approve such participation.

Collective Bargaining Rights
Many of the state and local public employees working under civil service provisions are represented by unions or professional associations. The Communication Workers of America (CWA) and the American Federation of State,

County, and Municipal Employees (AFSCME) have greatly increased their memberships among New Jersey civil service employees. The New Jersey Education Association (NJEA) represents the bulk of New Jersey teachers; others are represented by the American Federation of Teachers (AFT). Also serving state employees are the New Jersey Civil Service Association, the New Jersey State Patrolmen's Benevolent Association, and the New Jersey State Firemen's Benevolent Association.

Because of the vital nature of many of the services provided by government, the law has traditionally made a distinction between the rights of public employees and those of private employees. Whereas the state constitution gives private employees the right "to organize and bargain collectively," it gives public employees only the right to organize and make known "their grievances and proposals through representatives of their own choosing" (Article I, paragraph 19). However, the constitution does not specifically ban strikes by public employees.

To avert work stoppages by public employees the legislature enacted the New Jersey Employer-Employee Relations Act of 1968, which created machinery to help prevent and settle labor disputes between public employers and their employees. The seven-member Public Employment Relations Commission (PERC) is empowered to determine which units of employees are appropriate for collective negotiations and to resolve questions of the units' representatives.

Under this 1968 legislation the terms and conditions of employment, grievance procedures (which may include binding arbitration), and working conditions are considered negotiable. If negotiations reach an impasse, the commission may mediate at the request of either party. If this fails, PERC may conduct fact-finding sessions and recommend a final settlement. However, the law empowering PERC provides it with no penalties to impose for striking or for the failure of the parties to adopt its recommendations for settlement. Since its creation, PERC has tried to settle numerous disputes between public employees and their employers, including particularly bitter disputes between teachers' groups and their school boards.

In an opinion handed down following passage of the law creating PERC, the New Jersey Supreme Court ruled that, although strikes by public employees were not unconstitutional, they were presently illegal because the legislature had not yet made clear its intent to permit them. This ruling opened the door to legislation defining the limits within which strikes by public employees would be tolerated. No action has yet been taken by the legislature in this matter.

Appeals. The Civil Service Commission sits twice a month to hear appeals on such matters as disciplinary actions, examination challenges, and sick leave claims. All appeals to the Civil Service Commission involving major disciplinary actions and layoff situations go first to the Office of Administrative Law (OAL) for hearings that lead to an OAL report and recommendation. These are submitted to the Civil Service Commission for a final decision.

The Department of State

The Department of State, which is administrative home to the OAL, also performs other functions serving the executive branch as a whole. These include ceremonial matters such as custody and use of the Great Seal of the State of New Jersey; filing and certification of laws, proclamations, and executive orders; and publishing the *Official Directory* (an annual guide to functions, telephone numbers, addresses, and names of people in leadership positions in all state agencies).

Elections

The Elections Division, responsible for orderly elections in the state, operates through assistance to local and county elections offices, records petitions and other documentation for office seekers, certifies elections results, encourages voter registration, and advises on election laws. (See chapter 5, Election Procedures.)

Archives and Records

As the official depository for many state records, the Department of State maintains the state archives, permanent records of historical importance extending back to colonial times. Important records are microfilmed and stored; others, such as corporate filings, are stored for a set period of time before destruction. Assistance is provided to other government levels on record management, forms design, and archival matters.

Cultural Matters and Ethnic Affairs

Although not serving other state administrative agencies, the responsibilities of the Department of State for cultural matters and ethnic affairs will be discussed here to round out a description of the department's activities.

The New Jersey Council on the Arts recognizes and encourages art as a vital aspect of New Jersey culture and heritage. The council makes grants to various arts organizations and develops programs to foster excellence in the arts.

The cultural contributions of New Jersey's many ethnic communities are recognized by the Office of Ethnic Affairs which, with its citizens' council, sponsors festivals at Liberty State Park, the Garden State Arts Center, and other locations around New Jersey.

The New Jersey State Museum is housed in a complex consisting of the main museum, a planetarium, and an auditorium. The museum gathers and exhibits information on the geological and natural history of New Jersey, its plant and animal life, archaeology, fine arts, and decorative arts and crafts.

3.
The Legislative
Branch

L aws made by our state legislature—within certain federal and state constitutional limits—control and foster the health, safety, and welfare of the people; control municipal, county, and other organs of local government; regulate labor and conditions of work; establish civil and criminal law; manage public education; charter corporations; regulate political parties and elections; and protect the environment. In spite of the vast expansion of federal government activity over the years, the powers reserved to the states by the United States Constitution are still of great importance to the daily lives of American citizens.

The primary roles in the policy-making activities of the state are played by the legislature and the executive. Assessing needs, formulating proposals, deliberating between alternatives, and electing certain programs are dependent on the interaction of these two governmental branches. The role of the executive was discussed in the previous chapter; this chapter is devoted to the New Jersey Legislature.

Functions and Powers

A state legislature's function is to determine public policy in that state by making its laws, appropriating funds for government activities, determining how to raise the necessary revenues, and seeing that its wishes and those of its citizens are carried out by the executive branch of the government.

Beyond the general law-making function, the legislature has other specific roles:

■ The legislature has the authority to allocate the functions, powers, and duties of all executive and administrative offices and departments, with the constitutional limitation that not more than twenty major departments be established.

■ The legislature appoints the state auditor, whose duty is to see that the state funds are spent in accordance with the legislature's intention.

■ The legislature has investigatory powers and can subpoena witnesses as long as the legitimate public purpose of obtaining information as a basis for remedial or corrective legislation is present.

■ Constitutional amendments must originate in the legislature and be approved by the voters in a general election.

■ The New Jersey Legislature is required to make appropriations for the support of state government in one general bill that covers one fiscal year. (See chapter 6, The Annual Budget, for a discussion of the budget and appropriation process.)

■ The legislature is responsible for redrawing congressional districts after each decennial federal census.

Each legislative house is granted some individual powers.

■ The New Jersey Senate shares the appointive power with the governor by being required to approve or reject most nominations to posts in the executive and judicial branches.

■ All fiscal bills or new proposals for raising revenue must originate in the lower house, the general assembly.

■ The legislature has the power to impeach and try judicial and executive officials; the general assembly serves as the impeaching agent, and the senate sits as the trial court.

The other two branches of government "check and balance" the legislature: the governor with the use of veto power, and the judiciary with the power to determine the constitutionality of laws passed by the legislature.

Constitutional Restrictions

As discussed in Chapter 1, New Jersey's constitution has limited some of the areas in which the legislature would otherwise be able to act. One of the most important restrictions prohibits the legislature from passing private, special, or local laws in such categories as the laws of inheritance, taxation or exemption from taxation, the salaries or terms of tenure of public officials and employees, the management and control of public schools, the appointment of officers or commissions to regulate local or municipal affairs, and (except as otherwise provided in the constitution) the regulation of the internal affairs of municipalities and counties. The legislature can pass only general laws affecting all cases within any of these categories. However, the legislature may group any of these categories into classes and then legislate separately for each class. The legislature has used this procedure, for example, in regulating counties, after grouping them into six classes. Outside the prohibited categories, private, special, or local laws may be passed only when proper notice has been given in a manner specified by law.

Apportionment

Each New Jersey citizen is represented in the legislature by one senator and two assembly members elected from forty legislative districts drawn by the New Jersey State Apportionment Commission. This current system of districts, many of which cross county lines, from which one senator and two assembly members are elected, was designed after the 1964 United States Supreme Court ruling in the case of *Reynolds v. Sims*. The decision stated that representation in both houses of state legislatures must be solely on the basis of population to satisfy the "one person, one vote" requirement of the United States Constitution. Before this ruling each county, regardless of population, elected one senator—an important political factor in the balance of power in the New Jersey Legislature and in the political culture of the state.

The apportionment commission, reconstituted after each decennial federal census, establishes new senatorial and assembly districts and apportions the number of senators and assembly members among the districts. The state chairmen of the two major political parties each appoint five members of this ten-member group, giving due consideration to the various geographical areas of the state.

In the event of an impasse, the Chief Justice of the New Jersey Supreme Court appoints an eleventh member. The commission then has one month to produce a plan.

Legislative Membership

In New Jersey, state senators must be at least thirty years old, citizens of the United States, and residents of the state for four years and of the district from which they are elected for one year. Assembly members must be at least twenty-one years old, citizens, state residents for two years, and residents of their districts for one year. Assembly members and senators must be eligible to vote. According to the constitution, each house is the sole judge of the qualifications of its members and the validity of their elections.

Membership in the legislature is considered a part-time job, although the time required for legislative, caucus, and committee meetings, the study of proposed bills, meetings with constituents, and campaigning for office can make it virtually a full-time post.

Terms of Office

Legislative elections are held in November of each odd-numbered year, and members assume office at noon on the second Tuesday of the following January. Members of the assembly serve two-year terms. Members of the senate serve four-year terms, except that the first senatorial term at the beginning of each decade is only two years long. This "2–4–4" cycle allows senators to be elected from new districts as soon as possible after each reapportionment following the decennial census.

Vacancies

Vacant seats in the legislature can occur by resignation, assignment to another government post, election to another office, dismissal, or death. Upon a resolution adopted by the house in which the vacancy is declared, the presiding officer will issue a writ calling for a special election to fill the seat for the remainder of the unexpired term. If a vacancy occurs with less than three months remaining in a legislator's term of office, the house need not call for a special election. The existence of a vacancy has no effect on the requirement that a majority vote of the total authorized membership is needed to take a formal action.

Salary, Expenses, and Space

The legislators' salaries are fixed by law and may be changed by the legislature, provided that the change does not take effect during the term of the legislature that enacted it. In 1984 the annual salary of a legislator was twenty-five thousand dollars. The president of the senate and the speaker of the general assembly each receive an additional annual payment equal to one-third of the regular salary. This extra compensation is specified in the constitution in recognition of the additional duties undertaken by the presiding officers.

The state pays for the rental and basic furnishings and supplies of a district office for each legislator. In 1984 the maximum rent was about six thousand dollars and the supply allowance another four thousand dollars. In addition, each legislator receives an allowance for hiring staff to operate the district office and to assist the legislator in constituent and policy work. In 1984 the staff allowance was thirty thousand dollars per year. The legislator may decide how many aides to hire with this money; those engaged in full-time work may be eligible for fringe benefits, including a pension plan available to state employees. Legislative delegations from the same district are encouraged to establish a combined district office to increase efficiency and reduce cost to the state. The constitution bans allowances for expenses that legislators incur beyond those enumerated here.

The legislative branch occupies space in the State House and its adjoining building, the State House Annex. The senate and general assembly chambers, leadership offices, conference rooms, lounges, cloak rooms, and majority and minority staff offices are located in the State House. Committee rooms and the facilities of the Office of Legislative Services are in the Annex. The senate majority conference room and the bill room are also situated in the Annex. Offices are not provided for legislators other than the leadership.

The State House. Part of the State House was first built in 1792–1794, making New Jersey's state capitol the second oldest in continuous use. State Archives and Bureau of History and Public Information Office, Governor's Office.

The General Assembly Chamber. This wing was added to the State House in 1891. The Department of Environmental Protection

Ethics and Behavior

Members of the legislature enjoy certain limited constitutional immunities. Senators and assembly members may not be officially questioned in any other place for any statements they make in either house or at any meeting of a legislative committee. In addition, in all cases except treason and high misdemeanor, they are immune from arrest during attendance at the sittings of their respective houses and in traveling to and from these sittings. However, the attorney general has ruled that a legislator's immunity does not extend to the issuance of a summons for a traffic violation while going to or returning from a legislative session.

Following the approval of casino gambling in Atlantic City in 1976, detailed provisions were added to the legislative code of ethics forbidding a multitude of financial contacts between members of the legislature and their families and members of the casino gambling industry.

Legislation was also passed mandating financial disclosure of numerous categories of income received by legislators, their spouses, and their minor children. These disclosure statements are filed with the Joint Legislative Committee on Ethical Standards. After reviewing the statements, the committee may issue an advisory opinion stating that, in the committee's opinion, a particular category of income, reimbursement, or gifts give rise to an appearance of conflict with the member's service in the legislature. Failure by a member to file a disclosure statement is reported to the president of the senate or the speaker of the general assembly.

There is no legislative or constitutional requirement providing for the impeachment or recall of a legislator. The constitution simply states that each house may expel any member by a two-thirds vote of its authorized membership. There are laws, though, that require forfeiture of a legislative seat if a legislator is convicted of a crime of the third degree or greater or of an offense "involving dishonesty" or "involving or touching" upon the office, unless a court orders a stay of forfeiture for good cause shown.

In addition, the constitution and statutory law prohibit a legislator from holding any of the following offices while serving as a member of the legislature: membership in

Congress, any federal or state position of profit, membership in the electoral college, county clerk, registrar of deeds and mortgages, surrogate, or sheriff. A legislator automatically forfeits the legislative seat upon acceptance of any of these positions. It is lawful, however, for a legislator to hold any other elective or appointive office, position, or employment in county or municipal government.

Organization

While New Jersey's legislature operates under specified procedures that govern its activities, many of its practices depend less on these written rules than on tradition and the pragmatic realities of party politics.

The New Jersey Constitution places relatively few restrictions on the operation, organization, and internal procedures of the legislature. It provides simply that each house choose its own officers, determine the rules of its proceedings, and meet and organize separately at noon on the second Tuesday of January each year. The first annual session of each legislature accordingly begins at noon on the second Tuesday in January in each even-numbered year. This is the prescribed time each house meets, elects officers, appoints committee chairmen, assigns committee members, and proposes and adopts its rules.

The length of a legislative term was extended from one year to two as of January 1970. Thus each house needs to organize only every two years, and bills introduced during the first session of a term need not be reintroduced the following year.

Leadership

Each house elects its officers by majority vote. The presiding officer in the general assembly is the speaker; in the senate, the president. A speaker pro tem and president pro tem, who take over in the absences of the respective presiding officers, are also elected.

The powers of the president of the senate and the speaker of the general assembly are considerable. They include:

- presiding at all sessions,
- appointing the chairmen and members of all com-

mittees and commissions whose membership is not otherwise prescribed by law or rule,

- referring all bills and resolutions to reference
committees or ordering them advanced without committee reference
- listing the schedule of bills and order of events for
each legislative session,
- certifying the passage of bills and resolutions,
- maintaining order and decorum in the chambers,
- and generally supervising the administration of daily
business by the legislature.

The actual selection of legislative leadership is conducted by the political party caucuses, the legislative
members of each house meeting with the other members
of their party in private sessions. The majority party caucus selects the presiding officer for their legislative house
along with the other party leaders who call and preside at
party conferences and who supervise the work of the respective partisan staffs. This leadership includes the majority leaders (usually elected presiding officers of the legislative houses), the minority leaders, assistant leaders, and
party whips. Whips are responsible for counting votes
and making sure party members are in their seats for crucial votes.

In the 1970s the long-held tradition of rotating with
each new session the top two leadership positions, the
president of the senate and the speaker of the general assembly, was abandoned. By the 1980s continuity in these
offices had become common practice. By remaining in office from one legislative session to the next, these leaders
have increasingly become figures with whom governors
must deal in order to achieve their legislative agendas. Often, when the governor's party is not in control of one or
both houses of the legislature, the legislative leadership
presents their own legislative agendas in competition with
that of the governor.

Partisan Staff

Party leadership and members are aided in their work by
a full-time professional partisan staff, operating under the
direction of the party leadership. These aides conduct research, oversee public relations, and provide administra-

tive services for their respective party leaders, committee chairmen, and individual legislators. Each of the four partisan staffs, one for each party in each of the two houses, is headed by an executive director.

Caucuses

Despite the existence of the committee structure, for many years the real legislative action in New Jersey took place in majority party caucuses in each house. There, behind closed doors, bills were debated and decisions made. The caucuses, not the committees, would, by majority vote, decide which bills would be sent to the floor for a vote and how and if they would be amended. Floor debate was often lengthy and heated, but the crucial decisions usually had already been made. Voting on the floor normally followed strict party lines, with objections indicated by abstentions rather than "nay" votes. Bills were almost never defeated once they came up for a vote.

Under this system, reference committees in the legislature barely functioned. Beginning in the 1970 session, however, an effort was made to use the committees more, particularly in the assembly. Now the committees have become an important part of the legislative process. In fact, many bills not deemed matters of party policy are permitted to come up for votes without first receiving caucus approval. One of the most visible signs of the more open approach of the party caucuses and the effectiveness of the committee system has been the increase in the number of bills defeated after open debate on the floor of the assembly.

Despite the strengthened committee system, however, caucuses remain important to the legislative process. Bills are examined for their political implications and their compatibility with party philosophy, and strategies for dealing with the bills are devised in the caucuses. Debates within the party thus take place in the privacy of the caucus room, before the open floor debate is held in public view.

Committees

The number, names, and sizes of the committees are specified in the rules adopted by each house. (See figure 3.1).

Figure 3.1

Standing Reference Committees in The Legislature in 1984

Senate

Education

Labor, Industry and Professions

Natural Resources and Agriculture

Energy and Environment

Revenue, Finance and Appropriations

Institutions, Health and Welfare

Transportation and Communication

County and Municipal Government

Judiciary

Law, Public Safety and Defense

State Government, Federal and Interstate Relations and Veterans Affairs

Revenue, Finance and Appropriations

Corrections, Health and Human Services

Transportation and Communication

County Government and Regional Authorities

Municipal Government

Judiciary

Law, Public Safety and Defense

State Government, Civil Service, Elections, Pensions and Veterans Affairs

Independent Authorities and Commissions

Housing and Urban Policy

Assembly

Aging

Education

Higher Education and Regulated Professions

Labor

Commerce and Industry

Banking and Insurance

Agriculture and Environment

Energy and Natural Resources

Joint Committees and Commissions

Joint Appropriations Committee

Joint Committee on Ethical Standards

Law Revision and Legislative Services Commission

Legislative Oversight

Filling the committees is done by the party leadership. After the various leadership positions are filled, party legislative leaders in each house meet to make committee assignments. Considerations include the preferences of the individual legislators and their backgrounds, length of service, and home districts. The majority party in each house chooses the chairmen of the various committees and determines the number of majority and minority members on each committee, in proportion to their total numbers in the house. The majority traditionally honors the minority's preferences for committee assignments. Those districts which turn out the most votes for the majority party receive the better positions. Since committee assignments are based on partisan alignment, independents receive little consideration with regard to committee choice. After this background work is done by the party leadership, the presiding officer of each house, at the opening session, officially appoints the committee chairmen and members.

Each standing reference committee (a permanent committee to which bills are referred) works in specific subject areas. The committee function is to consider bills and resolutions referred to it by the presiding officer and to report the bills to the house; to review the operations of departments and agencies of the state and its political subdivisions; and to study whether an agency's implementation of a law is in accordance with the legislative intent.

The emergence in recent years of a strong committee system, aided by professional staff from the Office of Legislative Services, has resulted in more carefully drafted bills and in more citizen access to the legislative process. Committee hearings are open to the public in most instances; on very important bills hearings may be held at different locations around the state to increase citizen participation. Such hearings provide an opportunity for those who have an interest in the topic to supply information and express their opinions. A record of testimony is maintained. In the assembly, a measure on which a public hearing has been held may not be considered for third reading or final passage until a record of the public hearing is available to members of the house.

Advance notice of committee meetings, including agendas and written statements furnished to explain the bills to be considered, must be made available to the public. Committee reports on attendance and voting are also public record.

Study Commissions

The legislature creates a great number of study commissions to investigate special issues and to make recommendations for legislative or administrative action. The size, activity, and value of their work vary considerably. Current topics of study range from the effects of Agent Orange on Vietnam veterans to the New Jersey Commission on Sex Discrimination in the Statutes, which has worked since 1978 to uncover and change discriminatory state laws.

Commissions are usually made up of legislators appointed by the speaker of the assembly and the president of the senate; many also have citizen members appointed by the governor, the speaker of the assembly, the president of the senate, or by interest groups designated for representation. Some commissions are given funds for staff; more often staff is provided by the Office of Legislative Services.

The Office of Legislative Services

With the heightened activity of legislative committees and study commissions came an increased need for professional staff. The personal aides to the individual legislators are expected to be busy handling the interests of the home district. The partisan professional staff has duties in support of the party leadership and caucuses. In the early 1970s the professional nonpartisan staff of the legislature was greatly expanded to meet needs for legal advice, budgetary and audit information, research on the substance of the laws, and staffing for reference committees and study commissions.

A 1979 law called for reorganization of the legislative staff under the direction of the Legislative Services Commission. This commission consists of eight members from each house appointed for terms concurrent with their legislative terms. The president of the senate and the speaker of the general assembly appoint the members and currently include themselves on the commission. This group directs and supervises the Office of Legislative Services (OLS).

OLS consists of an executive director and administrative unit along with the Divisions of Legal Services, State Auditing, Budget and Program Review, and Information and Research. The staff is hired by the commission on the recommendation of the division directors; they serve at the pleasure of the commission. Staff members may not engage in any political activities that would conflict with their positions as employees of the legislature as a whole. By law all communications between legislators and OLS personnel are confidential.

Legal Services

The legislative counsel heads this division, which advises the legislature with respect to parliamentary procedure and legal matters. The division performs bill-drafting services for legislators and reviews all bills prior to introduction for compliance with proper technical form. The legislative counsel serves as counsel to the Joint Legislative Committee on Ethical Standards and is available to advise legislators and staff on questions regarding possible conflicts of interest.

State Auditing

This division is headed by the state auditor, a constitutional officer, appointed for a five-year term by the legislature meeting in joint session. This exception to the constitutional rule that the legislature acting alone cannot appoint any executive, administrative, or judicial officer, was made to maintain legislative control over the review of state finances.

The Division of State Auditing performs comprehensive financial audits of state agencies and, on the request of the legislature or the Legislative Services Commission, conducts studies of the operation of state and state-supported agencies with respect to their economy, internal management control, and compliance with applicable laws and regulations.

Budget and Program Review

The legislative budget officer heads this division which provides staff to the Joint Appropriations Committee as well as to the Legislative Oversight "watchdog" Committee. Staff is also provided to other committees as assigned. The division assists the legislature in analyzing expenditures, revenue, and tax issues. It also administers the fiscal note process, in which an estimate of the fiscal impact of proposed legislation is prepared.

Information and Research

Headed by a research director, this division provides staff for legislative standing reference committees, except those concerning fiscal matters. In this capacity it schedules hearings and meetings and records their proceedings. In its research function the division produces briefing materials, research reports, and drafts of bills.

The division also records public hearings and operates a public information service that answers inquiries about legislative activities and procedures. It distributes legislative documents such as bills, legislative calendars of events, records of public hearings, and legislative reports. It maintains a toll-free number that citizens may use to obtain legislative information and track the progress of bills that they are following. (See Sources for Further Information, Bill Watching and *Legislator's Handbook.*)

Sessions and Procedures

The New Jersey Constitution provides that each legislature is formed for a term of two years, divided into two annual sessions. Because the constitution also specifies that all business from the first year may be continued in the second year, the distinction between the two annual sessions is more ceremonial than practical.

The annual legislative session begins at noon on the second Tuesday in January, when both houses meet in joint session to hear the governor deliver the annual "State of the State" message. Thereafter, the legislature traditionally meets each Monday and Thursday until the governor's budget is received, as required by law, twenty-one days from the beginning of the session (although this date is frequently changed). Both houses then adjourn for eight to twelve weeks while the joint appropriations committee holds hearings on the budget. (See Chapter 6, The Annual Budget.) Reconvening in April or May, the legislature continues its regular meetings until agreement can be reached to adjourn.

The New Jersey Legislature is free to meet seven days a week, fifty-two weeks a year, should it choose. Constitutional limitations on the length of legislative sessions and the number of calendar days permitted a state legislature, common in other states, are absent in New Jersey.

In nearly all other states legislatures meet in concentrated sessions, either annually or biennially, for periods of two, three, or four months, or longer. As a rule, legislators in such states spend the weeks at the state capitals and return to their home districts for weekends. In New Jersey, however, the legislature has been in the habit of meeting only one or two days a week because its members can commute to one-day meetings. No part of the state is more than a two-hour drive from the State House in Trenton, traffic permitting. In recent years each house has held more than forty meetings a year. In addition, other days are often devoted to various committee meetings or public hearings.

The custom of the legislature in the past decade has been to meet year-round, even through the summer months. Each year the budget must be passed by July 1, when the new fiscal year begins. Otherwise there are no set deadlines during the two-year session. As a result, action frequently is postponed until the last few months of the session. Then hundreds of bills are passed and sent to the governor for action.

Since 1954 the legislature has always adjourned to a specifically set day except at the end of the term; it thus avoids invoking constitutional provisions regarding the amount of time the governor has to act on bills. Because the legislature always sets a day to reconvene, the traditional concept of a special legislative session called during a recess no longer applies. The constitution does require, however, that the legislature hold a special session on the next to the last day of the two-year session (the Monday before the second Tuesday of January of each even-numbered year) to receive and consider for override motions any bills enacted within the last forty-five days of the session and vetoed by the governor.

The senate and assembly meet in joint sessions a few times during the year for such purposes as receiving the governor's annual State of the State and budget messages, for additional addresses by the governor and other distinguished visitors, to hold special commemorative ceremonies, and to appoint the state auditor. Joint sessions are usually held in the assembly chambers.

Procedural Routine

Session days are frequently busy with overlapping schedules for committee meetings which generally begin in the morning, party caucuses which convene late in the morning to consider actions to be taken in the formal session, and the legislative session which is called to order early in the afternoon. Party caucuses and, with the permission of the house leadership, committee meetings may take place while the house handles the routine business which does not require the presence of a quorum—a majority of the authorized membership of the house.

A typical legislative meeting begins with the call to order and other opening ceremonies. Next come the speeches welcoming visitors and the resolutions marking events of momentous or, more aptly, momentary importance. Routine business of bill introductions, referrals to committee, committee reports, and such non-voting matters follow.

In preparation for consideration of bills, all members receive printed copies of proposed legislation. However, when amendments are made on the floor or in the majority caucus, amended copies of bills may not be available until the morning of the final vote. Notice of which bills are scheduled to come up for final passage (generally far more than are actually brought up for a vote at the session) is sent to members by telegram a few days before each session meeting.

Rules

Each house independently establishes rules of internal organization, operation, and procedure and, in concur-

rent action with the other house, institutes uniform joint
rules governing matters of mutual interest. It is customary for each house to adopt the rules of the preceding
year on a temporary basis until a permanent set of rules
is approved.

The rules of the general assembly and of the senate establish the order of precedence on the day's agenda and
the conduct of debate. Questions as to proper procedure
are decided by the presiding officer in each house, who
may be overruled by a majority vote. The presiding officers may not speak on an issue unless they relinquish
the chair.

Debate. Unlike the United States Senate, which allows
unlimited debate and filibustering on any matter, both
houses of the New Jersey Legislature impose precise limits
on the oratory of their members. In the general assembly
members may speak three times on each bill or motion
—fifteen minutes the first two times, five minutes the
third. A senator may also speak three times on each bill—
thirty minutes the first time, fifteen the second, and five the
third. Nonetheless, each house provides for "moving the
previous question," whereby debate can be cut off by a simple majority vote regardless of whether or not each member
has used all the allowed speaking time. A majority vote can
suspend any standing rule.

Voting. In the New Jersey Constitution, and in the rules
of both houses, when a majority of either house is required
to establish a quorum for passage of a bill, resolution, or
motion, it is a majority of the total authorized membership
that is meant. The total authorized membership of the general assembly being eighty, forty-one votes are required to
pass a bill or resolution. In the senate twenty-one votes out
of a possible forty constitute a majority. This stricture
applies regardless of any vacancies, temporary absences, or
abstentions. When a larger fraction of the membership is
required to pass certain measures, such as the three-fifths
required in the case of calls for constitutional amendments,
the fraction is again that of the total authorized membership, not that of those present and voting. (See figure 3.2.)

Both houses have electronic voting boards mounted on
the walls. The number of the measure under consideration
is posted, and the members' votes are recorded and auto-

Figure 3.2

The Votes It Takes . . .

Action	Requirement	Eighty-Member Assembly	Forty-Member Senate
to pass a bill . . .	majority	41	21
to amend a bill on the floor . . .	majority of those present and voting		
to demand a roll call vote . . .	$1/5$	16	8
to put a constitutional amendment on the ballot . . .	$3/5$*	48	24
to override a veto by the governor . . .	$2/3$	54	27
to approve a nomination . . .	majority of the senate only		
to move a bill on emergency procedures . . .	$3/4$	60	30
to adopt a motion on the floor . . .	majority of those present and voting (in most cases)		
to reconsider a bill or any action taken . . .	needs the same number of votes as required to pass the bill or take the action in the first place		

* or it must pass both houses by a majority in two successive legislative years

matically tabulated. Members cast an "aye" (green light) or a "nay" (red light) by operating a switch from their desks. Both houses require the presence of the legislator on the floor for his or her vote to be recorded. Both houses may be placed "under call," an action that prohibits legislators from leaving the floor. Legislators recorded as present when the house is under call will have their votes registered as negative to the measure if they abstain or leave their desks.

Volume of Bills

The purpose of the legislature is to assess needs, formulate proposals, deliberate various alternatives, and elect certain programs setting forth the policies of state government. Yet the sheer volume of bills introduced in the New Jersey Legislature (7100 in the 1982–83 session) makes assessing, formulating, and deliberating difficult. (See figure 3.3.)

This deluge of bills may be divided into several categories. Many are noncontroversial, of concern to individual members, or needed for the routine operation of state government. These "consent" bills may bypass the committee system (called "no reference" because they are not referred to committee) and go directly to the floor for easy passage.

Many other bills are essentially duplicates, presented separately for political reasons. Still others are trivial or have no chance of being passed; they are introduced largely to please some constituents. These may be weeded out by the committee chairmen, who simply fail to schedule them for consideration, or by the house leadership, who do not post them for floor votes.

Finally, there are the substantial bills, which affect the lives of many citizens of the state. These move through the system with more scrutiny, more media and citizen attention, and more controversy. *If* they are scheduled for consideration by the committee chairman, *if* they are reported out of committee favorably, *if* they are posted for floor consideration by the leadership, *if* they are approved and survive the same process in the other house, then they move to the governor for consideration. Only a small percentage of the substantive bills complete this process. (See figure 3.4.)

Figure 3.3

Types of Legislation and Resolutions

A bill is a proposed law. It is the vehicle for undertaking formal action such as establishing a new state program, making an appropriation, authorizing or prohibiting an activity, changing the language in an existing statute, or repealing a section of law. Each bill is assigned a number and prefixed with an "A" or "S" depending on its house of origin. Thus bills are referred to as S.000 (Senate Bill 000) or A.0000 (Assembly Bill 0000). Bills must pass both houses and be signed by the governor before they become law.

A joint resolution is a formal resolution separately adopted by both houses. These require the same procedure for passage as do laws, therefore they have the effect of laws. They are used in lieu of a bill when enactment is temporary or for the purpose of initiating a study or memorializing (recommending) something to the United States Congress. Funds may be appropriated only in a bill, not in a joint resolution. Joint resolutions are referred to as AJR.00 (Assembly Joint Resolution 00) or SJR.00 (Senate Joint Resolution 00).

A concurrent resolution is an expression of the will of the legislature, adopted by both houses. No funds may be appropriated through this means. A concurrent resolution expires at the end of the two-year legislative term in which it was adopted. It can be used for memorials, commendation, and legislative organizational matters, or to set up a study commission not involving gubernatorial appointments. It is also the procedure used to propose constitutional amendments. Concurrent resolutions are referred to as ACR.00 (Assembly Concurrent Resolution 00) and SCR.00 (Senate Concurrent Resolution 00).

A one-house resolution is a formal resolution adopted by one house expressing the policy or opinion of that house. It is also used for regulating that house's internal organization and procedures or for establishing a study committee under the sole jurisdiction of that house. One house resolutions are referred to as AR.00 (Assembly Resolution 00) or SR.00 (Senate Resolution 00).

A ceremonial resolution offers a means for a house to honor an individual or organization upon a significant occasion or for a notable achievement, or to pay tribute to the memory of a decedent. Formal rules of procedure are not required for passage of ceremonial resolutions.

Oversight

Once a bill has passed both houses and been signed by the governor, the responsibility of the legislature does not end. It has oversight responsibilities to see that the intent of the law is carried out and that it is indeed achieving the policy goals intended.

While the statute sets the broad policy, the details of how it will be applied are set forth by the appropriate executive department in the form of rules and regulations. These "regs" are reviewed by the substantive legislative committees. If they feel the regulations are not in line with the intent of the original law, the committee can draft further legislation to correct the situation. The legislature may not veto the regulations, however, because that would violate the separation of powers: only the executive branch has the power to administer the laws. To aid in the supervision of the rule-making process the legislature has assigned various oversight functions to the Office of Administrative Law, part of the executive branch. (See chapter 2, The Office of Administrative Law.)

In our system of government, legislatures were originally designed to be the source of laws; the executive existed to administer them. The revision of the New Jersey Constitution in 1947 caused a shift of power to the executive. Within this new framework the governor may propose a legislative program for the senate and general assembly to consider and revise. The dominance of the governor in formulating the legislative program was especially clear during the second term of the administration of Richard J. Hughes (governor 1962–1970) and continued to a lesser extent under William T. Cahill (governor 1970–1974). The leadership of the governor has usually been strongest when the legislative majority is of the same party as that of the governor. When the legislature is dominated by the opposing party, the legislative leadership may choose to formulate its own legislative program.

The predominance of gubernatorial influence in the legislature diminished during the administration of Brendon T. Byrne (governor 1974–1982), when the issue of major

Relationships between the Legislature and the Governor

THE PATH OF LEGISL

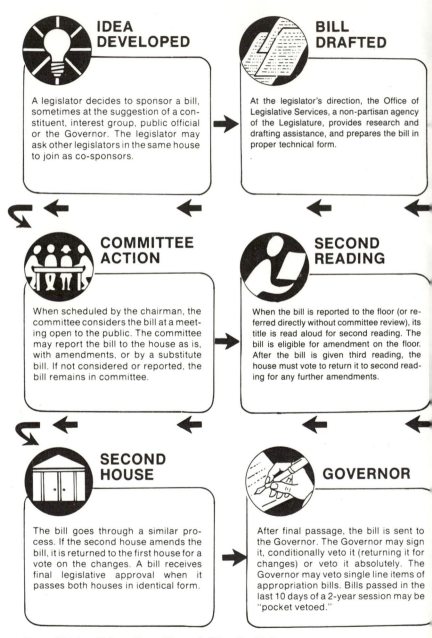

IDEA DEVELOPED

A legislator decides to sponsor a bill, sometimes at the suggestion of a constituent, interest group, public official or the Governor. The legislator may ask other legislators in the same house to join as co-sponsors.

BILL DRAFTED

At the legislator's direction, the Office of Legislative Services, a non-partisan agency of the Legislature, provides research and drafting assistance, and prepares the bill in proper technical form.

COMMITTEE ACTION

When scheduled by the chairman, the committee considers the bill at a meeting open to the public. The committee may report the bill to the house as is, with amendments, or by a substitute bill. If not considered or reported, the bill remains in committee.

SECOND READING

When the bill is reported to the floor (or referred directly without committee review), its title is read aloud for second reading. The bill is eligible for amendment on the floor. After the bill is given third reading, the house must vote to return it to second reading for any further amendments.

SECOND HOUSE

The bill goes through a similar process. If the second house amends the bill, it is returned to the first house for a vote on the changes. A bill receives final legislative approval when it passes both houses in identical form.

GOVERNOR

After final passage, the bill is sent to the Governor. The Governor may sign it, conditionally veto it (returning it for changes) or veto it absolutely. The Governor may veto single line items of appropriation bills. Bills passed in the last 10 days of a 2-year session may be "pocket vetoed."

Source: **Division of Information and Research, Office of Legislative Services.**

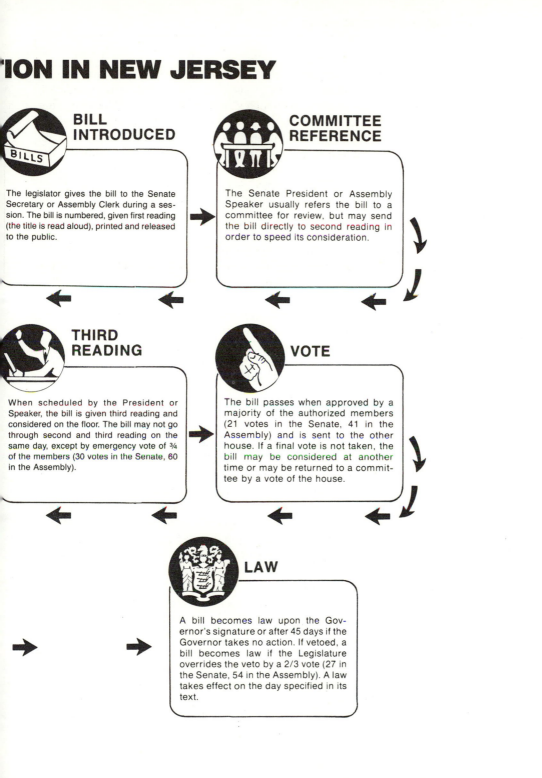

BILL INTRODUCED

The legislator gives the bill to the Senate Secretary or Assembly Clerk during a session. The bill is numbered, given first reading (the title is read aloud), printed and released to the public.

COMMITTEE REFERENCE

The Senate President or Assembly Speaker usually refers the bill to a committee for review, but may send the bill directly to second reading in order to speed its consideration.

THIRD READING

When scheduled by the President or Speaker, the bill is given third reading and considered on the floor. The bill may not go through second and third reading on the same day, except by emergency vote of ¾ of the members (30 votes in the Senate, 60 in the Assembly).

VOTE

The bill passes when approved by a majority of the authorized members (21 votes in the Senate, 41 in the Assembly) and is sent to the other house. If a final vote is not taken, the bill may be considered at another time or may be returned to a committee by a vote of the house.

LAW

A bill becomes law upon the Governor's signature or after 45 days if the Governor takes no action. If vetoed, a bill becomes law if the Legislature overrides the veto by a 2/3 vote (27 in the Senate, 54 in the Assembly). A law takes effect on the day specified in its text.

tax reform in 1976 changed the New Jersey Legislature's confidence in its ability to take the initiative in formulating legislation. Although Governor Byrne was a Democrat, the Democratic majority in the legislature acted as the governor's opposition party. In the agony of attempting to create a school funding formula to comply with the ruling of the New Jersey Supreme Court, the legislators rejected the governor's income tax proposal and wrote their own. Since then there have been many indications that the legislature has become a less willing follower of the governor's leadership in making policy.

The legislature's position vis-à-vis the governor was also strengthened by the increase in the size and activity of the Office of Legislative Services, which provides the legislature with a source of information and analysis of fiscal and substantive issues independent of the administration. The increased activity of the committee system, the addition of a legislative oversight committee, and the decision to maintain the same legislative leadership from one session to the next have all added to the strength of the legislature.

Presentation of Bills

One area of power traditionally exercised by the governor has been removed by constitutional amendments, passed in 1981 and 1983, that limit the governor's formal and pocket veto powers. The 1947 constitution gave the governor considerable veto power over legislation—the outright veto, the conditional veto, and the line item veto for the appropriations bill. In addition, the governor could pocket veto bills by not taking action during the time period stipulated.

The tradition of gubernatorial courtesy added another power to the governor's control of legislation. By custom the constitutional time limits imposed on the governor to take action on a bill were computed not from the date of passage in the legislature, but from the time the bill was "presented" to the governor. Out of "courtesy" the legislature presented bills to the governor for consideration only when "called" for. This permitted the governor's staff to deal with a few bills at a time after the closing days of a spring session, the period when traditionally a large number of bills were passed. However, the governor could refrain from calling for certain bills or delay until favorable action was obtained on other desired legislation. In turn, a hostile legislature could waive the custom of courtesy and present a clutch of bills all at one time.

The constitutional amendment of 1981 provides that a bill that has passed both houses be presented to the governor before the close of the next working day. It also limits the pocket veto power by providing that a bill passed before the last ten days of the session shall become law if the governor does not return it to the house of origin with any objections before the expiration of the period allowed for the governor's consideration.

The 1983 constitutional amendment requires the governor to take action on all bills passed in the last ten days of the session within seven days of the final meeting of the legislature. If the governor does not sign within that time period, the bill receives a pocket veto. That the system is still not perfect was evident in January 1984, when the governor was faced with consideration of over four hundred bills passed in the last days of the session. As a result, Governor Kean vetoed many bills that he was unable to examine carefully. (See figure 3.5.)

Action on Nominations

The senate's power to confirm or reject most of the governor's nominations to offices in the executive and judicial branches provides one of the most potent and public arenas for political maneuvering between the legislature and the governor. Adherence to the long-standing tradition of senatorial courtesy gives senators from a nominee's home county the veto power over that nomination. Nominations are sent to the senate judiciary committee, making a position on that committee a source of extreme power for a senator in dealing with the governor or with other senators. Another senatorial courtesy is the automatic confirmation of the nomination of a former state senator to an office, whether or not that person belongs to the majority party. The senate judiciary committee may go into executive (closed-door) session to consider nominations.

The custom of senatorial courtesy is annually attacked when a new legislative session begins and rules must be

Figure 3.5

Ins and Outs of the Governor's Veto Power

THREE KINDS OF VETO

Absolute veto: The governor returns a bill with objections to the house of origin. The bill cannot become law unless the legislature overrides the governor's veto by a vote of at least two-thirds of the members of each house.

Conditional veto: The governor returns the bill, setting forth objections and proposing amendments that would make it acceptable. If the legislature re-enacts the bill with the recommended amendments by a majority vote in each house, the bill is presented again to the governor. It becomes law if the governor signs it within ten days.

Line-item veto: This applies only to appropriations bills. The governor may approve the bill but veto specific items or approve the bill only with deductions made in various line-items. The deleted or reduced items, with a statement of the governor's objections, are returned to the legislature, which may restore them only by a vote of at least two-thirds of the members of each house.

THREE TIME FRAMES FOR THE GOVERNOR TO TAKE ACTION ON A BILL

Situation 1: Bills passed up to the 45th day prior to expiration of the legislative session.

Bill becomes law: upon the governor's signature

or

after 45 days if the governor takes no action

Exception: If the house of origin is not in session on the 45th day, the bill becomes law on the first session day thereafter.

Situation 2: Bills passed between the 45th day and the 10th day prior to the expiration of the legislative session.

Bill becomes law: upon the governor's signature

or

unless the governor vetoes it before noon of the day prior to the expiration of the legislative term, i.e., the second Monday in January. The legislature convenes on that day to consider any such vetoes.

Situation 3: Bills passed within the last 10 days of the legislative session.

Bill becomes law: upon the governor's signature only.

Pocket veto: The governor has until noon of the seventh day following the end of the term. If the bills are not signed by the deadline, they do not become law. This is the governor's limited "pocket veto" and is the only situation in which a bill can be vetoed without being returned to the legislature for reconsideration. Of course, these bills may be subject to a conditional veto provided that option is exercised prior to the end of the term.

adopted by the senate. Debate also erupts whenever a senator exercises the privilege. This device is the source of a long-standing controversy between the New Jersey Bar Association and the senate. A proposed rules change stated that after a certain number of days, if an appointment had not been considered by the judiciary committee, it would be brought to the entire senate for discussion. When brought before the senate, the rule change failed miserably, and it is unlikely that it will ever be passed. Senatorial courtesy is considered a useful tool for patronage and power, and an effective means to restrain, contain, and discipline the executive. There is much talk of change but no effective challenge to its practice.

Legislative Liaisons from Executive Departments

Most executive departments (and the judicial system) employ a staff member as a liaison between the department and the legislature. The role of the legislative liaison is to report to the head of the department any activities of the legislature that affect the department and to provide the legislature with technical expertise and information about the department.

Lobbyists and Campaign Financing

Lobbyists are a source of influence on the formation of public policy, especially on laws and the regulations implementing those laws. They perform this role through contact with legislators and public officials, providing them with information and opinions. As representatives of special interest groups, lobbyists have customarily been a major, though not necessarily objective, source of information for legislators. When opposing lobbyists argue, more than one side of a complex issue may be aired.

Because of the volume of legislation regulating business and industry and directly affecting labor, organizations representing these interests lobby actively. Prominent among the lobbies are business and professional groups such as the New Jersey Business and Industry Association, the trial lawyers' group, the dentists, and other health care professionals, to name a few. Labor is also represented through its unions (the New Jersey State AFL-CIO, for example), as are associations of public employees—the Communication Workers of America (CWA), representing a large proportion of the unionized state employees, the American Federation of State, County, and Municipal Employees (AFSCME), and the New Jersey Education Association (NJEA), among others. So that their interests will be heard, associations of hospitals, school boards, farmers, and other groups lobby the legislature. Issue-related lobbies—anti-abortion and pro-choice, National Rifle Association and handgun control groups, advocates of various environmental issues, supporters of the fine arts, lobbies for the rights of tenants and for the interests of welfare recipients—all join the bustle in the halls of the capitol. Other groups such as the League of Women Voters, Common Cause, and the New Jersey Taxpayers' Association are public interest organizations. As such they lack the financial clout of other lobbies, but they are able to provide substantive information to legislators and voters on a variety of issues and to focus public attention on legislative activity.

While lobbyists are an important source of information for legislators, they certainly are neither disinterested nor impartial participants in the legislative process. To help legislators identify and evaluate lobbyists, the Legislative Activities Disclosure Act was passed in 1964 and revised in 1971. Under this statute lobbyists must register with the state attorney general, disclose whom they represent, and report four times a year which pieces of legislation they tried to influence.

This law defines "lobby" as the organization seeking influence and the "legislative agent" (lobbyist) as the person hired to carry the lobby's message to the legislators. Legislative agents must register with the state if they receive any compensation, including expenses of more than one hundred dollars per quarter, or lobby as a significant part of their employment. They must wear badges while in the State House, and they are not allowed on the floor of either house while it is in session—a rule usually, but not strictly, observed.

Less attention has been paid to the internal lobbyists,

those legislators themselves who, in their private roles, are associated with special interest groups. For this reason, the 1971 conflict-of-interest law specifically provides that a legislator must reveal any personal interest in a matter being considered by the legislature before participating in discussion or voting.

As part of their effort to influence legislation, lobbyists have traditionally entertained legislators, and lobbies have contributed to the campaign finances of friendly candidates for the legislature. The 1973 New Jersey Campaign Contributions and Expenditures Reporting Act was designed to furnish a clearer picture of lobby-legislature relationships.

One major provision of this law calls for all lobbyists and political information groups to file detailed financial statements. Due, however, to a long legal battle over the constitutionality of this provision and debate over the regulations implementing the law, the first financial disclosure statements were not filed until 1982. Early in that same year the law was amended to eliminate the disclosure requirement except when direct communication took place at the time of the lobbying expenditures. Thus lobbyists could "wine and dine" legislators one evening, call them the next morning to discuss pending legislation, and have no need to report the cost of the dinner.

4.
The Judicial
Branch

The courts keep the peace by administering justice under laws and legal principles. The courts permit individuals to resolve disputes; they decide whether or not there have been violations of laws and administrative regulations; they determine whether or not laws and regulations meet federal and state constitutional standards. Courts serve justice even when there are no disputes—as in their supervision of the administration of the estates of minors and incompetent persons.

But a court is more than merely a mechanism for the administration of law and justice. Even in judicial circles, the New Jersey Supreme Court is acknowledged as a policy-making as well as an adjudicating body. The court's landmark decisions have had a significant impact on shaping state policy.

While New Jersey's highest court and the state's entire court system are now regarded with respect, this was not always so. The judicial article of the 1947 New Jersey Constitution accomplished a major revision of what had been an archaic, intricate, and self-defeating network of courts. As a result of the new constitution and further amendments, the state now enjoys a modern, effective, and unified judicial system—a system that has been used as a model for court reform throughout the country. Significant constitutional innovations involved the creation of a trial court of state-wide jurisdiction, the granting of the administration of the court system as a whole to the chief justice, and the vesting of the rule-making power in the state supreme court. (See figures 4.1 and 4.2.)

Figure 4.1

The Judicial Branch

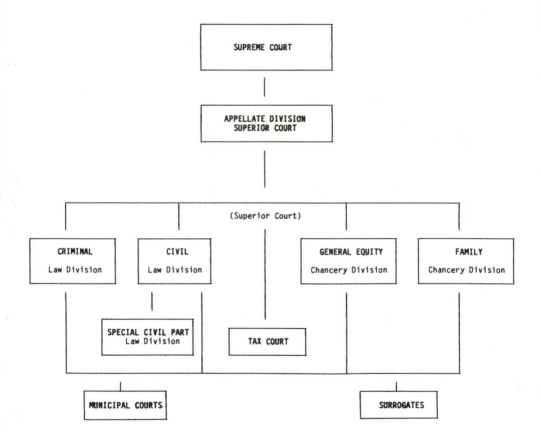

Justices, Judges, and Jurisdictions

SUPREME COURT:

Chief Justice and 6 Associate Justices. Initial term of 7 years with tenure on reappointment. Mandatory retirement at 70. Final Appeal in:

1. Constitutional questions

2. Issues where dissent in Appellate Division

3. Capital causes

4. Certification

5. In such causes as provided by law

SUPERIOR COURT:

329 Judges authorized. Term, tenure and retirement same as Supreme Court.

Appellate Division Appeals from:

1. Law and Chancery Divisions

2. State Administrative Agencies

3. Tax Court

4. As provided by law

Law Division: Criminal and Civil

1. General jurisdiction in all causes, civil and criminal

2. Proceedings in lieu of prerogative writs, except review of state administrative agencies

3. Appeals from Municipal Courts and Wage Collection Section, Office of Wage and Hour Compliance

4. Probate

Law Division: Special Civil Part

1. Contract, penalty, and tort actions at $5,000

2. Landlord and tenant

3. Small claims at $1,000

4. Concurrent criminal and quasi-criminal jurisdiction with municipal courts

Figure 4.2

Figure 4.2 (continued)

Chancery Division: General Equity and Family

1. General equity

2. Probate

3. Family

   a. Exclusive jurisdiction over juvenile delinquency

   b. Juveniles and families in crisis

   c. Domestic violence

   d. Divorce and separation

   e. Custody of children

   f. Support

   g. Paternity

   h. Child abuse

   i. Child Placement Review

   j. Adoption

Tax Court: 12 authorized judges. Term, tenure and retirement same as Supreme Court. The Tax Court reviews the determinations of agencies and officials charged with administration of state and local taxes and in particular:

1. Local property tax assessments

2. State tax assessments

3. Equalization tables promulgated by the director of the Division of Taxation or the County Boards of Taxation

MUNICIPAL COURTS:
359 Judges. Term: 3 years.
1. Traffic and motor vehicle violations

2. Ordinance violations

3. Disorderly persons offenses

4. Fish and game and navigation violations

5. Other specified crimes (where penalty does not exceed 1 year incarceration or $1,000 fine) and offenses (where value of property does not exceed $500), including some crimes where indictment and trial by jury can be waived.

6. Probable cause hearings on indictable offenses.

SURROGATES' OFFICES:
21 Surrogates. Elected. Term: 5 years.
1. Uncontested probate matters

2. Deputy clerk of the Superior Court for probate matters

The process of unifying the courts, begun with the 1947 constitution, was largely completed following voter approval of a constitutional amendment in 1983 that abolished the county district court and the juvenile and domestic relations court, integrating their functions into a single superior court system. This same amendment created a family court within the chancery division of the superior court.

The State Courts

The New Jersey Constitution provides for a supreme court, a superior court, and other courts of limited jurisdiction that can be established, altered, or abolished by the legislature. The constitution further provides for the surrogates' offices, which perform quasi-legal functions such as probating uncontested estates. In 1979 the legislature established the tax courts, which join the municipal courts in being courts of limited jurisdiction. Most recently, according to the 1983 constitutional amendment abolishing the county district courts, the superior court is divided into an appellate division, a law division, and a chancery division that includes a family court.

There is, of course, a separate federal court system for trying alleged violations of federal laws, regulations, and provisions of the United States Constitution. The federal courts also resolve disputes in certain categories of civil cases such as controversies between citizens of different states. The United States Attorney for New Jersey, located in Newark (see chapter 14, The United States Attorney), is part of this federal court system. The scope of this chapter, however, is limited to the state court system.

Supreme Court

New Jersey's highest court, the supreme court, is composed of a chief justice and six associate justices. The supreme court serves as the court of last resort for cases involving substantial constitutional questions, dissent in the appellate division, or imposition of the death penalty at the trial court level (death penalty cases bypass the appellate division). In certain other cases the supreme court may agree to grant certification (i.e., hear appeals) because of the public importance of the question involved. The Mount Laurel zoning case was such an issue.

The supreme court also admits attorneys to practice and, when appropriate, disciplines them. A program to certify trial attorneys in order to improve the quality of trial advocacy and to inform the consumer about those members of the bar who have achieved a certain level of skill, knowledge, and experience in trial representation, is also administered by the supreme court.

In addition, the supreme court promulgates the rules that govern the administration, practice, and procedure in all courts in the state. The chief justice appoints and supervises the director of the Administrative Office of the Courts in administering these rules of court.

Superior Court

The superior court is divided into three divisions: the appellate division, and the two trial divisions, law and chancery.

The appellate division receives appeals from the law and chancery divisions, from the lower courts, and also from the final orders and decisions of state agencies. The chief justice assigns judges from the law and chancery divisions to sit in panels of two or three judges to hear appeals. After deciding each case, the panel issues a written opinion.

Since the revision of the criminal code in 1979 and the institution of mandatory prison sentences for many crimes, the number of criminal appeals brought before the appellate court has increased dramatically. To deal with this a special five-judge panel was established in 1983 to hear only criminal appeals. As a result the majority of the appeals judges were freed to hear civil cases, and the backlog in both criminal and civil cases has been reduced.

In the law division, a single judge presides over a trial court either with or without a jury. At least one law division judge sits in each county seat. The criminal part handles all indictments and accusations in criminal cases following initial filings of the complaint in municipal court. The civil part handles general civil cases, while the special civil part handles issues such as landlord/tenant disputes and small claims. These disputes were the responsibility of the county district courts before the constitutional amendment of 1983 eliminated that level of the judiciary.

In the chancery division a single judge presides over the trials, which are generally without juries. The chancery division is divided into the general equity and the family parts. The general equity cases involve issues such as preventing the continuance of a wrong (injunction) or completing the performance of a contract (specific performance), as well as probating contested estates. The family part deals with a wide range of issues concerning families as a whole. Under the jurisdiction of the family part comes juvenile delinquency, juveniles and families in crisis, domestic violence, child abuse, review of cases involving placement of children outside of their homes, adoption, paternity, separation and divorce, and support and custody of children. Within this system all cases related to a family will be heard in the same court, often by the same judge. Greater coordination, access to information, and comprehensive court services for the families involved are the goal. However, funding for many of the supportive services for families has yet to be appropriated.

Superior courts of the law and chancery divisions are grouped geographically into vicinages (judicial districts made up of one or more counties, currently fifteen in all). Administration in each vicinage is the responsibility of the assignment judge, appointed by the chief justice. On the recommendation of the assignment judge, the chief justice also appoints a presiding judge for each of the functional units—criminal, civil, general equity, and family parts—of the law and chancery divisions. These judicial administrators are assisted by professional court administrators.

Tax Court

The Tax Court of New Jersey is a trial court having statewide jurisdiction. It was established by the legislature in 1979 as a court of limited jurisdiction to review state tax and local property tax assessments. The court reviews the actions and determinations of the assessors and the county boards of taxation with respect to local property tax matters, and of the Director of the Division of Taxation and the Director of the Division of Motor Vehicles and other state officials with respect to state taxes. The annual caseload is six to seven thousand, the bulk of which involve local property taxes. Homestead rebate cases account for the next largest group.

Surrogates' Offices

Under the state constitution, a surrogate is elected in each of the twenty-one counties for a five-year term. Not really courts, since disputes are not adjudicated, the surrogates' offices handle the great volume of probate matters that are routine and uncontested. The surrogates admit wills to probate, appoint guardians for minors, and issue certificates of authority to executors, administrators, guardians, and trustees of estates.

Municipal Court

Each municipality is authorized to establish a municipal court either individually or jointly with one or more other municipalities. Currently the municipal court judge, formerly called a magistrate, is appointed for a three-year non-tenured term by the governing body of the municipality or, in the case of a joint municipal court, by the governor with the consent of the senate. In municipalities with populations over 100,000, from one to five additional judges may be appointed. The post of municipal judge is almost always part-time, and the judge may continue in private legal practice. All the expenses of the court and the salary of the judge are borne by the municipality.

Municipal courts handle more cases than all other courts combined. Their jurisdiction includes traffic and motor vehicle violations; ordinance violations; disorderly persons offenses (with domestic violence cases going to the family part of superior court); fish and game, and navigation violations; and other specified crimes where the penalty does not exceed one year's incarceration or one thousand dollars fine, and offenses where the value of the property involved does not exceed five hundred dollars. Municipal courts also hear some cases where indictment and trial by jury can be waived. Probable cause hearings on indictable offenses are held in municipal courts before being sent to the superior courts for trial.

The various types of court cases and the procedures and terms involved in a criminal case are outlined in "A Glossary of Judicial Terms" (See figure 4.3.) Changes in the state criminal code since 1979 are found in figure 4.4.

Grand and Petit Juries

The laws of New Jersey are explicit in directing the workings of both the grand jury, which screens criminal charges before a case goes to trial, and petit juries, which decide the facts in a trial. This system of involving citizens in the judicial system is an important part of the legal tradition of English-speaking people.

Jury selection is handled by the court clerk, assisted by two jury commissioners for each county. These commissioners, who may not belong to the same political party, are appointed by the governor for one-year terms and may be reappointed to additional terms not to exceed seven years in office. The lists of prospective jurors are selected at random from a combined list of registered voters and licensed drivers. Twenty-three prospective jurors are chosen for the grand jury and as many for the petit jury. Questionnaires are then sent to these prospective jurors concerning their qualifications to serve. Any individual not responding may be held in contempt of court.

To qualify as a prospective juror, an individual must be a citizen of the United States, a resident of New Jersey for two years, and a resident of the county in which he or she is to serve. The prospective juror must be between eighteen and seventy-five years of age, must never have been convicted of a crime, must read and write English, and must have no physical or mental disability that will prevent serving properly. Under recent changes in the system, very few people are automatically exempt from jury duty. Because of the random selection a citizen may be called to serve more than once, although not for a period of twelve months after service.

Grand Jury. The right to have a serious federal criminal charge screened by a grand jury is guaranteed in the Fifth Amendment of the United States Constitution. This right to indictment by a grand jury is also guaranteed by the New Jersey Constitution for those facing state charges. However, a defendant may waive this right.

Figure 4.3

A Glossary of Judicial Terms

Courts are forums assembled for the administration of justice. There are two types of courts, trial and appellate (review).

Trial courts conduct *adversary proceedings* (two opposing sides argue the case) to resolve factual disputes and to apply the law to the facts. If the case is tried before a jury, the judge rules upon points of law; the jury decides the facts. If the case is tried before the judge alone, he or she will both determine the facts and rule on points of law.

Appellate courts act on applications to review trial court decisions. Should the appellate court believe more facts are required, it may send the case back to trial.

Civil actions in court are those not involving criminal offenses.

Actions at law are civil suits brought by one or more persons (including corporations) against one or more persons, usually seeking monetary compensation (*damages*) for committing a wrong (*tort*) or for breaking a contract. Personal injury negligence cases resulting from automobile accidents are actions at law.

Actions at equity are civil suits brought by one or more persons where actions at law do not apply. Equity covers such matters as preventing the continuance of a wrong (*injunction*) or completing the performance of a contract (*specific performance*). By historical precedent there are not juries in equity trials.

Matrimonial actions in equity are civil actions seeking a change in status (such as divorce or legal separation) and are heard in the family part of the chancery division of the superior court.

Actions in probate are civil actions involving the property of deceased persons, incompetent persons, and minors. By tradition there are no jury trials in probate matters. Uncontested probate matters are handled on the county level by an elected *surrogate* who is deputy clerk of the superior court for probate matters. Contested probate matters are handled by the superior court.

Criminal action is taken against a person violating a criminal law of the state or an ordinance of a municipality.

Minor offenses are those in which the penalty does not exceed one year's incarceration or $1,000 fine, or where the value of the property involved does not exceed $500. Municipal court judges sit without juries to dispose of these cases.

Figure 4.3
(continued)

Disorderly persons offenses are petty offenses not considered serious enough to be classified as crimes. As nonindictable offenses, they are tried before municipal court judges. A defendant has all the procedural safeguards of a criminal trial except the right to a grand jury hearing and the right to a trial by jury. Disturbing the peace is an example of a disorderly persons offense.

Indictable offenses are more serious crimes and are disposed of in the law division of the superior court. The New Jersey Code of Criminal Justice classifies these crimes and establishes degrees of varying severity: crimes of the first, second, third, and fourth degree.

A first court appearance takes place within a reasonable time after arrest before a municipal court judge. The judge reads the *charge* (the accusation against the defendant), informs the defendant of his or her rights, and then conducts a *preliminary hearing* to determine whether there is *probable cause* to believe that a crime was committed and that the defendant committed it. If probable cause is found, the defendant is bound over to await final determination of the case. The judge must set bail for the defendant in accordance with court rules.

A grand jury indictment is a formal written statement charging one or more persons with an offense. The grand jury bases its indictment on the evidence presented by the prosecutor and serves to weed out frivolous criminal cases and to guard against over-zealous prosecutors. The right to indictment by a grand jury may be *waived* (relinquished).

The arraignment proceedings follow an indictment. Appearing before a court in the law division of the superior court, the defendant enters a *plea of "guilty" or "not guilty."* The court accepts a guilty plea only if the judge is satisfied that the plea is made voluntarily and with an understanding of the consequences of the plea.

Bail is set at the arraignment. Bail is money or property deposited with the court to assure that the accused will appear for trial. Failure to appear causes the bail to be forfeited. Bail, unlike a fine imposed upon conviction, is not supposed to punish. In some instances a judge may release a defendant on his or her own *recognizance* (pledge) until the trial.

The defense will be handled by a staff member of the Office of the Public Defender or by a lawyer designated by that office if the defendant is unable to afford counsel. A defendant, in consultation with counsel, may decide to *plea bargain*, a highly controversial practice by which a defendant pleads either guilty to a lesser offense or pleads "no defense" in return for a consideration of leniency in sentencing. As a result, a trial is not needed.

The trial may be before a *petit or trial jury* made up of twelve citizens chosen at random or before a judge, if the defendant waives the right to trial by jury. If the *verdict* (the jury or judge's decision on the truth of the charges) is "guilty," the defendant is *sentenced.* This is the formal pronouncement by the court, following conviction, of the *"sanctions"* (punishment) to be imposed on the defendant. There are five basic sentences: fines, probation, partial confinement, total confinement, and death.

Appeal of the conviction may be made to the appellate division of the superior court whose role it is to review the procedures used in the earlier court action and rule on the fairness of those proceedings.

Figure 4.4

Changes in the State Criminal Code Since 1979

Revision of the state criminal code resulted in crimes being ranked according to their seriousness and sentences being defined for each degree of offense. In most cases the judge is required to give a prison term within a specified range of years. Additional amendments and legislation have expanded mandatory sentencing.

Mandatory Sentencing Laws

First degree crimes, such as armed robbery, carry presumed sentences of fifteen years, with the judge required to give a sentence of from ten to twenty years.

Second degree crimes, such as arson, that purposely put a person in grave danger, or bribery involving a public official, carry presumed sentences of seven years with the judge required to give a sentence of from five to ten years.

Crimes committed while in possession of a gun carry a mandatory three-year prison term without parole, added to any other prison terms imposed.

Sex offenses carry a mandatory sentence of at least five years for a person convicted of a second or subsequent sex offense.

Shoplifting carries a mandatory minimum sentence of thirty days for anyone convicted of a third or subsequent shoplifting offense.

Halloween offenses, purposely or knowingly offering, giving, or enticing a person to take or accept any treat, candy, gift, or food which is poisonous, deleterious, or harmful, carries a minimum term of six months.

Reinstatement of capital punishment not only provides for the death penalty but also for mandatory thirty-year prison terms for capital crimes not punished by death.

Sentencing leeway, allowing a judge to increase or decrease a prison term, is provided for in some instances. In addition, if the reasons for leniency are strong, the judge may, under certain conditions, for sentencing purposes reduce a first degree crime to a second degree crime and so forth. The judge may also, under certain circumstances, give a noncustodial term in which the offender would not be incarcerated.

Revision of juvenile justice laws includes a mechanism making it easier for county prosecutors to try youths under age sixteen as adults.

A grand jury is not a trial jury. Rather, it reviews cases to ensure that only substantial criminal charges go to trial. A grand jury decides whether or not the evidence presented by the county prosecutor is sufficient to require a defendant to stand trial. Thus the grand jury can also serve as a check on an over-zealous prosecutor. Grand jury hearings are closed to the public, and jurors are bound to keep matters before them in strict confidence (although witnesses before the grand jury are not so constrained). If twelve jurors vote that sufficient evidence has been submitted to warrant a trial, they return an indictment (which is not in any way an assertion of guilt).

A grand jury has other powers as well. For instance, it may hand up a presentment, that is, a statement calling attention to public affairs or conditions that it finds in need of correction. The grand jury may also censure public officials if their conduct has contributed to a situation needing correction, but which is not itself a criminal offense. Like an indictment, a presentment usually results only from the evidence presented by a prosecutor, although a grand jury has the power to initiate investigations and subpoena witnesses and records relating to any matter that, in its opinion, requires indictment or correction. In the past, the opportunity for a county prosecutor to manipulate a grand jury was great, and the grand jury's power to hand up a presentment was occasionally abused. Therefore, new rules have given public officials named in a presentment the right to challenge, in a private hearing prior to the presentment being filed and publicized, the reference to their names.

One grand jury serves at all times in each county; counties with populations over 250,000 may have two grand juries simultaneously. The twenty-three members of a grand jury serve for four months but may serve longer in certain circumstances.

Statewide grand juries were authorized under a 1968 law. They may be called at the request of the attorney general and with the permission of a superior court judge designated by the chief justice. No more than one-fourth of the jurors may come from one county. Such a jury's indictment is returned to the judge, who then sets the county for the trial. Since the first state grand jury was empaneled in 1969 to hear testimony presented by a newly created organized crime unit under the direction of the attorney general, testimony presented to the state grand juries has led to convictions for such crimes as extortion, gambling, and bribery of public officials, to name a few. (See chapter 14, Criminal Justice, and The State Commission of Investigation.)

Petit or Trial Jury. The right to trial by a jury of one's peers dates back to the Magna Charta. It is guaranteed in the United States Constitution and in New Jersey law since the 1776 constitution. Generally, prospective jurors are summoned for a period of one week or less; if this period ends while they are sitting in a trial, they continue to serve for the duration. Several counties operate a jury system whereby a juror sits for one trial (however long) or one day and is then excused.

A petit jury sits in criminal and civil cases to determine facts that are in dispute. The jurors are chosen by lot from panels of prospective jurors. The first one selected becomes the foreman. In criminal cases the jury is composed of twelve jurors. If a trial is expected to be lengthy, however, fourteen or even more jurors may be selected. In this situation, all sit during the trial; at its end jurors are selected as alternates until twelve remain to participate in the jury deliberations. A conviction in a criminal case must be by unanimous vote; lack of unanimity is called a "hung jury." In civil cases, the jury consists of six to twelve jurors; affirmative votes by five-sixths of the jury are necessary for a verdict.

A jury trial is never mandatory except when the prosecutor is seeking the death penalty. A defendant in any other criminal case may waive the right to a jury trial. In a civil case allowing trial by jury, there is a jury trial only if one or more of the parties request it.

Judges

Judges of the state judicial system are appointed by the governor with the consent of the senate. The governor must give seven days public notice of judicial nominations before sending them to the senate for confirmation. An equal number of Democrats and Republicans are customarily appointed to courts, usually on the recommendations of the county political chairmen.

The initial appointment is for a seven-year term. After reappointment, which also requires senate approval, tenure is granted, conditional on good behavior. Judges serve until age seventy and, upon meeting certain requirements, are eligible for pensions upon retirement. The judges are subject to impeachment or to disability retirement if incapacitated; and all judges, except supreme court justices, may be removed from office for such causes as misconduct in office, other conduct evidencing unfitness for judicial office, or incompetence.

Numerous constitutional provisions and state laws pertaining to the various judgeships are intended to provide for a qualified and competent judiciary having a large measure of political and economic independence. Once appointed, a judge is barred from partisan political activity, and members of the judge's family may engage only in limited political activity. State court judges must resign from the bench if they become candidates for public office, and they cannot hold any other employment. They are prohibited by the constitution from practicing law or engaging in any other "gainful pursuit," but they are assured that their salaries will not be reduced during their terms. All judges must be attorneys, and those in the state court system must also have been admitted to the New Jersey bar at least ten years prior to appointment.

While New Jersey, unlike many states, neither elects judges nor votes on reappointment of judges, avenues do exist for citizens to have a voice in the selection of judges and prosecutors.

A Judicial Appointments Committee has, since 1969, screened the qualifications of judicial and prosecutorial candidates, as a service to the governor. Under this system, names of possible appointees are sent to committees of both the New Jersey Bar Association and the bar association of the county involved. Although the findings of both committees are confidential, the state association has the right to comment if its committee's recommendations are not followed.

While the Judicial Appointments Committee only reacts

to names suggested by the governor, a six-member committee of the New Jersey Bar Association, formed in 1984, may recommend highly qualified people, specifically including women and minorities, to the governor for consideration. The need to appoint more women and minorities to the bench and as county prosecutors was highlighted in the 1983 report of the New Jersey Supreme Court's Task Force on Women in the Courts.

Both processes for helping the governor select highly qualified people for appointment to the bench and as prosecutors are, of course, only advisory, since the constitutional power to appoint judges and prosecutors rests solely with the governor, with the consent of the senate.

A pilot program operating at the present time evaluates judges once they are appointed. The program aims towards helping judges improve their skills from the beginning of their seven-year terms. The program, overseen by a supreme court committee, is built around evaluations by assignment judges and appellate judges, and by questionnaires filled out by members of the bar. The program has won national attention and is seen as a valuable model for other states.

The Advisory Committee on Judicial Conduct investigates charges of ethical impropriety against judges and makes recommendations to the chief justice for disciplinary action. The committee, composed of retired judges, lawyers, and three representatives from the general public, was formed in the mid-1970s. Since that time it has found a small number of judges "guilty of unethical conduct warranting the filing of a presentment with the Supreme Court"; most so charged have resigned, been publicly reprimanded, or been removed from the bench.

Judicial Policy

The supreme court has broad powers over the state's judicial system. It makes the rules governing the administration, practice, and procedures of all courts, including the municipal courts. Recommendations for new policy come from a broadly based system of standing committees and task forces reporting to the supreme court. Together, these permanent committees make up the Judicial Conference of New Jersey.

Membership on the committees includes not only members of the state judiciary but also municipal court judges and lay people. One such committee, the Child Placement Advisory Council, is made up of representatives from the volunteer Child Placement Review Boards, which operate in each county to review out-of-home placements of children and to make recommendations to the court on the appropriateness of those placements.

The standing committees continuously study areas such as civil practice, criminal practice, municipal courts, judicial opinions, judicial performance, and media relations. Task forces have been appointed from time to time to study, on a short-term basis, such issues as women in the courts, interpreter and translation services, and mental commitments. Members of the standing committees meet in convention once a year to review the recommendations of the committees. Usually one issue is the focus of attention for each meeting—for example, probation and family courts have been the main topics in recent years.

Recommendations made by the committees, if adopted by the supreme court, become the rules and procedures for the judiciary. Other recommendations that involve legislative changes are circulated to the appropriate legislative committees as suggestions for their consideration.

Administrative Office of the Courts

According to the constitution, "The Chief Justice of the Supreme Court shall be the administrative head of all the courts in the State. He shall appoint an Administrative Director to serve at his pleasure" (Article VI, Section VII).

The Administrative Office of the Courts was created as a management and control agency with a number of responsibilities:

- to assist the Chief Justice in assignment of judges,
- to attend to the financial arrangements of the courts,
- to supervise the clerks and support personnel,
- to conduct investigations concerning complaints against the courts,
- to assemble statistics concerning the operations of the judicial system.

The management abilities of the Administrative Office of the Courts have been challenged in recent years as high crime rates and new legal protections for defendants have caused an increase in criminal cases. Complicated new laws and regulations dealing with such matters as consumer and environmental protection have caused a jump in the number of civil cases as well. And automobile accidents continue to offer ample opportunity for thousands of negligence cases. The court Committee on Efficiency made recommendations to the Administrative Office of the Courts resulting in that office instituting a system of case management.

The case management system attempts to apply modern management techniques to an overburdened court system, thereby increasing its efficiency and effectiveness. Working under the direction of the judges, professional managers handle scheduling, paper work, supervision of record keeping and clerical staff, court volunteers, and so forth. Each year since its institution the case management system has helped the courts resolve more cases than were added to the docket—this is called "clearing the calendar."

In addition to the case management system, the courts established a Speedy Trial Coordinating Committee to reduce delays in criminal cases. Working with the State Police, representatives of local police, the municipal courts, and the academic community, this committee has streamlined the criminal justice system, initiated screening and diversion programs to reduce the number of cases coming to trial, and taken action to speed up those cases sent to trial.

A major breakthrough in increasing procedural speed and reducing personnel is expected to come from computerization of much of the scheduling and paper work for the court system. The program for computerization of the courts is expected to be implemented within the next decade. With a case load of over 700,000 cases for the state courts and 4.5 million cases for the municipal courts in the mid-1980s, the need to use modern technology to handle information and generate useful data is pressing. Because so many court cases are also cases for the Corrections Department, the Office of the Public Defender, the Department of the Public Advocate, and the Department of Human Services, linkages between the government departments for information sharing are being explored. The need to maintain security for this information has presented additional challenges in designing the system.

Following the lead of United States Chief Justice Warren E. Burger, who urged lawyers to look beyond the courtrooms and think in terms of mediation, arbitration, and conciliation, New Jersey has developed a number of creative alternatives to court action. (See figure 4.5.)

Probation

While probation, as an alternative to incarceration, could well be discussed as part of New Jersey's corrections program, administratively it is part of the judicial system. Traditionally the probation system has been county based and county financed in New Jersey. However, in light of the continuing unification of the court system, there is movement toward a more centralized approach. Performance standards for the twenty-one county probation offices are currently being developed, special probation projects are being funded and run by the state in conjunction with the county offices, and a statewide advisory council on probation has been formed with similar councils expected to be started on the county level. Increasingly, supervision of the probation offices is also coming under the state court system, with both superior court judges and court administrators having supervisory responsibilities for probation department functions.

The chief probation officer for each vicinage is appointed by the director of the Administrative Office of the Courts, on the recommendation of the assignment judge for that vicinage, with the approval of the chief justice. Upon the recommendation of the chief probation officer, the assignment judge appoints the probation officers, who must be college graduates. Movement is underway to raise the pay of these probation officers and to develop a career ladder, thus allowing experts in field work to advance without leaving for administrative posts.

Supervision of Offenders

Probation as an alternative to incarceration is based on the theory that society may be helped best by having certain offenders who are not convicted of violent crimes and who

Figure 4.5

Alternatives to Court Action

Non-binding arbitration as a means of resolving no-fault automobile accident disputes involving pain and suffering damages of less than $1,500 is called for in a 1983 law. The assignment judge appoints a lawyer to sit in judgement on these cases. If either party is not satisfied with the arbitration settlement, it can be appealed through the courts. (If even a small percentage of these automobile insurance cases are settled by arbitration, the savings in tax dollars and in caseload pressure on will be considerable.)

Out-of-court resolution for family conflicts is proposed in the legislation establishing the family part of the superior court.

Family crisis intervention teams will, when funded, take action in cases of juvenile-family crises. As 24-hour, on-call services, these units will focus on the family problems which led to the crisis. Only if the crisis continues, despite the services of the unit and appropriate community resources, will a petition be filed to bring the family before a judge. The goal is to keep as many family crises as possible out of the courtroom.

Juvenile conference committees (community-based volunteer boards composed of six to nine citizens) and intake officers serving the court will deal with juvenile delinquency complaints diverted to them by a judge. Any obligations imposed by a juvenile conference committee or an officer at an intake conference will be set forth in writing and will be enforced by the judge if the juvenile and the parents fail to comply with the agreement.

Judicial settlement conference checklists are a tool for narrowing down the issues in dispute in matrimonial (divorce and separation) cases. When economic issues are involved, the case may be referred to the local county bar association's Early Settlement Panel. Many custody cases are referred to a mediator. In cases in which all issues are resolved in these conferences, a consent agreement is drawn up, signed, and presented to the judge.

Municipal dispute resolution committees to deal with conflicts on the local level are recommended by the New Jersey Supreme Court's Committee on Alternative Dispute Resolution. The committee also recommends establishment of a mechanism for resolving more complex disputes out of court. Two of the committee's recommendations—arbitration of civil claims of less than $1,500 in damages and mediation of family disputes—are already being implemented.

Pre-trial intervention in criminal cases is a program aimed at keeping certain nonviolent offenders out of the court system. If the defendant is willing to enter the program and completes the prescribed education and/or work activities, the charges against him or her will be dropped.

The Office of Dispute Settlement in the Department of the Public Advocate uses mediation in resolving disputes over housing, local government, state agencies, and environmental matters. Under contract with the Department of Community Affairs, the office provides mediation and conciliation services for the New Home Warranty Program. Also the office maintains training programs in negotiation and mediation for agencies and interested citizens.

are not considered "hardened criminals" remain in the community under supervision. This is done by having the sentence to a correctional institution "suspended" in favor of probation.

The conditions of probation are set by the court and presented in writing to the offender. Since probation is aimed at helping the offender learn to live productively in the community, the terms of probation often include responsibilities such as supporting one's family, working or furthering one's education, receiving medical or psychological help, obtaining treatment for addiction to drugs or alcohol, maintaining residence in a prescribed area, and refraining from consorting with undesirables or known criminals or frequenting certain forbidden places. Often probation requires making restitution or reparation for the crime committed. Violation of these conditions of parole can result in revocation of the sentence suspension; the offender then is sent to a correctional institution.

Investigations

While the term "probation" refers to one function of the probation offices—the supervision of convicted criminals and of juveniles—another function is investigation. As disinterested professionals, probation officers conduct investigations for the judges. A pre-sentence investigation is made of every person who has entered a plea of guilty or been found guilty in a trial. The report, containing prior police records and social background, is submitted to and discussed with the judge before sentencing. The probation officers also make home and social investigations as directed by the family part judges and by other judges of the superior courts. Such investigations are mandatory in cases involving the custody of children.

Administration

The third major function of the probation office is enforcement and bookkeeping—collecting fines, restitution monies, and various support and alimony payments. Persons under court order for these obligations are required to make their payments to the probation office, which records them and sends them on to the appropriate parties. A person who falls behind in payments and disregards notices may be required to show cause why he or she should not be found guilty of contempt of the support order. A more business-oriented, computerized system of handling these monies is being instituted. In cooperation with the Department of Human Services and with funding from a federal grant, the probation section of the Administrative Office of the Courts has developed a single computerized system for handling child support payments and searching for those persons who are delinquent in meeting child support responsibilities. In addition, recent legislation has provided for automatic wage garnishment procedures to be included in divorce settlements.

Other Programs

A number of innovative programs are managed by the probation departments also. Volunteers in Probation offers counseling services to youthful and adult offenders. The Intensive Supervision Program handles offenders released from correctional institutions after a short period and places them under rigorous supervision by specially trained probation officers. Other programs, still in the pilot stage, involve rehabilitative services, such as education and recreation for various groups of juveniles in trouble with the law.

5.

Political Parties
and Elections

Political parties play an enormously important role in state and national government—a role far greater than simply nominating candidates for public office and campaigning to get them elected. Instead, political parties are an integral part of the process of government. Their role is defined in our state election laws and in the rules under which state government is organized.

New Jersey is a two-party state—a fact of great significance both to the parties themselves and to the citizens. Within New Jersey there are definite enclaves of party strength: Democratic strength is centered in Hudson, Essex, Mercer and Middlesex counties, while Republican power is most evident in Cape May and Ocean counties in the south and in Hunterdon and Morris counties in the north.

New Jersey functions as a "swing" state on the national political scene, giving evidence of its two strong political factions. From 1900 through 1984 Republican presidential candidates carried the state in fifteen contests and Democratic contenders in seven. While these statistics might imply a preference for the Republican party, they more probably indicate that New Jersey reflects national trends, since this state has voted on the winning side in all but three presidential elections in this century. Only New Jersey's own Woodrow Wilson in 1916, Harry Truman in 1948, and Jimmy Carter in 1976 won the presidency without carrying New Jersey.

Voting Patterns

An examination of the voting returns for candidates for the New Jersey legislature shows a curious picture: although the governor has more often been a Democrat than a Republican during this century, the state legislature has been overwhelmingly Republican—usually by two-to-one or three-to-one majorities. This is probably because representation in the state senate was determined on a county basis until 1966, that is, each county was entitled to one senator regardless of its population. This enabled the heavily Republican rural counties, with a small percentage of the state's population, to dominate the senate. The large Democratic pluralities in more urban counties, while important in statewide elections, had little effect in state senate races. The United States Supreme Court's "one person, one vote" decision forced reapportionment on the basis of population in 1966. (See chapter 1, Constitutional Issues.)

Thus, while New Jersey had clearly defined voting patterns in the past—rural Republicans dominating the senate and urban based Democratic political machines exerting strong influence on the assembly and the governor—these patterns no longer exist. (For listings of names and party affiliations of current and past elected representatives to congress and to the legislature see the current year's edition of the annual *Fitzgerald's Legislative Manual: State of New Jersey*.) The Democratic urban strongholds diminished in power with the passing of the political bosses and with shifts in population. The more educated children of the white middle class moved to the suburbs. The cities not only suffered from declining population, they became increasingly poor, and racial problems interfered with the harmonious workings of the city political organizations. Charter reforms led to changes in the power structure in a number of cities: Essex County, for example, changed to an elected county administrator who controls both budget and jobs, the traditional tools of the political bosses

With the movement of population to the suburbs came a more complicated political picture; suburban Democrats joined suburban Republicans. With the increasing mobility, family voting patterns and traditional approaches also weakened; voters became increasingly independent. By the 1970s polls repeatedly showed only about half of New Jersey voters considered themselves *either* Republicans or Demo-

crats. Those who did affiliate with a party were often more
interested in influencing party decisions and stands on issues than in receiving patronage jobs. All these factors play
a part in the increasingly unpredictable game of New
Jersey politics.

Political parties are the mechanism through which candidates are nominated, elections conducted, party policies
and platforms promulgated, political appointments made,
and, most importantly, through which the orderly change
of government following elections is accomplished.

> **Political Parties**

The primary function of the political parties is the selection and election of candidates at the local, county, state,
and national levels. Since nominees in primary elections
are for the most part selected or recommended by political
clubs and county committees, it is obvious that the support
of those who make these decisions is extremely important
for the potential candidate.

Political party membership in New Jersey operates on
two distinct levels. The great majority of people who belong
to a party are passive members, who declare their affiliation
in order to qualify for voting in primary elections. This is
the full extent to which most citizens take part in partisan
politics. It is estimated that only twenty out of every one
hundred registered voters participate in the primaries. Of
those twenty, fewer than five voting citizens participate in
what has been termed the "gladiatorial activities" of the
party—working for a party, joining a political club, and attending political meetings. It is these few party activists who
actually pick candidates, raise campaign funds, and run the
campaigns and elections. A major political party, according
to New Jersey election laws, is one that polled at least 10
percent of the total vote cast in the state in the most recent
general election held for all the members of the general assembly. Only the Democratic and Republican parties meet
these statutory requirements. Their nominees are entitled
to party lines on the ballot. It is easy, however, for a candidate of a minor political party or even an ambitious independent candidate to have his or her name placed on the
general election ballot by presenting a petition in keeping
with the statutory requirements.

Political Party Organization

The legal basis for New Jersey's political party system is out-lined in Title 19 of the New Jersey State Statutes. The law enumerates four levels of political party structure in the state—the district, the municipality, the county, and the entire state.

The grass-roots units are the election districts, small geographic areas specified by the county boards of elections to facilitate handling of elections within each county. An election district usually consists of three hundred to five hundred voters. The number of districts varies with population shifts, but totals around fifty-seven hundred throughout the state. Each election district annually elects one committee-man and one committeewoman to serve on a county committee. This county committee determines the units into which the county is to be divided for purposes of representation in the county committee. In general the election districts within the county are used as the basis of representation. In some counties each district may be an entire municipality. Thus it is possible for one municipality with a small population and another with a much larger population to have the same representation on the county committee. There may be variations not only from county to county but within a county between the two party structures. Recently both parties have been attempting to make this representation more equitable.

All the elected county committee members living in one particular municipality constitute a municipal committee. This committee meets on the first Monday following a primary election to elect a municipal chairman. The county committee in turn meets the first Tuesday following the primary election to elect a county chairman. The man or woman elected chairman need not be an elected member of that committee, only some suitable person. Often this chairman holds the post for several years; this powerful position, once achieved, is not lightly surrendered.

The County Chairman

The traditional focus of political strength in New Jersey was the county chairman. Until the 1966 constitutional convention reapportioning senate districts on the basis of

Figure 5.1

Major Political Party Organization

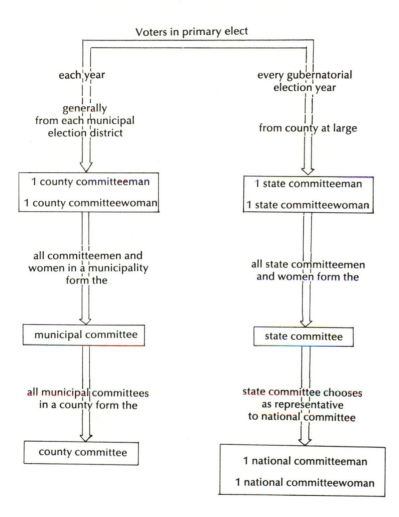

Voters in primary elect

each year

generally from each municipal election district

every gubernatorial election year

from county at large

| 1 county committeeman |
| 1 county committeewoman |

| 1 state committeeman |
| 1 state committeewoman |

all committeemen and women in a municipality form the

all state committeemen and women form the

| municipal committee |

| state committee |

all municipal committees in a county form the

state committee chooses as representative to national committee

| county committee |

| 1 national committeeman |
| 1 national committeewoman |

population and the 1972 New Jersey Supreme Court decision (*Scrimminger v. Sherwin*) mandating that state legislative districts be drawn without considering county boundaries, the county chairmen had considerable power not only within their counties but also in state politics. After this ruling, candidates for the legislature were no longer as dependent on county chairmen for nomination, financing, and volunteers for their campaigns. In multi-county districts, of which there are many, legislative candidates often choose to run independently of the county political organizations.

Within the county political realm, however, the county chairman still has considerable power. The county political organization is the vehicle for nominations to elected county offices. The county committee collects and provides funds for campaigns, organizes and directs campaigns, and staffs the polls with party election board members and party challengers. It works through municipal committees or political clubs (depending on the community), which maintain party cohesion, stimulate registration, get out the vote, and maintain contact with voters.

The county chairmen also have considerable influence over patronage. They are consulted on virtually all appointments from their counties, including those made by the governor with the approval of the senate. Posts ranging from state board and commission members, from judges to assistant county attorneys, are within the domain of the county chairmen.

Patronage dispensed by the county chairmen is not limited to political appointments: jobs; contracts for goods, services, and construction; personal favors such as arranging for admission to state institutions or expediting the usual requirements for local or county services—all are within the power of the county chairmen.

The State Committees

State committee members for each party are elected for four-year terms in the primary election in which candidates are nominated for governor. The Republican State Committee consists of one woman and one man from each county. The Democratic State Committee makeup provides for no fewer than two and no more than nine members from each county, the number reflecting county population. These state committees have a number of duties.

They select from their committee one national committeeman and one national committeewoman to serve on the national party committee. The state committee selects party nominees for governor, United States senator, and, in certain circumstances, for congressional districts. The state committee also calls the state party convention.

State Party Conventions

According to New Jersey law, state party conventions are to be held in the years in which all members of the general assembly are elected, i.e., in odd-numbered years, and are held in Trenton the week after the primary election. The law defines the delegates: all party nominees for national and state office, all party members incumbent in those offices, members of the state committee, New Jersey members of the national committee, and the county chairmen. There are no elected delegates.

Because candidates are chosen in the primary elections, the state conventions are concerned only with drafting and adopting the party platform. After the introduction of all proposed planks, the convention adjourns to reconvene not later than ninety days after the initial adjournment. Meanwhile, the resolutions committee prepares a tentative platform and furnishes a copy to each member of the convention. The convention then reassembles to vote on the adoption of the platform.

Campaign financing at all levels of government is an ever-increasing problem intensified by steeply rising costs and the use of lavish and sophisticated campaign techniques. Candidates in statewide elections, specifically gubernatorial and congressional candidates, have an especially costly job of reaching the voters. The state is served primarily by both New York City and Philadelphia network television, which give little regular coverage to New Jersey news. Only WOR-TV and New Jersey Network (see chapter 9, The New Jersey Broadcasting Authority) make an effort to offer

Campaign Financing

New Jersey Campaign Contributions and Expenditures Reporting Act

Figure 5.2

Contributions in excess of $100 must be reported, including the name and address of the contributor along with the date of receipt and the amount of the contribution.

Contributions in cash above $100 are prohibited, thus removing one area susceptible to abuse.

Political action committees (PACs) and other continuing political committees, including state, county, and municipal party committees, must file quarterly reports instead of annual reports and election campaign reports.

Campaign treasurers and continuing political committees must, within forty-eight hours, disclose contributions greater than $250, if they are received in the last days of the campaign, after the last pre-election report or quarterly report has been filed.

Joint campaign committees spending less than $4000 and single candidates spending less than $2000 (local candidates usually) have a much simplified reporting procedure.

statewide coverage, yet they are seen only in part of the state or require cable access. As a result voters are often unfamiliar with both the faces and the issues involved in New Jersey elections. The candidates must remedy this by purchasing radio and television time in two of the nation's most expensive media markets.

Both major political parties have made attempts to broaden the base of their financial support. Most campaign funds are raised by the political organization through solicitation of its membership, elected and appointed public officeholders, persons having government contracts, labor unions, business corporations, political action committees, and wealthy individuals. (See chapter 3, Lobbyists and Campaign Financing.)

The New Jersey Campaign Contributions and Expenditures Reporting Act

In 1973, at the height of public concern over the abuses of campaign finance monies revealed by the Watergate scandal, New Jersey passed a tough and comprehensive campaign finance disclosure law. In 1984 the act was amended to reflect the experience gained since passage of the original law. (See figure 5.2.)

Enforcement of the New Jersey Campaign Contributions and Expenditures Reporting Act is the task of the New Jersey Election Law Enforcement Commission. This body consists of four members appointed by the governor for three-year terms. They receive per diem payments for meetings rather than salary. A professional staff assists the commission. The 1984 amendments incorporated many of the commission's recommendations.

Public Financing of Gubernatorial Primary and General Elections

Amendments to the Campaign Contributions Law also established a system of partial public funding of the gubernatorial primary and general election campaigns. The stated purpose of the legislation is to provide adequate funds so that candidates "may conduct their campaigns free from improper influence, and so that persons of limited financial means may seek election to the state's highest office."

Public financing was first used at the federal level in the 1976 presidential campaigns. New Jersey followed suit in 1977 and was the first state to conduct a gubernatorial campaign with public funds. As in the federal system, New Jersey taxpayers may check off funds for gubernatorial campaign financing when they file their state income tax returns. The funds received in this manner are supplemented with money from the general fund.

Under the New Jersey system gubernatorial candidates who choose to receive public funding must also limit their campaign expenditures to a certain amount per vote cast in the last presidential election. The spending limit is smaller for the primary election—greater for the general election. No spending limits are imposed on candidates who do not choose to receive public financing. Matching funds from public money are provided after the qualified candidate has raised a certain amount in contributions. Amendments to the Campaign Contributions and Expenditures Reporting Act have changed the amount of the spending limits and the matching funds several times.

While there are generally no restrictions on how a candidate may spend funds raised from contributors, the public matching funds may only be used for media advertising, printing and mailing campaign literature, telephone bills, and the legal and accounting costs of complying with the public financing law. In addition to direct financial assistance, the legislation also provides for free broadcast time on the stations of the New Jersey Public Broadcasting Authority for gubernatorial candidates.

Election Procedures

Qualifications for voting in New Jersey are a matter of citizenship, age, residence, mental competency, and registration. Since its beginnings as a colony in 1664, New Jersey has bestowed the franchise more liberally than many other states. Literacy was never a requirement for voting, and voters were never excluded on religious grounds, although an oath was sometimes prescribed. Property ownership, once a common prerequisite for voting in early United States history, was completely abolished in New Jersey in 1844 as a voting qualification. Moreover, voting laws were often so loosely worded and enforced that at times slaves, free Negroes, non-property holders, aliens, minors, convicts, and non-residents were able to vote. This last category might even include the dead; according to newspaper columnist Art Buchwald, this practice has not disappeared from the American scene. Speaking of a certain county (not in New Jersey) he says, "Tradition has it that even after you die you don't lose your right to vote." Charges were made in one New Jersey county following the 1968 general election that vacant lots and boarded-up buildings had produced some voters.

Women were allowed to vote in New Jersey under laws passed in 1790 and 1797, but that right was taken away from them in 1807 after a wildly fraudulent election. The franchise was permanently extended to Negroes in 1870 and to women in 1920.

Nomination for Public Office

Nominations for partisan public office are made by petition, signed only by qualified voters who are members of the same political party as the nominee. Signers must assert that in the last general election they voted for a majority of the candidates of that political party and that they intend to affiliate with the same party at the ensuing election. The minimum number of signers needed varies from twenty-five to one thousand, depending largely on the particular office sought. Petitions must be filed by the fortieth day preceding the primary election with the secretary of state, the county clerk, or the municipal clerk, again depending on the office sought. There is no filing fee.

Requirements for independent candidates, i.e., candidates for a public office who do not want to run as Democrats or Republicans, are somewhat different. For example, the signers' party affiliations are immaterial and fewer signatures are required. Independent candidates file their petitions at the same time and place as other candidates, but their names do not appear on the ballot until November, since they are not involved in the primary election.

Candidates who run for municipal office in nonpartisan elections also follow somewhat different procedures. They must file petitions signed by registered voters of the community, the required number of signatures ranging from ten to a percentage of the total number registered. Filing dates vary depending on the office involved.

Nomination for Party Office

Petitions are also used to nominate candidates for party office; the signers must not be members of the other party. Three types of party posts are filled by the voters in a primary: county committeeman and committeewoman, elected yearly; state committeeman and committeewoman, elected in gubernatorial election years; and delegates and alternates to the parties' national nominating conventions, elected in presidential election years. The number of necessary signatures ranges down to ten for county committeepersons, but the filing requirements are the same as those for public office. The primary election is the only election at which party officials run and may be elected.

Role of the Political Parties in the Election Process

In New Jersey primary and general elections are run by the two major parties. The county and district boards of elections—whose members (two from each party) are selected by the county chairmen of the two parties—supervise every detail of both primary and general elections, from registration through the counting of the ballots. Order is maintained at the polling places by these party officials, and challengers named by each candidate may be present to check possible violations by voters of the opposite party. The proponents and opponents of public questions may have challengers as well.

Predictably, there are sometimes efforts by each party to weigh the balance in its favor. The opportunity to do this often seems to be grasped at the crucial drawing for ballot position. Although the election laws stipulate methods designed to insure a fair draw, it has become a matter of some fascination to note that in certain counties the party currently in power is able to confound the laws of chance and draw the desired Row A position year after year. The county clerk (or municipal clerk in appropriate cases) draws lots from a closed box that, according to law, is to be "turned over to thoroughly intermingle the cards." In some counties compliance with the law has been met by turning the box laterally in such a way that the cards remained in the position in which they were placed at the outset, making it a simple matter to draw out the name of the "right" party. Occasionally, the party in power has been so confident of the outcome of the draw that they printed "Row A all the way" campaign posters even before the selection took place.

Primary Election

A primary, so called because it is the first election, the second being the general election, is a party election. Prior to the adoption of New Jersey's direct primary laws in 1903 and 1911, the selection of party candidates and officials was solely within the control of the parties themselves. But election scandals then rocking the state pointed up the corrupting power of the political machines. In response the primary was devised as a means of giving the voters direct control of the parties.

New Jersey has a "closed" primary in which a voter must declare his political affiliation in advance of election day and then can vote only for candidates from the party of his declared choice. The voting machine is locked for each voter in such a way that he cannot vote for candidates of the opposing party.

Registered voters may qualify to vote in the party primary elections several ways. The first is to declare one's party preference (Republican, Democrat, or Independent) in writing at the time of registration. One's name on the voter roll then has an "R," "D," or "I" next to it. Voters who have not declared a party affiliation and have not voted in a previous primary may declare their affiliation at the polling place at the time of the primary. After that, their names will be identified by the letter of the party declared.

To change party affiliation or to change from declared independence to party affiliation, the registered voter must file the appropriate form with the municipal clerk or commissioner of registration at least fifty days before the primary. How a person votes in a primary has no binding effect on how that person may vote in a general election.

How to Register

Figure 5.3

1. In person: Voters may register at a county board of elections or municipal clerk's office by signing (or making a mark upon) a registration form.

2. By mail: Mail registration forms are available from the commissioner of registration, the municipal clerk, or the League of Women Voters. These forms must be returned by the twenty-ninth day preceding the election.

3. Timing: Voters may register in person at any time of the year during the appropriate registrar's office hours or by mail up to and including the twenty-ninth day prior to any election. Registration of voters is accepted during the twenty-eight days prior to an election, but the registered voter may not vote in that election. Voters do not join a party when they register in New Jersey, although they may, at that time, declare a party affiliation.

110

The primary election is actually two types of election at one time; it results in both the election to office of party officials and the nomination of party candidates for public office. A primary victory gives the successful nominee the right to enter the general election as the official party candidate, that is, the regular organization candidate. A defeated primary candidate may not run in the general election.

Primary elections for state and local offices may or may not offer the voter a choice. If party differences are resolved and a party slate is agreed upon, a single slate of candidates is presented on the ballot. However, if there is disagreement within the party that cannot be resolved, the dissidents may withdraw and form their own slate of candidates, often under the "reform" Democratic or Republican label. Voters then have a choice. There is no single lever to vote a straight party line in these elections.

Primaries for statewide office—the governor and United States senators—have become an important means of selecting candidates. Since the decline of the county chairmen's political powers, the roles once played by political parties are now being filled by political consultants, media specialists, public financing, and funding from political action committees (PACs).

The National Primary Election

Every four years New Jerseyans also vote in a presidential primary, traditionally in June. There are two parts to the contest. First, in a "beauty contest," voters indicate the candidate they prefer as the presidential nominee of their party. The second, and decisive part, is the choice of delegates to the party's national convention. They are chosen from eighty districts (two in each assembly district). The delegate slate receiving the most votes in each district is elected on a "winner-take-all" basis. Then those elected choose additional statewide delegates. In 1984 the New Jersey primary was critical in Walter Mondale's winning of the Democratic presidential nomination.

The Elections Division in the Office of the Secretary of State is responsible for orderly elections in the state. It operates through assistance to local and county elections offices.

A Guide to New Jersey Elections

The division also records petitions and other documentation for office seekers, certifies election results, encourages voter registration, and advises on election laws.

Registration

Registration is required in order to vote in New Jersey. To register, prospective voters must be citizens of the United States, eighteen years old or older by the time of the next election, residing in the district in which they intend to vote, and residents of their county for thirty days by the time of the next election. No "idiot" (the election laws are very old and include some archaic language) or insane person is eligible to vote, nor are persons convicted of certain crimes. Registration is permanent unless a voter fails to vote in any election for four consecutive years, moves out of the county, changes his or her name (by marriage, divorce, or court decree), or is convicted of a disqualifying crime.

Responsibility for voter registration lies with the county commissioner of registration, a post filled by the superintendent of elections in counties having that office (it is mandatory in first-class counties and permissive in certain other counties) and by the secretary of the county board of elections in all other counties. The commissioner must submit to the secretary of state, by mid-February, a plan for evening registration prior to the primary election and, by July first, plans for evening and out-of-office registration for the general election. Plans for out-of-office registration may include door-to-door or mobile registration. Notices of sites and times must be published in a locally circulated newspaper within seven days of the registration date. The commissioner of registration in all counties is required to arrange for and conduct registration in each public and private high school in the county each year during the month of March. School officials are required to cooperate in such efforts to register their students.

Registration practices vary from county to county because some election laws are permissive, and the authority for administration lies at the county level. Thus registration of voters can be encouraged or hampered, depending upon the decisions of the county board of elections.

Election Machinery

The actual election at the polling place is conducted by the district board of elections, which is, in turn, supervised by the county board of elections.

The *county board of elections* is composed of four voters, two from each political party, appointed for two-year terms by the governor, who selects from lists provided by the county chairmen of both parties. In March of each year the board organizes and elects a chairman and a secretary, who shall not be members of the same political party. The board sets up the machinery for voting, is responsible for the administration of the elections, and has authority to settle controversial questions connected with elections.

The *district board of elections* is composed of four members (two Democrats and two Republicans) appointed for one-year terms by the county board of elections upon recommendation of the county committee members. Any voter residing in a county, who has voted for two consecutive years in the same party, is eligible to serve on a district board of elections and may make written application to the county board of elections to do so. District board members need not live in the districts to which they are assigned.

The board of education appoints election workers to supervise school board elections held in each school voting district.

Election Calendar

General elections are held the first Tuesday after the first Monday in November. These are open elections for all declared candidates for national, state, county, and some local public offices.

Primary elections are held the first Tuesday after the first Monday in June, although this date has been frequently moved by law. These elections allow voters to nominate party candidates for the general election, to elect county committee members from their respective election districts, to elect state committee members in gubernatorial years, and to elect delegates and alternates to the national conventions in presidential years.

Municipal elections are held with the general election, except in municipalities with a nonpartisan form of government. In these communities the municipal elections are held on the second Tuesday in May. If necessary in municipal elections, a run-off election for each office is held five weeks later among the 50 percent of the candidates receiving the highest number of votes.

Special elections are held for certain types of referendums when and as required.

School elections are held the first Tuesday in April; regional and local school elections are held at the same time. These school elections are to approve proposed budgets and to elect non-partisan boards of education.

Ballots

Sample ballots, which also include polling places and voting hours, are mailed to all registered voters before the primary and general elections. A sample ballot is also displayed at the polling place on election day.

Special sample ballots must be printed in English and Spanish in election districts where 10 percent of the registered voters are primarily Spanish-speaking. In those districts two additional members of Hispanic origin, fluent in Spanish, must also be appointed to the district board of elections.

Absentee ballots may be applied for by those registered voters who cannot be at the polls on election day because of travel, illness, religious observance, school, or work. Absentee voters must apply for their ballots no later than seven days prior to the election. A voter who fails to meet this deadline may vote "absentee" in person at the county clerk's office until three P.M. the day before the election.

A qualified voter who is bedridden may send a messenger to the county clerk's office to obtain and return an absentee ballot. The messenger's name must appear above that of the voter.

The absentee ballot contains a check-off box for permanent application for the permanently disabled. Upon such notice the county clerk enters the name on a list and that voter is automatically sent an application for an absentee ballot.

Military service ballots may be requested by the following persons who are qualified to vote, whether they are registered or not:

■ persons in the military service, their spouses and dependents;

■ patients in veterans' hospitals;

■ civilians attached to or serving with the armed forces out of the state and the spouses and dependents of these civilians.

Emergency voting forms may be obtained from the commissioner of registration by the above listed persons connected with the military if they have been released too late to register within the twenty-nine days prior to an election. If not previously registered, they may register at the time they apply for the emergency voting forms.

Citizen Participation

Democracy, it has been said, is the most difficult form of government because it requires active participation on the part of its citizens. Historically, there has been a great reluctance on the part of most citizens to become involved in political activity. The work of selecting candidates, financing campaigns, and conducting the business of government at every level has been left to the few. Even registration and voting, the minimal forms of participation in the rites of democracy, are not exercised by a sizeable number of the voting-age population.

For those who disapprove of a party's choices there is always a remedy. They may join the local organization of the party of their choice and use their influence there—where it counts the most—in picking candidates and deciding party policy. Membership is open to any citizen eligible to vote. If there is no political club of the party of a voter's choice, then he or she may join with a group of interested citizens to organize one. A voter may even choose to run for party or public office.

6.

Finances

In today's complex society, governments at all levels have come to assume a wide range of responsibilities. The state government in New Jersey, in addition to giving aid to local units of government and school districts, is concerned with human services, education, transportation, environmental protection, urban affairs, and many other aspects of daily life. The cost of meeting these responsibilities is figured in billions of dollars.

New Jersey raises money for operating the government through collecting taxes, licenses and other fees, and through lottery ticket sales. Revenue from these sources is allotted by the legislature, in the annual general appropriations bill, to the various government departments and agencies.

Long-term projects such as capital spending on roads, buildings, and state facilities may be financed through the sale of bonds. Issuance of these government backed bonds must be authorized by the voters in a referendum. The bonds are then offered for sale, and the revenues are placed in a special fund to be used only for the purposes authorized by the voters.

An alternative way of funding capital spending is through the creation of authorities. An authority is an independent public corporation set up for one purpose or several closely related purposes, such as the construction and/or operation of a turnpike, an airport, or a seaport.

The federal government is another major source of funds for the operation of state government. Federal aid, given either in the form of grants or as "matching funds" to be used in conjunction with money put up by the state, reached its zenith in the late seventies and has declined sharply in some areas since the Budget Reconciliation Act of 1981.

The rise and fall of federal funds is not the only major change in the New Jersey government's financial picture in the last two decades. The creation of new sources of revenue includes the general sales tax, the state lottery, the state income tax, and approval of casino gambling in Atlantic City. Together these make up well over half of the annual revenue budget.

The Annual Budget

The New Jersey budget is a balanced listing of estimated revenues (income) and proposed expenditures for a given fiscal year. In New Jersey the fiscal year runs from July first of the calendar year through June thirtieth of the following year.

Limitations

The New Jersey Constitution places certain limitations on the budget-making process. The budget must be balanced—the legislature cannot make appropriations in any fiscal year in excess of the total amount of revenue on hand and certified by the governor. The constitution further prohibits borrowing to meet more than one percent of the annual budget unless that debt is submitted to the people for approval and the revenue raised is applied to the specific use stated in the referendum.

The budget is also limited by constitutional amendments that have established special-use funds for specific sources of revenue. This is true for revenues from the lottery, from the income tax, and from taxes on casino gambling in Atlantic City. Despite these dedicated funds, the bulk of state revenues is still assigned to the general fund and may be appropriated at the legislature's discretion. The general fund budget combined with the special-use fund budgets makes up the annual budget.

The Executive Branch's Budget Proposal

While the constitution assigns the task of passing a general appropriations law each fiscal year to the legislature, the governor is reponsible for proposing an annual budget. By

Figure 6.1

The New Jersey Budget
Appropriations for 1985–1986
All State Funds (in thousands)

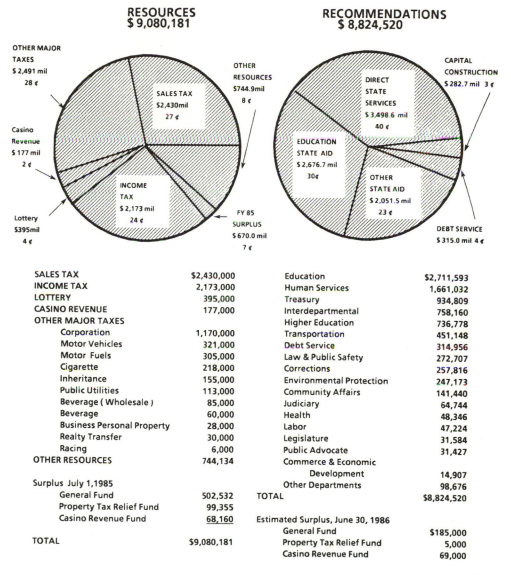

RESOURCES
$ 9,080,181

RECOMMENDATIONS
$ 8,824,520

SALES TAX	$2,430,000		Education	$2,711,593
INCOME TAX	2,173,000		Human Services	1,661,032
LOTTERY	395,000		Treasury	934,809
CASINO REVENUE	177,000		Interdepartmental	758,160
OTHER MAJOR TAXES			Higher Education	736,778
Corporation	1,170,000		Transportation	451,148
Motor Vehicles	321,000		Debt Service	314,956
Motor Fuels	305,000		Law & Public Safety	272,707
Cigarette	218,000		Corrections	257,816
Inheritance	155,000		Environmental Protection	247,173
Public Utilities	113,000		Community Affairs	141,440
Beverage (Wholesale)	85,000		Judiciary	64,744
Beverage	60,000		Health	48,346
Business Personal Property	28,000		Labor	47,224
Realty Transfer	30,000		Legislature	31,584
Racing	6,000		Public Advocate	31,427
OTHER RESOURCES	744,134		Commerce & Economic	
			Development	14,907
Surplus July 1,1985			Other Departments	98,676
General Fund	502,532		TOTAL	$8,824,520
Property Tax Relief Fund	99,355			
Casino Revenue Fund	68,160		Estimated Surplus, June 30, 1986	
			General Fund	$185,000
TOTAL	$9,080,181		Property Tax Relief Fund	5,000
			Casino Revenue Fund	69,000

statute the governor must present the budget to the legislature before the third Tuesday after the first meeting of the legislature each year; the budget message is generally presented during the last week of January and is accompanied by a comprehensive bound document detailing the proposed budget.

Long-range planning is an important prelude to the budget process. The budgetmakers take into account not only current estimated revenues, but also projections for revenues in a long-range context. These include such factors as intergovernmental, technological, and social trends —projections of federal aid, plans for computerizing various government functions, and future social needs, for example. The various departments work with the budget strategists to develop their long-range plans and their annual spending projections. The final document reflects not only these factors, but also the priorities for state services established by the governor.

The Legislature's Role

The legislature, in fulfilling its constitutional responsibility to pass a general appropriations law by the beginning of the new fiscal year, considers the governor's budget proposal. The process starts with scrutiny of every aspect of the proposed budget by the Joint Appropriations Committee aided by the fiscal affairs experts from the Office of Legislative Services. The committee holds public hearings so testimony by representatives of the administrative departments and by interested citizens may be presented. Any budget changes must be made by a majority vote of the committee. The budget bill then moves to the floor of the senate and the assembly where legislators, depending on their own priorities, increase some appropriations and cut others, while keeping in mind the need for the governor's signature for the budget bill to become law. The process of legislative budget review culminates in passage of a general appropriations bill.

The bill then goes to the governor for consideration. The governor may use a line-item veto (see figure 3.5), reducing or eliminating various line items in the appropriations bill. The legislature may override a line-item veto by a two-thirds majority vote in each house. Otherwise the bill becomes law without those items so vetoed. A balanced budget must be approved and signed by the governor by July first, the start of the new fiscal year.

The New Jersey Constitution requires that all monies for the support of the state government "as far as can be ascertained or reasonably foreseen" (Article VIII, Section II) be appropriated in a single bill for each fiscal year. While exercising all reasonable foresight in passing a balanced budget, the legislature usually finds it necessary to pass a supplemental appropriations bill covering unforeseen expenses sometime during the year.

The courts are not involved in the budget process except when they rule on the constitutionality of legislation. A notable example of court involvement occurred in the 1970s when the New Jersey Supreme Court ruled the current means of financing public education was unconstitutional. (See chapter 1, Constitutional Issues.)

Various Funds within the Annual Budget

While the 1947 constitution provided for only one general appropriations bill, which was interpreted to mean all revenues would go into one general fund, constitutional amendments and the legislature itself have established several other funds dedicated to specific expenditures.

The major funds are the General Fund, the Property Tax Relief Fund, the Casino Revenue Fund, and the Casino Control Fund. (See figure 6.2). Receipts from the state lottery, while constitutionally dedicated to education and institutions, are contained in the general fund.

The state treasurer also maintains smaller special purpose dedicated and trust funds, which are not available for general state use. Some receive monies from the sale of bonds; others, such as the Unemployment Compensation Tax Fund and the Disability Benefit Fund, are essentially insurance funds. They receive payments from payroll taxes and use the funds to pay off claims as they arise.

One of the oldest dedicated funds, the School Fund, dates back to 1903 when New Jersey first assumed responsibility for free public education. As reconfirmed in the 1947 constitution, the School Fund is the depository for proceeds

Figure 6.2

Major Funds Included in the Proposed Budget for Fiscal Year 1984–1985

General fund. Most revenues and expenditures flow through this fund. It also contains the state lottery revenues which are designated for aid to education and state institutions. There are four sections of the general fund:

Direct state services. These are funds for the administrative departments and for state-run programs and services, in addition to the operating expenses of the legislature, the judiciary, and the office of the governor.

State aid. These are appropriations from the general fund that deliver revenues to other New Jersey governmental units including school districts, counties, municipalities, and the Hackensack Meadowlands Commission. The largest amount of state aid goes to education, followed by human services and community development programs.

Capital construction. Funds for minor construction projects, renovation, and equipment for state facilities are included here. More expensive projects are funded through bonding and authorities.

Debt service. Payments on the principal and interest due on the state's outstanding debt from bond issues are made from this fund.

Property tax relief fund. Revenues from the state income tax are used to reduce or offset local property taxes.

Casino revenue fund. A tax on gross casino revenues is dedicated to property tax reductions and various services, especially health and transportation, for eligible senior and disabled New Jersey citizens.

Casino control fund. License fees from casinos fund regulation of the industry.

Note: Transportation trust fund. Dedication of 2½ cents of the existing 8 cents-a-gallon state gasoline tax to be spent exclusively on transportation through the remainder of this century was approved by the voters in November 1984.

from sales and rents of riparian lands (lands on the banks of tidal waters).

Other separate funds receive monies from unclaimed bank deposits, life insurance, and other personal property that has no known owners (usually because the owner dies without heirs). These escheat (revert) to the state after a length of time prescribed by law. From time to time transfers are made from these funds to the state general fund.

Dedication of Revenue

Dedication of taxes, especially the earmarking of highway-user taxes for the construction and maintenance of highways, is the custom in many states. Although many cogent arguments are advanced by the proponents of dedicated taxes—chiefly for transportation and school use—most authorities on state administration feel the practice of constitutional dedication of revenue and the establishment of separate funds and budgets for those revenues (as opposed to legislative earmarking of revenues maintained in the general fund) is unwise. Since needs cannot always be determined in advance and since revenue yields fluctuate, the efficiency of overall fiscal management is hampered by the existence of constitutionally dedicated funds; and, in any case, it is seldom that the revenue from a given source exactly matches the purpose for which it is dedicated. Despite these problems, the legislature and the voters have shown, in the last decade, an increasing willingness to approve dedication of revenues.

State Revenues

The tax structure of New Jersey shows the influence of the state's history. Colonial New Jersey was primarily an agricultural region, in which the most important form of wealth was land. A tax of half a penny per acre for the support of the colonial government was the earliest tax, imposed on its citizens in 1670. Personal property became subject to taxation in 1716. The colonial assembly soon delegated part of its taxing power to the counties and later to the towns, which taxed property for their own support. Thus the tradition of home rule in New Jersey—the emphasis on the assessment and collection of local taxes to be spent locally—began early and remains a dominant factor in its political climate today.

Public education, as a responsibility of the local governments, was instituted in New Jersey in the early nineteenth century. The state government gradually withdrew from the taxing of property, leaving the revenue to the local taxing districts, whose expenses were greatly increased by the necessity of supporting the schools.

The gap in the revenue at the state level was filled by taxes paid by the newly established railroads; the first railroad in the state—the Camden and Amboy—was chartered in 1830. The taxes levied on railroads produced so much revenue that in some years in the mid-nineteenth century the entire budget was met by railroad taxes alone. The existence of such an ample source of funds meant that for many years there was no need to impose broad-based general taxes at the state level, and it became a tradition in New Jersey that state taxes should be as few as possible, and those that were levied should be chiefly of the excise or special-purpose type.

The heyday of the railroads had passed by the early twentieth century, and the taxes they paid, which by this time were being shared with the municipalities, were no longer adequate to meet the increasing needs of an expanded state government. Even so, the slogan "no new taxes" for years remained part of every political campaign in New Jersey.

A sales tax, briefly instituted in 1935, aroused so much antagonism that it was repealed only a few months later. Other attempts to impose a broad-based tax were consistently defeated by the legislature until the needs of the state became so pressing that the present sales tax was successfully instituted in 1966. Voters approved a constitutional amendment permitting a state lottery in 1969 and casino gambling in Atlantic City in 1976. Also in 1976 the legislature, forced to comply with a New Jersey Supreme Court order to find a more equitable way to fund public education, finally enacted an income tax. Thus New Jersey, in a period of ten years, instituted major new sources of revenue: the broad-based sales and income taxes and the lottery and casino gambling revenues raised from those who choose to participate. Governor Kean has appointed the State and Lo-

cal Expenditure and Revenue Policy Commission composed of 32 members including government officials, legislators, and representatives of citizens groups to study state
and local finances and make a report of their findings and
recommendations by January of 1986.

Gross Personal Income Tax

Since 1976 New Jersey has had a state income tax. The revenues from this tax are dedicated exclusively to reducing or
offsetting property taxes. Monies generated are deposited directly into the Property Tax Relief Fund. From this fund
come grants to the counties, municipalities, and school districts. In addition, direct payments of homestead tax rebates
are made to homeowners to offset a small part of their property tax bill. The loss to municipalities for property tax exemptions granted veterans, their spouses, senior and disabled citizens, are also reimbursed by grants from this fund.

The New Jersey personal income tax is a gross income
tax on individuals, estates, and trusts. In computing the tax
return, very few deductions are allowed. The income tax
was increased in 1982 to raise additional revenue.

Sales and Use Tax

Initiated in 1966, New Jersey's sales and use tax brings in
revenue roughly equal to that of the personal income tax.
Together, the sales and income taxes contribute about 50
percent of the state's annual revenue. Unlike the income
tax, the sales tax goes into the general fund and can be appropriated for any purpose designated by the legislature.
Twice the sales tax has been increased to raise additional revenue.

Clothing, food, paper products, over-the-counter drugs,
fuel oil, and other specified items were all made exempt
from the sales tax in an effort to reduce the effect of this tax
on low-income citizens.

Corporation Business Taxes

New Jersey levies a flat rate corporate income tax on all
corporations conducting business in New Jersey. The tax
is levied on net earnings—the corporation's revenues
less expenses.

Public Utilities Gross Receipt Tax

Public utilities (telephone and telegraph, water, sewer, gas, and electric) are exempt both from corporation business taxes and from local property taxes on their equipment. Instead utilities pay a franchise and gross receipts excise tax. Part of the tax is distributed to municipalities on a per capita basis; the remainder is usually distributed to economically distressed communities.

Realty Transfer Tax

Recording of deeds that transfer title to real property in New Jersey is subject to the Realty Transfer Fee Tax. The proceeds are shared between the county where it is collected and the state.

Other Major Taxes

■ Cigarettes and alcoholic beverages are exempt from the general sales tax but are subject to selective sales taxes called excise taxes.

■ Gasoline, diesel, and other motor fuels are taxed at a set rate per gallon.

■ Motor vehicle license and registration fees are another important source of revenue.

■ Inheritances of five hundred dollars or more from a New Jersey resident's estate and inheritance of New Jersey property worth five hundred dollars or more are subject to taxation. The amount is based on the size of the inheritance and the beneficiary's relationship to the deceased. There are many exclusions and exemptions to this law, and it is currently being gradually phased out. It is believed that such a law encourages New Jersey residents to move after retirement to states with lower or no estate taxes.

Gaming Revenues

With passage of constitutional amendments approving a state lottery in 1969 and casino gambling in Atlantic City in 1976, gaming revenues have increased dramatically as a source of income for New Jersey government. Pari-mutuel betting on thoroughbred and harness races is a third source of gaming revenue.

State Lottery. A constitutional amendment approved the state lottery and dedicated the revenues to education and state institutions. The lottery is the largest source of gaming revenues for New Jersey and is administered by the Division of the State Lottery in the Treasury Department. A State Lottery Commission advises the director of the division.

Casino Gambling. Income from a tax on the gross revenue from the casinos in Atlantic City goes into a separate fund to be used for reductions of property tax and utility charges and for expanded health and transportation services for senior and disabled citizens. Additional uses of these revenues must be approved by the voters in the form of a constitutional amendment. Casino gambling is regulated by the New Jersey Casino Control Commission located within the Treasury Department. (See chapter 14, Regulation of Gambling and Gaming Activities for a discussion of enforcement of gaming laws.)

Pari-Mutuel Betting. The state receives a percentage of the pari-mutuel betting pool at the racetracks. Revenue also comes from license fees and fines. All horse races conducted in New Jersey are regulated by the New Jersey Racing Commission, a division of the Department of Law and Public Safety. (See chapter 14, The New Jersey Racing Commission.)

Other Revenues

In addition to these major sources of revenue, the state derives funds from a large number of minor taxes, payments collected by various departments, and user fees. Tuition at state colleges, patient fees at state institutions, and fees paid for use of state recreation facilities are all user fees. Another source of income is interest on the investment of bond funds.

Surplus

A surplus, beyond that included in each budget as a reserve fund in case revenues are lower than normal, can come about either because expenditures were lower than appropriated or because revenues were unexpectedly high, or both. It is customary for the Joint Appropriations Committee to recommend that any remaining surplus for one year be applied to the next year's budget; in years when the surplus is large, it becomes, in effect, an additional source of revenue. (For a concise and current detailing of the method of collection, the rates, and the revenues of each of the major New Jersey taxes, see the current year's edition of the annual *Fitzgerald's Legislative Manual: State of New Jersey* under the Treasury Department heading.)

Long-Term Capital Financing

While the annual budget and the major revenue sources discussed in the preceding pages deal with the annual operating expenses of the New Jersey government, capital spending for roads, buildings, state facilities, recreational and conservation land acquisitions, to name a few, are often financed through long-term bonded indebtedness.

Commission on Capital Budgeting and Planning

In 1975 the Commission on Capital Budgeting and Planning was created to coordinate the long-range planning and the budgeting process for New Jersey's capital needs. The commission is a twelve-member bipartisan group consisting of four legislators, four citizens, and four representatives from the executive branch. The commission is responsible for the annual preparation of a state capital improvement plan which includes a three-year projection of all capital projects recommended to be undertaken or continued, forecasts of the capital requirements of state agencies for the next four fiscal years, a schedule of possible appropriations from bond funds, and a review of current capital projects.

Along with preparing the state capital improvement plan, the commission also is responsible for proposing the capital spending section of the annual budget, those less expensive projects which are funded by appropriations from the general fund each year. These projects include capital outlays for minor construction, repairs, and equipment for state facilities such as the hospitals, prisons, and state parks. In addition, the commission evaluates proposed bond authorizations and decides which they will endorse. The commission's endorsement is generally respected by the legislature, which votes on placing bond issues on the ballot, and by the voters, who approve or reject bond issues at the polls. The commission uses the following criteria in deciding which bond issues to endorse:

■ Proposals must be well planned.

■ They must be for capital expenditures, including re-habilitation projects.

■ They must address critical needs and be capable of implementation within three to four years.

■ Those that are cost effective, consider on-going operating costs, and can attract federal funds are given preference.

Bond Financing

Bond financing provides a way of borrowing large sums of money immediately for necessary capital construction proj-ects, as distinguished from pay-as-you-go financing by an-nual budget appropriations. Such borrowing provides that the cost be repaid gradually, over the lifetime of the projects (for example, state institutions and highways).

Critics of bond financing point out that the pay-as-you-go method may be more economical—depending on the level of interest rates at the time the borrowing is done —because it does not involve the payment of interest charges, and it does not commit future voters to the pay-ment of debts about which they were not consulted.

Proponents of bond financing counter that building a capital fund so that improvements can be made on a pay-as-you-go basis has serious problems. First, it takes a number of years to accumulate enough capital to fund major proj-ects. Second, the easiest item to eliminate when the current budget is under stress may be a reserve fund for future ser-vices. Proponents also argue that it is appropriate for proj-ects with useful lives extending for a number of years to be paid for by the generations that use them.

Most people agree that some expenditures should be paid out of current expenses and others either from borrowing or a capital reserve fund. Projects such as construction of high-ways, schools, and hospitals are such long term undertak-ings and require so much money that they necessitate bor-rowing or a capital reserve fund. Maintenance of highways, on the other hand, and the cost of materials and supplies are commonly considered operating expenses of the current budget. Decisions to borrow become more subjective when they fall in the gray middle area where financing could be either from current expenditures, from long-term borrowing, or from a capital reserve fund. A new furnace for a small building might be financed out of operating expenses, but a new heating system for a large institution would probably be financed through borrowing.

Quite apart from these arguments, it is generally agreed that there are many unmet capital needs in New Jersey. Assuming that they are to be met by long-term financing, how is this done by governments?

The New Jersey Constitution limits the debt that the legislature may incur without voter approval to less than one percent of the total appropriation for that fiscal year. Additional debt may be incurred through voter-approved general obligation bonds backed by the state's credit, or through authorities created by the legislature to sell bonds and carry out a specific mandate.

General Obligation Bonds

General obligation bonds are authorized by the voters for a specific purpose. The monies raised by sale of the bonds are deposited in a special fund and used only for the purpose designated or for repayment of the debt. The state government is not subject to limits on the amount of debt it can incur—the public in effect sets that limit by approving or rejecting bond referendums. Once passed, the authorization of the debt cannot be repealed, but the bonds need not be issued.

The bonds are backed by the full faith and credit of the state which, based on taxation, are legally and unconditionally pledged. In New Jersey each bond authorization has a specific tax pledged to support it. This simply means that if the general budget is insufficient for the debt service, the tax pledged must be used for that purpose. As a last resort, local property taxes must be levied to pay off the debt.

New Jersey voters have approved general obligation bond issues for a variety of purposes.

■ Bricks and mortar projects: buildings for corrections, higher education, the mentally ill, the mentally and physically handicapped.

■ Infrastructure projects: highways and bridges, mass transportation, public water supplies, and sewage treatment facilities.

■ Environmental projects: Green Acres and farmland preservation programs, beach, shore, and harbor projects, flood control projects, and the identification and cleanup of hazardous waste sites.

Revenue Bonds and Authorities

While general obligation bonds are used to finance many capital projects in New Jersey, those projects that produce income—the tollroads and the Meadowlands sports complex, for example—can be built with revenue bonds issued by authorities. These are independent public corporations established to construct and/or operate revenue-producing facilities. Examples of authorities in this state include the New Jersey Turnpike Authority, the Sports and Exposition Authority, and, on an interstate level, the Port Authority of New York and New Jersey. Local districts may also create authorities to build and manage such facilities as parking lots and sewage treatment systems.

The cost of the project (i.e., the debt) is paid from the revenue. Because the debt created by authorities (the cost of the projects) is repaid with revenue from the projects themselves and not through taxes, such undertakings do not require approval by referendum. However, voters must approve any bond issue backed by the state's credit. The state may, and often does, appropriate funds to help an authority begin its operation. A general obligation bond issue may be used for this purpose.

Because the revenue produced from the projects undertaken by authorities is less certain than the full faith and credit of the state which backs general obligation bonds, interest rates tend to be higher for the revenue bonds sold by authorities. Nevertheless, the rate is lower than that for the corporate bond market because revenue bonds, like general obligation bonds, are tax exempt, thus increasing the actual return netted by the purchaser.

Most authorities have broad powers, within the stated purpose of the enabling legislation, both to decide what projects they will undertake and to incur debt by selling bonds to raise the necessary capital. While the authorities are highly autonomous entities, there are limited checks on their power: the actions of some are subject to the approval of the governor (for example the New Jersey Turnpike Au-

Major New Jersey Authorities

Figure 6.3

New Jersey Turnpike Authority

New Jersey Highway Authority (Garden State Parkway and Garden State Arts Center)

New Jersey Expressway Authority

New Jersey Sports and Exposition Authority (the Meadowlands)

South Jersey Port Corporation

New Jersey Housing and Mortgage Finance Authority

New Jersey Educational Facilities Authority (constructs academic and residential facilities)

Rutgers, the State University

New Jersey Health Care Facilities Financing Authority

New Jersey Economic Development Authority

Hackensack Meadowlands Development Commission

New Jersey Building Authority (constructs office facilities for state agencies)

New Jersey Water Supply Authority

thority); all statewide authorities come under scrutiny from the Joint Legislative Oversight (watchdog) Committee; and each is subject to an annual audit. In recent years the legislature has built more accountability into the authorities that it creates by requiring greater legislative review of authority actions and, in some cases, by adding a "sunset" clause setting a date for the end of that authority's active life.

Moral Obligation Bonds

In the 1960s an additional assurance—the moral obligation of the state—was added to the debt-creating powers of some authorities. It was used particularly with those authorities or agencies whose revenue was less certain. For moral obligation bonds a debt service fund is set up using revenue from the project, earnings from investment of bond revenue before that money is needed to pay bills for the project, and finally money from state appropriations. The fund is set to equal the following year's payment of debt service (that is, the principal and interest). If at any time the fund falls below that amount, the state is asked to replenish the fund through further state appropriations. These obligations are not legally binding on the state, hence the name moral obligation bonds.

During the 1960s and early 1970s moral obligation bonds were popular for financing projects. However, their overuse, especially in New York City, was a major cause for the decline in confidence in the revenue bond market. Since 1974 the New Jersey Legislature has not authorized any new moral obligation bonds. New Jersey's experience with moral obligation bonds has been mixed; the New Jersey Sports and Exposition Authority was financed with moral obligation bonds, but in 1978 following a voter referendum, the authority was allowed to issue state-guaranteed, full faith and credit, bonds. The sports complex refinanced its debt with these new bonds and now has no moral obligation debt outstanding. The South Jersey Port Corporation is also backed by moral obligation bonds; some years the revenues cover the debt service, other years appropriations from the general fund are needed.

Short Term Bonds

In the search for a stable funding source for highway and mass transit construction, the Department of Transportation, in conjunction with Wall Street advisors, developed a hybrid form of bond financing. Under the plan approved by the governor and the legislature in 1984, the Transportation Trust Fund authority will sell ten-year bonds over the four years of the program—fiscal years 1985 through 1989. The bond revenue, along with other revenue sources, will be used to match the more than $600 million in federal funds expected to be available each of those four years. These bonds will not be general obligation bonds and thus do not need voter approval, nor are they conventional revenue bonds. Payback will be from state appropriations including a proposed dedication to transportation needs of two and one-half cents of the existing eight-cents-a-gallon gasoline tax. The legislation creating the authority includes legislative review both of the sale of bonds and of the selection of projects. A sunset provision is also included in the proposal.

Funding Maintenance of the Infrastructure

The Transportation Trust Fund agreement evolved from Governor Kean's original concept of an infrastructure bank. The goal was to have a dependable source of funding for financing the construction and repair of New Jersey's infrastructure—the highways, bridges, mass transit, sewers, and water systems, for example—which are essential underpinnings of a healthy economy.

The essentials of the plan for an infrastructure bank included getting the most out of the dwindling supply of federal capital grant money by combining those funds with state bond revenues in a centrally administered state fund. These monies would then be lent to local authorities and governments which would agree to repay the loans. Once repaid, the money would be lent out again for other projects. While the plan was defeated by the legislature, which passed the bill authorizing the infrastructure bank but did not appropriate funds for its operation, the concept has stimulated national discussion of the problem. Since the basic problem of funding the infrastructure construction and repairs remains, the citizens of New Jersey can expect to see continuing debate on solutions.

State Debt

Because New Jersey still maintains the highest possible credit rating (AAA) and debt service as a percentage of the annual budget remains in the acceptable 3 to 4 percent range, the financial community is not alarmed by the level and growth of state debt.

The Treasury Department

In addition to the General Services Administration (described in chapter 2), the Treasury Department has broad responsibilities for assessing and collecting taxes and investing state monies. The department is also home for the Division of the State Lottery and the New Jersey Casino Control Commision.

The Division of Investment manages state revenues for the annual budget and invests billions of dollars of pension monies, both for state workers and for many county and municipal workers as well.

The Division of Taxation supervises the assessment and collection of most state taxes, with the notable exception of the motor vehicle fees which are collected by the Division of Motor Vehicles. (See chapter 14.) The division also collects some taxes that are distributed to municipalities, namely the Public Utility Gross Receipts Tax. Another important responsibility is providing assistance to local governments in the administration of the property tax.

The Property Tax

While property taxes are not a source of state revenue in New Jersey, they do affect the state budget and state taxes. This was most evident in 1976 when passage of the state gross personal income tax was tied to property tax relief.

Property taxes are the principal source of local revenue, far greater than state and federal aid and other income sources. The property tax is entirely assessed, collected, and spent at the local level. Although used largely for local services, some property tax money is used to support state functions that are administered locally, for example, certain costs of running the judicial system.

State Mechanisms Affecting the Property Tax

The New Jersey Constitution specifies that "property shall be assessed for taxation under general laws and uniform rules." Amendments specify certain exceptions to this rule. (See figure 6.4.) These exceptions, approved by the voters, reflect public concern with the issue of equity in assessing property taxes.

Assessment

Throughout the long history of property taxation in New Jersey, as in all states, there have been many difficulties in achieving assessed valuations that are fair, impartial, and consistent—among various areas within a community as well as from municipality to municipality.

Property is assessed (assigned a value for tax purposes) by the assessor or board of assessors of the municipality in which the property is located. To improve the fairness of the assessment, municipal tax assessors, who formerly had to meet no qualifications at all, are now required to take courses and pass an examination. Assessors certified in this way serve for four years and then receive tenure, regardless of whether they were originally elected or appointed. In addition, provision is made for reassessment of property every five years or when property values rise above a set percentage, whichever comes first.

A property owner pays only one tax bill to his municipal tax collector. However, the bill includes the taxes needed to support three separate bodies: the municipal government, the school district, and the county government. In some cases a special district, such as a fire district, also requires taxes.

Municipal and county government needs are determined and reflected in the budgets their governing bodies adopt each year. The school budget is prepared by the district's board of education and approved by the voters, usually at the time of school board elections in April, or is adopted by a board of school estimate. The property tax to be raised is the amount remaining when all other revenue sources, such as state and federal aid, have been applied to

Exemptions and Rebates on Property Taxation

Special assessment for farmland used for agriculture or horticulture

Exemption from the property tax for real property used exclusively for religious, educational, charitable, or cemetery purposes and owned by a not-for-profit corporation or association

Rebate for veterans and spouses with additional benefits for disabled veterans and spouses

Rebate for senior and disabled citizens who own their homes or who own a mobile home

Property tax credit for homeowners and tenants

Tax abatement for buildings in certain distressed municipal areas

Tax exemption, for a limited time, for any municipal, public, or private corporation authorized to clear and redevelop a blighted area

Figure 6.4

these budgets. Thus the property tax is a "remainder" tax—the rate is set according to the remaining financial need.

Once these budgets are established, the final tax rate, calculated in dollars per $100 of assessed valuation, can be computed. This is accomplished by dividing the amount to be raised by the assessed property value. If a local rate is $3 per $100 of valuation and a piece of property is assessed at $50,000, the owner's tax bill would be $3 times 500 ($100s) or $1500. Each "penny" in the tax rate is called a point; an increase from $3.00 to $3.15 would be a fifteen point increase.

The actual rate is certified later by the county's board of taxation. The total tax rate is often subdivided into a municipal rate, a school rate, and a county rate to indicate how much of the total tax goes for each of these purposes. The taxes collected on behalf of the school district and the county are turned over to these units by the municipality.

County Boards of Taxation

Determining how much each municipality must raise for the county is somewhat complicated because it involves property valuations in a number of communities. The task is carried out by the county board of taxation, appointed by the governor with senate consent and paid for by the state. Each board is charged with seeing that each municipality in its county "bears its full and just share of taxes." This is done by preparing county equalization tables in which the actual ratios of assessed valuation to true value are computed for each municipality by comparing the sale prices of properties that changed hands during the year with their assessed valuations. The ratables of each municipality are then converted to the same standard, called equalized net valuations, which is used to apportion the county taxes. As a result, each community contributes a share of the county taxes that is proportionate to its share of the true value of all the ratable property in the county. All counties must assess 100 percent of true value. Tax maps must be updated before re-evaluation. Electronic data processing of tax lists has been updated, and a uniform petition-of-appeal form is now available for use by taxpayers.

In addition to apportioning the county taxes, the county

boards of taxation sit as courts of appeal for individuals who are dissatisfied with their municipal assessments. Appeals from decisions of the county board, both by individuals and by municipalities, may be made to the Tax Court of New Jersey. This statewide trial court was established in 1979 to review the actions and determinations of the county boards of taxation with respect to local property tax matters (which make up 90 percent of their case load). The Tax Court's other function is to review the actions and determinations of the Director of the Division of Taxation and other state officials with respect to state taxes.

PART II

THE ADMINISTRATIVE
DEPARTMENTS

7.
Education

Until 1966 the Department of Education handled all primary, secondary, and higher education matters. At that time the legislature split the department into the Department of Education (primary and secondary schools) and the Department of Higher Education. The goal was to focus public attention and administrative energy on the rapidly expanding system of public higher education in New Jersey. Both departments attempt to balance a perceived need for statewide organization and standards with a strong home rule tradition.

The two abiding characteristics of public education in New Jersey—home rule and the public school—have been strongly influenced by the state's heterogeneity. New Jersey's early settlers came from many countries and represented various creeds. The religious sects wanted to be free to impart their own beliefs in their own schools. For two hundred years this situation worked against the concept of a common school supported by public funds and available to all. However, as local and religious schools became unable to serve the needs of an expanding population, religious leaders increasingly gave their support to a system of public education. But communities, having grown accustomed to addressing their own needs, insisted upon a great degree of home rule within the framework of a statewide system of free public schools.

PRIMARY AND SECONDARY EDUCATION

During the nineteenth century a sustained effort was made to establish free public education for everyone. Provisions of the 1844 constitution secured this effort. Government support culminated in a constitutional amendment of 1875 mandating the legislature "to provide for the maintenance and support of a thorough and efficient system of free public schools for . . . all," a provision incorporated verbatim into the 1947 constitution (Article VIII, Section IV). The implications of this rather obscure provision remained unexplored until the 1970s, when education in New Jersey took on a new direction.

In 1972 the suit *Robinson v. Cahill* (William T. Cahill, governor 1970–1974) was brought against the state charging that Robinson, the plaintiff, was not receiving an educational opportunity equivalent to that existing in other communities, and that reliance on property taxes as a means of financing schools contributed to that inequality of opportunity. In 1973 the New Jersey Supreme Court found that it is the state's responsibility to provide a thorough and efficient educational system for all public school children. The court ruled that the state must define "thorough and efficient," must see to it that all school districts provide such a thorough and efficient educational system, and must develop a plan of financing the constitutional mandate that would avoid the present heavy reliance on local property taxes.

Two years after the court's decision, the legislature still had not met the court's original deadline for legislation, largely because it could not agree upon a taxation method that would fulfill the state's financial responsibility. Finally, after an agonizing, arduous session that lasted from summer 1975 to summer 1976 and included a court-ordered withholding of education funds starting July 1, 1976, the legislature passed the Public School Education Act of 1975. This act has two parts: it defines "thorough and efficient" and the process for achieving it, and it sets up a method for distributing state aid to provide a thorough and efficient educational system.

Before detailing the Public School Education Act provisions, however, it is helpful to look briefly at the structure of

the New Jersey Department of Education and at the local
school systems which the department supervises.

The New Jersey Department of Education was created by
the legislature to exercise general supervision and control of
public education. It consists of the state board of education,
which supervises the department, the commissioner of education, and the departmental staff.

The New Jersey State Board of Education has thirteen
voting members. Twelve are appointed by the governor and
serve without pay for overlapping terms of six years. Of the
twelve, not more than one may be appointed from any one
county, and at least three must be women. The thirteenth
voting member is a representative of the state board of
higher education.

The state board adopts rules and regulations that have
the effect of law and are binding upon local school districts.
The board decides on appeals from decisions made by the
commissioner on matters of school law or board rules and
regulations. It can issue subpoenas compelling the attendance of witnesses and the production of papers at hearings.

The commissioner of education is appointed by the governor with the consent of the senate for a term of five years.
He or she is secretary to the state board of education and enforces its rules and regulations, exercising general supervision over all schools. In actual practice most of the board's
rules are based on the commissioner's recommendations.
The commissioner also has the power to appoint assistant
commissioners and the professional staff, subject to state
board approval.

The commissioner has broad responsibility for the work
of the department, although many actual duties are delegated to staff. The commissioner renders decisions on controversies and disputes arising under school law, following
formal hearings before and recommendations by an administrative law judge. (See chapter 2, the office of Administrative Law). The commissioner meets with county and local
superintendents to discuss ways to improve public education and has the authority to recommend the withholding

The Department of Education

of state financial aid for failure to comply with state recommendations or standards. The commissioner's consent is required for authorization to sell school bonds that exceed the debt limit of a district. The commissioner may also set the amount to be raised by taxation in a local district when a budget has been defeated and the municipal governing body has failed to act upon it. In addition, the commissioner appoints and chairs the New Jersey State Board of Examiners, a fourteen-member group of educators that issues, suspends, or revokes state certificates to elementary and secondary teachers and other school professionals. This board also has the authority to determine whether alternative experience meets course or study requirements for certification and may recommend certification standards and requirements to the state board of education.

The commissioner of education has the authority to take over control of a school district's fiscal or programmatic affairs and to appoint a department official to oversee the district's fiscal affairs until the problem is resolved and sound fiscal management is restored.

The extent of the commissioner's power was evident when Commissioner Saul Cooperman completely reorganized and refocused the Department of Education in the early 1980s.

Regional and County Services

County superintendents are appointed by the commissioner, each county providing office space and staff. The superintendents act as arms of the department and enforce rules pertaining to certification of teachers. financial reporting, and pupil registers. Three of the county superintendents' offices are designated to house and administer Regional Curriculum Services Units (RCSUs), serving each of three seven-county areas. The RCSUs provide instructional materials, training, and followup activities to school districts. They also house specialists for specially funded projects on equal educational opportunity, drug and alcohol education, nutrition, and special education. Child Find, a statewide project to help identify and serve preschool handicapped children, is located at the RCSU for the central New Jersey counties.

Local School Districts

Although by law district boards of education are arms of the state legislature, they are generally highly responsive to local needs and interests. Each municipality in the state constitutes a separate school district unless, by a vote of the people, two or more municipalities decide to unite and form one district. Thus, even though a school district is coterminous with one or more cities, boroughs, towns, or townships, it is a separate and independent legal entity, subject to the control or supervision of the municipality or municipalities only in certain budget requirements or restrictions.

School districts in New Jersey are divided into Type I and Type II districts, as well as into vocational school districts. In Type I school districts, the mayor appoints the members of the board of education, and a board of school estimate fixes the annual school budget. In Type II districts, the members of the board of education are elected, and the annual school budget is submitted for approval by the voters at a school district election. Each city is automatically a Type I school district unless the people have noted to be governed by Type II provisions—which all but a few school districts have chosen. The City of Newark voted for such a change in the early 1980s, leaving only abut 30 Type I districts among the state's 558 school districts.

The state has set only three qualifications for local school board membership. The board member must be literate, have lived in the district for a minimum of two years directly preceding becoming a member, and not be concerned directly or indirectly in any contract with or claim against the board.

Special School Districts

Consolidated districts are formed through the merger of two or more existing districts into a single district.

Regional districts, by contrast, are formed when two or more districts unite to provide educational services, but each retains its own identity. The two types of regional districts are limited purpose (high school or vocational school, for example) and all-purpose (kindergarten through twelfth grade). These regional districts are created by a referendum in which each local district involved must vote approval. In subsequent school elections, however, the total vote of the entire regional district determines the result. Most of these districts operate with an elected board of education.

Vocational schools may be maintained by a local or regional school district, or they may be created by the freeholders as countywide vocational schools. County vocational schools have a separate board consisting of the county superintendent of schools and four appointed members. County funds for these vocational school districts are appropriated annually by the freeholders.

The Public School Education Act of 1975

To fulfill the court mandate to provide a "thorough and efficient" education to all children in the state, the legislature passed the Public School Education Act of 1975 (Chapter 212, Laws of 1975), popularly called "T&E." Its legislative goal is "to provide to all children in New Jersey, regardless of socioeconomic or geographic location, the educational opportunity which will prepare them to function politically, economically, and socially in a democratic society."

Under this law a thorough and efficient school system includes ten elements:

1. Educational goals of each district, set by the local school board, compatible with state standards

2. Encouragement of public involvement in setting goals

3. Reasonable level of pupil proficiency in basic skills with verbal and computational skills singled out for priority

4. Sufficient breadth of program to develop individual talents and abilities

5. Programs and supportive services for all students, especially those who are educationally disadvantaged or who have special needs

6. Adequately equipped, sanitary, and secure physical facilities with adequate materials and supplies

7. Qualified instructional and other personnel

8. Efficient administrative procedures

9. Adequate state programs of research and development

10. Evaluation and monitoring of programs by state and local districts

The procedures delineated to implement these elements and ensure their incorporation into every school district include having each school district write specific goals, objectives, and standards for education; report its annual progress in meeting these goals; and submit a copy of its proposed budget for review and assessment each December to the state. In addition, the procedures call for uniform statewide testing in basic skills and for review of the state goals and standards every five years.

Monitoring

In 1982 implementation of the T&E law was reviewed; as a result, the system for monitoring compliance was simplified. Stress was placed on more effective local planning, helping local school districts share information about successful instructional programs, certifying for five-year periods those school districts that successfully met the requirements (thus eliminating constant state monitoring of these school districts), and concentrating more resources on helping those local school districts that have deficiencies.

To gain certification, a school district must be rated acceptable in the ten major elements and fifty-one indicators developed by the chapter 212 monitoring committee, appointed by the commissioner of education. Districts that are not approved enter level II monitoring. Under the level II program, a district self-study team must analyze and develop a plan to correct deficiencies. If the district is successful in correcting those deficiencies, it is recommended for certification. If it is not, the county superintendent appoints a level II review team to produce and implement an improvement plan. Upon successful completion of that plan, the district may be recommended for certification. However, if the district still cannot meet state standards, the commissioner has the authority to intervene.

To help the local school districts obtain certification, the county superintendent's office offers technical assistance, information, and help in determining education goals. The county office also conducts periodic progress checks and analyzes the budgets of the individual districts.

Testing

A 1976 amendment to the Education Act of 1975 established a Minimum Basic Skills (MBS) test in reading and mathematics to be given in grades three, six, nine, and eleven. Further legislation in 1979 established high school graduation requirements and set the MBS test taken in grade nine as one of those requirements. A writing test was also required for graduation, but was not funded at that time.

In 1982 Commissioner Saul Cooperman pointed out the shortcomings of a test that measured minimum and basic skills instead of mastery. By 1983 a new Statewide Testing System was adopted which included a grade nine High School Proficiency Test (HSPT) in reading, mathematics, and writing. The writing test included a student essay. This test becomes part of the high school graduation requirement in the 1985–86 school year. The local districts are required to administer a standardized test meeting state standards in grades three through eleven and to submit results from testing in grades three and six to the department for analysis. These results are announced publicly. The goal of the Statewide Testing System is to establish higher educational standards and to test for the skills and competencies a student needs in order to become a productive citizen.

State Aid to Public Schools

The financial outlay necessary to maintain public education in New Jersey is considerable. The court decision ordering the state to assume a greater financial role in local school support has made the administration of school budgets increasingly intricate.

A major goal of the T&E legislation was to decrease the gap in spending between wealthy school districts and poor school districts. Yet eight years later the issue was back in the courts in the case of *Abbot v. Burke*. The nonprofit Education Law Center, representing the parents of children attending schools in urban areas, argued that the gap between rich and poor school districts had increased rather than decreased since passage of T&E. To see how this might be possible, it is necessary to look at the components of state aid to education and at the function of the budget caps.

The Level of State Aid. Although neither the court nor the legislature set a specific state share for the cost of education, it was generally expected in 1975 that state aid would rise to about 40 percent of educational costs within two years and stabilize at that level. While state funding has come close to the 40 percent mark, since the T&E legislation, there has not been a strong, ongoing commitment on the part of the legislature and the governor to fund in full the statutory formula for state aid. The national average for state funding for education in the early 1980s was 49 percent. Many argue that New Jersey should increase its share of funding to at least the national average.

Equalization Aid. About half the state aid to local school districts is for their current expense budgets and is given on a sliding scale according to the wealth of a given district as measured by property value in relation to the resident school population. The poorer the district, the more state aid. By contrast, many school districts have so much property wealth per pupil that they are eligible to receive little or no equalization aid. For these districts a minimum aid formula is used.

School Building Aid. Those districts eligible for current expense equalization aid are also eligible for capital outlay and debt service aid (for capital expenditures such as new buildings and playgrounds and major repairs to these facilities). However, there is no minimum aid formula in this category for wealthy districts.

Categorical Aid. The state provides nonequalized aid for the extra costs of providing education to children who have special needs or who are enrolled in special programs. However, each district may be aided in only one category for each student, even though that child may be receiving services in several categories. The classifications are special education, compensatory education (remedial programs), bilingual education, and local vocational education. Often the urban areas with the least tax wealth have the most children needing one or more categories of aid, especially in compensatory and bilingual education.

Transportation Aid. The state reimburses the district for a percentage of the transportation costs for handicapped children, for elementary pupils who live more than two miles from school, and for secondary pupils who live more than two and one-half miles from school. If a district provides transportation for public school pupils, it must also provide transportation for private school pupils who attend classes within the state not more than twenty miles from their homes; this transportation aid to private school students may not exceed an established amount per year.

Teachers' Pension and Annuity Fund (TPAF). The state contributes the entire local districts' share of both the Teachers' Pension and Annuity Fund and social security for all teaching and professional staff in local school districts. It has been argued that this part of state aid tends to widen the gap between wealthy and poor districts, because wealthy districts tend to have smaller class sizes and pay higher salaries.

TPAF payments accounted for about one quarter of all state aid monies in the first half of the 1980s, the cost growing at over 13 percent per year for the 1977–1983 period. At that rate, it will take an increasingly larger share of state aid to education in the future. Various reforms of the teachers' pension system are being debated at the present time.

Aid to Nonpublic Schools. State law provides that, upon request, the board of education in any school district shall have the power and duty to purchase and lend textbooks to all students living in the district who are enrolled in either public or nonpublic schools.

School Lunches. The state supplements federal funds provided under the National School Lunch Program to provide school districts with reimbursement for lunches that meet federal nutritional standards.

District School Budget Caps

The amount that a district's new current expense budget can grow from one year to the next is limited by the T&E law. The purposes for this cap include limiting future state aid, assuring that some of the state aid is used to provide property tax relief, holding down the growth of expenditures in higher-spending districts while enabling lower-spending districts to catch up, and preventing inefficient use of funds, which might show up as an extraordinary increase of expenditures in any one year.

The cap is based on the growth in the statewide equalized property values and also on the state average cost per pupil. Those districts that spend below the state per pupil average for their grade level types (K–12 districts versus high school only districts) are permitted a higher rate of budget growth than districts that spend at or above the state average. A cap waiver process allows districts to spend more than the permissible level, if that level would be insufficient to meet the goals, objectives, and standards of the T&E legislation, or if increased enrollment is anticipated.

While the cap has provided some property tax relief and limited state aid to education, it has apparently done little if anything to decrease the spending gap between wealthy and poor districts. One possible reason is that the budget cap is based on the previous year's enrollment; therefore, school districts with declining enrollment rates are able to increase their spending per pupil more than the cap might suggest. Those school districts with high declining enrollment rates (usually suburban districts) can benefit more than those with lower declining enrollment (usually city districts).

Educational Standards

Since both the Department of Education and the school districts receive their powers from the state legislature, neither can act to change its own powers or trespass on the powers of the other. The effect of these restrictions is to achieve a balance between local initiative and home rule on the one hand, and state control and assistance on the other. The following examples illustrate that balance.

Employment of Teachers

Local boards employ teachers, but they may hire only those with the professional and academic credentials entitling them to certification by the New Jersey State Board of Examiners. Before the alternative certification method went into effect for the 1985–1986 school year, if no qualified candidates were available for an opening, local school boards could hire someone not properly qualified under the "emergency certification" program. Now emergency certification may be used only in limited cases where there is a serious shortage of qualified teachers, English as a Second Language or bilingual education, for example. A local board may set its own salary guide (pay scale), but only if it

Figure 7.1

Educational Initiatives for the 1980s

Operation School Renewal. As part of the state's Urban Initiative, the department chose three districts—Trenton, East Orange, and Neptune Township—to participate in a three-year pilot program for improving urban school performance. In return for the planning assistance and expertise of the department's School Renewal Team, as well as some financial assistance, these target districts have committed themselves to providing a range of resources and support for the program. In addition, the districts have committed themselves to meeting five objectives:

- Raising student attendance to the statewide average of 92 percent
- Raising basic text scores to the state average
- Increasing the effectiveness of participating building principals
- Reducing the incidence of disruptive pupil behavior by 40 percent
- Reducing youth unemployment through vocational education

The Academy for the Advancement of Teaching and Management. The academy, established by Governor Kean, will supplement graduate teaching and in-service courses with intensive hands-on learning experience in skills aimed at helping teachers improve the likelihood of student learning. In this program three to five experienced teachers and their principal will learn and practice teaching skills together and then support each other as the skills become part of their day-to-day teaching patterns.

Master Teaching Program. This program is designed to give recognition and support to outstanding teachers and thereby encourage them to remain in the profession, to increase learning opportunities for New Jersey students, and to enhance the teaching profession by allowing teachers to share their skills with their colleagues. Up to 5 percent of the teachers in a participating district may be selected for designation as master teachers and awarded $5,000 bonuses from the state. Newark and the Pinelands Regional (Ocean County) school districts are participating in the pilot program during the 1985–1986 school year.

Alternative Certification Program. In 1984 Commissioner Saul Cooperman proposed a plan allowing people with college degrees but without formal teachers' training to be hired by local school districts after the applicants pass a state subject matter test. Then the teacher candidates would undergo a year-long, paid state-approved training program. At the successful completion of this program candidates would be eligible for a permanent license. This alternative certification program was adopted in 1984 and implemented in the 1985–1986 school year. It replaced the emergency teaching licenses, which required only that the applicant be over eighteen years of age, hold a high school diploma, and be a resident of New Jersey. Such emergency certification now is available only in a few limited cases where there are serious shortages of qualified teachers, English as a Second Language or bilingual education, for example.

Teacher Seniority. As declining enrollments caused reductions in force (RIF) of the teaching staff, a review of the seniority rules for New Jersey teachers was in order in the early 1980s. Changes allowed teachers holding certification in more than one subject area to earn seniority only in that subject area or areas in which they actually taught. Thus senior teachers may no longer "RIF" junior teachers from subject areas in which the senior teachers were certified but had not taught for many years.

Higher Standards for Teacher Preparation. The departments of Education and Higher Education worked together to prepare new college standards for teacher preparation. The new standards shifted the focus for education students from professional education courses to a liberal arts program. Requirements now include an academic major, study in the behavioral sciences, and a field-based professional training component, in addition to a minimum of sixty credits of liberal arts courses. Students now need a minimum 2.5 average on a 4.0 grading scale and a passing grade on English and computational skills tests in order to enter the junior year of a college course for future teachers. All students must pass subject matter competency tests before graduation.

is equal to or higher than the salary guide adopted by the legislature. Furthermore, local boards must comply with laws on such employment policies as tenure, veterans' rights, sick leave, and labor negotiations.

School Calendar
Local boards may set their own school calendars, but their schools must be open at least nine calendar months and a minimum of 180 days.

Secondary Education
Local boards may establish high schools with the approval of the state board of education. The state may withhold or withdraw its accreditation whenever, in its opinion, the academic work, the facilities, the enrollment, or the maintenance is unsatisfactory. All public secondary schools must be visited by the department at least once every five years for reaccreditation purposes.

Curriculum
Although school districts may establish their own curriculums, the state mandates that health (including family life education), safety, and physical education be taught throughout the grades. Each elementary school must also offer courses in community civics, geography, New Jersey history and citizenship. High school requirements, in addition to health, safety, and physical education, include four years of communications; two years of computation (mathematics); two years of American history (including black history); one year of natural or physical science; and one year of fine, practical, or performing arts.

Buildings, Plans, and Specifications
Local boards, if the community makes funds available, may erect and equip school buildings after the design has been approved by the state Department of Education which has set criteria for adequate educational facilities.

Special Education
Each local board is required to conduct classes for the physically, mentally, or emotionally handicapped, singly or

jointly with other districts. Teams of specialists (the Child Study Teams) are responsible for the identification and placement of the handicapped and for establishing necessary programs to meet their needs.

Other Programs

The Department of Education is responsible for educating the severely hearing-impaired at the Marie H. Katzenbach School for the Deaf, a kindergarten through twelfth grade residential and day educational facility.

The department also works in conjunction with the Department of Corrections and the Department of Human Services to provide educational programs, training, and counseling services to institutionalized juveniles. A mix of state and federal funds is available for these programs.

Adult education needs are met through the department which sets standards and supervises programs for Adult Basic Skills, the General Education Development Test (GED), English as a Second Language ESL) programs, citizenship classes for immigrants, and skills training for refugees.

To supplement the special education programs conducted by the various school districts, the department established seven regional day schools for severely handicapped children. These facilities provide another choice, in addition to the private schools that have traditionally served this population, for school districts seeking these services.

Migrant workers are also served by the department through both summer and winter education programs. A model program in career education and counseling for children of migrants has been initiated.

The State Library

The state library, an administrative unit of the New Jersey Department of Education, offers a variety of services to the state government, other libraries in the state, and the public. An extensive law library serves the legal profession as well as the state government. Large collections of New Jersey material and genealogical reference works are available to researchers. The library reference staff meets the information needs of state government and of other libraries by using the library holdings and more than one hundred on-line data bases. In addition, the library distributes copies of state governmental publications to depository libraries throughout the state. A general book collection of more than one-half million volumes is maintained for loan and exhibition purposes. Access to this collection is gained through interlibrary loans to local public, school, or special libraries.

The statewide library network, composed of approximately three hundred thirty local public libraries associated with twenty-six area libraries, culminates in the New Jersey State Library. The state library provides professional advisory and consultative services on all aspects of library administration to these New Jersey libraries and also distributes aid to local libraries. The network is currently being enhanced by the creation of multi-type library cooperatives designed to work together to improve library services to all residents. Six new regional library cooperatives are expected to be operational in 1985 or 1986.

The New Jersey State Library also serves a large blind and handicapped population in a new building in Trenton, specifically designed to serve that population as a walk-in library.

HIGHER EDUCATION

After World War II the states of the Northeast, having been well served by scores of private institutions of higher learning, were slow to recognize that private colleges and universities could not indefinitely meet the growing student demand. The nationwide population explosion and the requirements of increasingly sophisticated sciences, technologies, and social institutions were rapidly bringing about the need for higher levels of education for greater numbers of people. As a result, new public colleges and universities proliferated everywhere but in the Northeast. Finally, in the 1950s, Eastern complacency began to crumble, and the governments of these states began to plan for new and expanded institutions of higher education.

Although least blessed with private institutions, New Jersey was among the slowest to recognize the coming student space crisis. Strong and organized anti-tax sentiment opposed the kind of broad-based state taxation being intro-

Figure 7.2

Access to Higher Education

Recommendation of the Joint Statewide Task Force on Pre-College Preparation:

Development of a high school graduation test, geared to the eleventh grade, to replace the Minimum Basic Skills Test. (See text for discussion of the replacement text, the High School Proficiency Test.)

Use of that test as a college admissions examination for New Jersey colleges and universities.

Elimination in public high schools of the traditional distinction between college-bound and non-college-bound students.

Eventual phasing out of remedial courses offered at the college level.

Instituting statewide tests for all college sophmores that would have to be passed before students would be permitted to continue on to their junior year. This would include county college graduates going on to four-year institutions.

Requirement of four years of English, emphasizing writing and the study of literary masterpieces for all high school students.

Requirement of three years of math, including elementary and intermediate algebra and geometry.

Implementing a new emphasis on critical thinking and writing skills in all courses.

The reinstatement of final examinations for most courses both in high school and college.

Requirement that all college students pass comprehensive examinations in their major fields of study before receiving a degree.

Statewide Plan for Higher Education—Recommendations for Access by Minority Students:

Each public institution of higher education should admit a minimum of 10 percent of its New Jersey freshmen through the Educational Opportunity Fund.

The Basic Skills Assessment Program should provide testing and then remediation to those educationally disadvantaged students from economically disadvantaged homes who need such help.

Figure 7.3

High Technology Initiatives in Higher Education
Recommendations of the Governor's Commission
on Science and Technology

High Technology Initiative Appropriation. State higher education monies were set aside for projects such as upgrading technical education and engineering programs through the purchase of state-of-the-art equipment and for integrating computers into college curriculums.

High Technology Research Centers. A bond issue approved by the voters in 1984 provides for, among other things, a biotechnology center for Rutgers and the University of Medicine and Dentistry of New Jersey, a hazardous and toxic substance management center at the New Jersey Institute of Technology, an industrial ceramics research center at Rutgers, and a food technology center at Rutgers' Cook College.

Center for Molecular Medicine and Immunology. This was recently funded at the Newark campus of the University of Medicine and Dentistry.

Center for Information Age Technology. The center, located at the New Jersey Institute of Technology, is modeled after the agricultural extension centers and exists to extend to government, business, and academia the expertise of faculty and researchers in computer, telecommunication, and information technology fields.

Summer Institutes for Mathematics and Science Teachers. Two-week summer institutes will be operated for elementary and secondary teachers in response to the recommendations of the Advisory Council on Math/Science Teacher Supply and Demand.

duced in other states to meet construction needs accumulated during two decades of depression and war. A few private college interests also opposed state support for public higher education. Thus, most postwar attempts to face up to New Jersey's mounting public college space problem were successfully thwarted.

Even after the establishment of Rutgers as the State University in 1956, state financial support of public higher education did not increase substantially until the 1960s and 1970s. In order to undertake a massive expansion of higher education the legislature, galvanized by organized public efforts, passed the Higher Education Act of 1966, creating a separate board and the Department of Higher Education.

The result was not only a new department, but also legislative and voter support for an aggressive program of building and expanding the higher education system. This expansion was financed in part by general obligation bonds approved by the voters to build college classrooms, revenue bonds used to build dormitories, and general funds to subsidize operating costs. Since 1969 lottery revenues have also been earmarked, in part, for higher education.

The Department of Higher Education

In 1966 the legislature transferred all functions, duties, and powers pertaining to higher education to the new Department of Higher Education, guided by a board of higher education and administered by a chancellor.

The New Jersey Board of Higher Education has responsibility for overseeing, planning, and coordinating higher education. Among its duties are development and maintenance of a master plan and review and coordination of budgets for the various public institutions of higher education. The board establishes new colleges, campuses, and programs. It sets general policies on such matters as minimum admission standards and minimum standards for educational programs and degrees. In addition, the board licenses and approves the programs of all private institutions in the state except those eight institutions established before April 1, 1887.

The Board of Higher Education

The eighteen-member board of higher education consists of nine citizen members, two of whom must be women, and nine institutional members. The latter are the chairmen of the boards of Rutgers, the University of Medicine and Dentistry of New Jersey (UMDNJ), and New Jersey Institution of Technology (NJIT); the chairmen of the Council of State Colleges and of the Council of County Colleges; the president of the New Jersey Board of Education; and a representative of the private colleges and universities of New Jersey. The chancellor of higher education and the commissioner of education are ex officio, nonvoting members. The citizen members, who are unsalaried, are appointed by the governor with the consent of the senate and serve six-year overlapping terms.

The board of higher education appoints the chancellor, with the approval of the governor, for a five-year term. The chancellor promulgates and enforces the rules and regulations prescribed by the board and organizes and administers the work of the department. The chancellor is a member of the governor's cabinet.

Introducing a greater degree of lay participation into the public education system was one purpose in the creation of the board of higher education. It was believed that lay people inject a general, citizen point of view desirable in a public profession like education. It also was felt that lay people would add a higher degree of credibility in stating the needs of higher education than had the professional educators alone.

To give the higher education system even further benefits from citizen participation and to provide the state colleges with more autonomy, the 1966 law also created a nine-member board of trustees for each of the state colleges, to be appointed by the board of higher education with the approval of the governor. Of the nine trustees on each board, at most three may live in one county and at least two must be women. Each board administers its college within policies and procedures established by the board of higher education. The governing boards of the other public institutions—Rutgers, NJIT, UMDNJ, and the county colleges—are also lay boards.

Figure 7.4

Public Institutions of Higher Learning

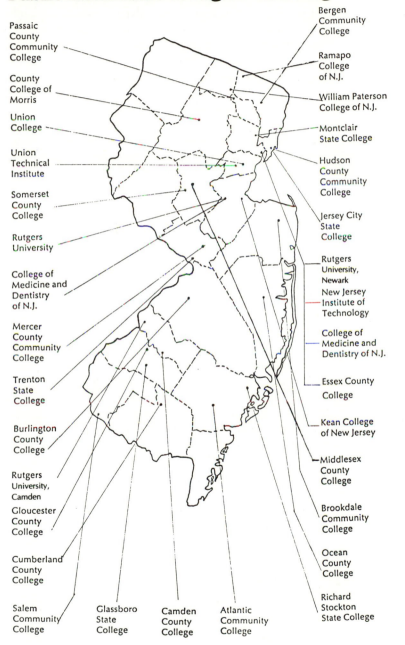

Passaic County Community College

Bergen Community College

Ramapo College of N.J.

County College of Morris

William Paterson College of N.J.

Union College

Montclair State College

Union Technical Institute

Hudson County Community College

Somerset County College

Jersey City State College

Rutgers University

Rutgers University, Newark

College of Medicine and Dentistry of N.J.

New Jersey Institute of Technology

Mercer County Community College

College of Medicine and Dentistry of N.J.

Essex County College

Trenton State College

Kean College of New Jersey

Burlington County College

Middlesex County College

Rutgers University, Camden

Brookdale Community College

Gloucester County College

Ocean County College

Cumberland County College

Richard Stockton State College

Salem Community College

Glassboro State College

Camden County College

Atlantic Community College

163

Institutions of Higher Education

Rutgers, The State University of New Jersey

Rutgers is the only American institution of higher learning that was founded as a colonial college, designated a land-grant institution, and developed into a state university. These three aspects of the university's history are of more than historical interest; they shape the objectives of the institution in conducting its programs of instruction, research, and extension service.

The principal campus, which is in New Brunswick, was founded as Queens College in 1766 and became a land-grant college a century later. A private institution until legislation in 1945 made it nominally the state university, Rutgers did not become a true state university until legislation in 1956 created a board of governors (six of whose eleven voting members are appointed by the governor and confirmed by the senate) and granted greater state financial support.

The State Colleges

Six public colleges were established in New Jersey between 1855 and 1929 for the sole purpose of preparing teachers for the state's public elementary and secondary schools. Today the state colleges, with the exception of Thomas A. Edison College, offer the general program of arts and sciences common to American four-year colleges.

The state colleges are Glassboro State, Jersey City State, Kean College, Montclair State, Ramapo College, Stockton State, Trenton State, and William Patterson College. In addition, Thomas A. Edison College of New Jersey is a non-traditional state "college without walls" that verifies and grants degrees for college-level learning experiences gained in non-traditional ways.

New Jersey Institute of Technology (NJIT)

NJIT is a publicly supported technological university in Newark. Engineering, computer science, industrial administration, management, architecture, engineering technology, applied sciences and related fields are the focus of this urban campus.

The University of Medicine and Dentistry of New Jersey (UMDNJ)

Newark is the home of the main campus of the University of Medicine and Dentistry, formed from a merger of the former Seton Hall College of Medicine and Dentistry and a two-year medical school at Rutgers. Additional programs include the School of Osteopathic Medicine, the Graduate School of Biomedical Sciences, and the School of Health-related Professions, including programs in nursing and toxicology. While there is no private medical school in New Jersey, Fairleigh Dickinson University operates a private dental school which receives some state funding on a per capita basis.

County Community Colleges

County community colleges, authorized in 1962 by state legislation and founded by the state and the respective county boards of freeholders, are two-year public institutions that offer three distinct types of programs: the first two years of college for transfer to a four-year institution, technical and paraprofessional courses leading directly to specific jobs, and a wide variety of community service courses. Two or more counties may participate in establishing a county college, but to date no such combination has taken place. There is, however, increasing cooperation between the colleges of neighboring counties to coordinate course offerings.

While construction costs for community colleges are shared by the county and the state, operating costs are also funded by student tuition. State aid to community colleges is based both on categorical aid and on differential funding to encourage significant programs which may be more costly to start up and operate.

The Department of Higher Education is responsible for the general oversight of the county colleges. The board of higher education approves each college's request to begin operations and to enter various phases of its development. The board also approves all new programs and all construction proposals.

Independent Colleges and Universities

New Jersey is served by Princeton University, Seton Hall University, Stevens Institute of Technology, and a score of other private institutions. The largest of these include Drew University, Fairleigh Dickinson University, Rider College, Upsala College, Monmouth College, and Bloomfield College. State aid is made available to sixteen of these private schools to aid them in providing higher education to New Jersey residents. (For a description of the colleges and universities in New Jersey see the current edition of the annual *Fitzgerald's Legislative Manual: State of New Jersey.*)

Financial Aid Programs

A portion of the cost of higher education is borne by the students in the form of tuition, in essence a user fee. For those who cannot afford this cost, there is a range of financial grants, scholarships, and loan programs.

Tuition

The board of higher education established the educational cost to the institution as the basis for setting tuition levels. Board policy calls for the gradual stabilization of state resident undergraduate tuition at 30 percent of average educational costs in each sector of higher education for the previous year. The recommended tuition levels for non-resident and graduate students are to be 45 percent of average costs. The goal is establishing a balance between payment by those benefiting from higher education and, at the same time, maintaining tuition low enough to attract New Jersey students. Of concern are statistics showing that many of the approximately 27,000 freshmen who go to out-of-state colleges each year, often New Jersey's gifted students, do not return to New Jersey after their education is finished. Various scholarship programs to cover all or part of college costs have been established to aid New Jersey students.

Grants and Scholarships

Tuition Aid Grants. This very large program provides non-repayable grants to students based both upon the individual's ability to pay and the cost of tuition at the New Jersey institution chosen.

Educational Opportunity Fund. This program is targeted at economically disadvantaged youths. In addition to direct grants made to the student, state funds are given to the college to support the additional special academic services necessary to help students succeed who are academically promising but educationally disadvantaged. The program also has funds for graduate study.

Garden State Scholarship. This program awards grants to students with superior academic abilities as well as financial need. The goal is to help keep New Jersey's most talented students in New Jersey. The program also has funds for graduate study.

Guaranteed Student Loans. This federal program is the largest source of financial assistance in New Jersey. The interest rate is fixed below the current market rate. Repayment of both principal and interest does not begin until after a post-graduation grace period. While the student is in school the federal government pays the interest.

Parent Loans for Undergraduate Students. This federal program supplements the Guaranteed Student Loan program, but it has a fluctuating interest rate, and repayment begins within sixty days of borrowing.

Public Loan Program. This state-funded program functions as the "lender of last resort" for students who fail to secure Guaranteed Student Loans from banks. The program is small but contains funds for graduate students as well as undergraduates.

8.
Transportation
and Labor

O ften called the corridor state, New Jersey serves as a passageway for almost all traffic moving north and south to and from New England and New York. New Jersey has more railroad and highway mileage in proportion to its size than any other state and the highest ratio of multi-lane highways to other roads among the states. However, it is as a commuter's state, with large numbers of New Jerseyans traveling daily to and from New York City and Philadelphia, that New Jersey captures the traffic trophy.

In fact, the estimated daily travel usage per mile of highway in New Jersey is close to four times the national average and much higher than any of the neighboring states. In addition, automobile registrations have increased faster than population—a result of suburban living and dispersal of business and industry.

The Department of Transportation

In 1966 the legislature created the Department of Transportation which absorbed the functions of the Highway Department and the aeronautical facilities functions of another department. This new department was charged with providing the state with the necessary structure for implementing a comprehensive and balanced transportation program encompassing all modes of transportation, including mass transit. The department is headed by a commissioner appointed by the governor with senate consent. Connected with the department are the autonomous authorities responsible for the toll roads and the New Jersey Interagency

169

Coordinating Committee which is composed of the heads of the turnpike authorities, the Port Authority of New York and New Jersey, and the Hackensack Meadowlands Development Commission.

History

The earliest roads grew from the network of Indian trails and were kept up with county taxes and compulsory road service, usually requiring six or eight days a year from all male inhabitants of the colony. In the early years of the nineteenth century the state legislature granted individual charters for turnpike companies. Thirty turnpikes were built, and tolls collected on the turnpikes repaid the investors. That era also saw the development of a system of canals to move freight through the state. The first one, the Morris Canal, operated for almost a century and brought anthracite from Pennsylvania to within reach of the emerging metropolitan area. Newark's growth as a major industrial and commercial center was due in considerable part to the existence of the Morris Canal. Part of its bed is now the Newark City Subway with Raymond Boulevard running above it. The Delaware and Raritan Canal, a thirty-two mile stretch at the narrow waist of New Jersey from the Delaware River to Raritan Bay, was opened in 1834. A prosperous operation, it was abandoned for navigation only in 1933. All lands and pertinent water rights were acquired by the state in 1934, and it is now being developed as parts of both the recreation system and the water supply system.

Steamboat service between New York and New Jersey and between Philadelphia and New Jersey ports on the Delaware dates from revolutionary times. It was the fight to break New York's hold on interstate service between New York City and New Jersey which lead to the landmark *Gibbon v. Ogden* decision establishing the principle that navigation on the interstate waterways is interstate commerce and therefore subject to the exclusive jurisdiction of the federal government. The sense of competition between the two sides of the Hudson continues to this day despite many joint projects.

The Camden and Amboy Railroad, the first important line in the nation, was granted a monopoly on railroad transportation across the middle of New Jersey in 1830. The company's shrewd political manipulations earned for New Jersey the nickname "the state of Camden and Amboy;" this monopoly was to last until 1869. Eventually this railroad joined forces with the New Jersey Railroad which then became part of the vast Pennsylvania Railroad system. A landmark in the history of commuter service to New York City occurred in 1910 when the Pennsylvania Railroad completed its tunnel under the Hudson River and provided direct rail service to Pennsylvania Station in midtown Manhattan.

Yet by the mid-twentieth century the railroad system was in deep decline. In 1976 the federal government formed Conrail, a corporation created from the remains of the seven bankrupt railroads serving the Northeast. On January 1, 1983 the commuter rail service was turned over to public agencies—New Jersey Transit Corporation (NJ Transit) took over the New Jersey lines, and the freight lines were offered for sale in 1984 to private investors.

History of Transportation Finance

The railroads helped shape not only the economic growth of New Jersey, but also the way state government financed itself. Until the railroads declined in the early twentieth century the railroad taxes produced so much revenue that in some years in the mid-nineteenth century the entire state budget was met by these taxes alone. The existence of such an ample source of funds meant that for many years there was no need to levy broad-based general taxes at the state level, and it became a tradition in New Jersey that state taxes should be as few as possible and those that were raised should be excise or special purpose taxes.

With the advent of the automobile came a shift in emphasis in the state transportation picture. As early as 1906 the New Jersey Legislature created the Department of Motor Vehicle Registration and Regulation. All funds from fees and fines were used for repair of roads. In 1917 the state Highway Department was created, and under the state budgets in those years highway funds were placed in a dedicated fund rather than in the general fund. Both the legislature and the department participated in spending these funds to lay out the state highway system. In an ambitious $200 million road building program the Pulaski Skyway, the George Washington Bridge, and U.S. Route 1 from the Holland Tunnel to Trenton were built.

Prior to 1945 New Jersey's Highway Department operated under a budget separate from that of all other state departments. Its resources included bond monies, the gasoline tax, vehicle registration fees, federal aid, and from 1917 to 1933 a real estate tax. During the Depression money was borrowed from the dedicated highway funds to help meet the crisis in the state general fund. But by 1945, in a reversal of this policy of dedicated funds, the department's budget was integrated into the state government's overall budget. As a result, after 1945 the Highway Department did not have the usual funds available for road construction and maintenance.

The last two decades have seen a steady decline in the percentage of the total budget devoted to transportation needs. In 1961 transportation received 28 percent of the total state budget, in 1971 12.5 percent, and in 1981 5.2 percent (as quoted in the *Regional Plan News*, January 1983). By the early 1980s state priorities had shifted away from transportation issues with the result that only about half of the revenue from the eight-cents-a-gallon gasoline tax and from motor vehicle fees was returned to the transportation budget.

After rejecting four bond issues during the 1970s, the voters of New Jersey finally approved a 1979 transportation bond issue which, combined with federal funds, state appropriations, and funds from the Port Authority of New York and New Jersey, generated over $2 billion for transportation improvements. About 40 percent was earmarked for mass transit, another 40 percent for state highways, and the rest went to state aid to county and municipal roads. The funds were to be spent between 1981 and 1987. It soon became apparent, however, that this bond issue fell far short of meeting the long-range funding needs for highway maintenance.

Bridge improvements became a highly visible issue when Connecticut's I-95 Mianus River Bridge collapsed in June 1983. In November of that year New Jersey voters approved

the $135 million Bridge Rehabilitation and Improvement
Bond Act of 1983. Federal funding was also received to rehabilitate the Pulaski Skyway—one of the nation's longest
stretches of raised super-highway.

By 1984 traffic congestion on unfinished parts of the
highway network and the deterioration of the existing highway system that was not receiving needed maintenance
funds prompted the legislature to return to a policy of separating funds for transportation—this time through the
Transportation Trust Fund. The Transportation Trust
Fund Authority will sell ten-year bonds over the four years
of the program (fiscal year 1985 through 1989). The bond
revenue along with other revenue sources will be used
to match the more than $600 million in federal funds ex-
pected to be available each of those four years. Payback for
the bonds will come from state appropriations including the
dedication to transportation needs of two and one-half cents
of the existing eight-cents-a-gallon gasoline tax, approved
by the voters in 1984.

The State Highway System

People who regularly travel the interstates and toll roads in
New Jersey can appreciate the advantages of road-systems
that have stable sources of long-term funding. Those who
commute on the state road system not included in the interstate and toll road network are often keenly aware of funding deficiencies—deficiencies that translate into poor
maintenance, overcrowding, and the stop-and-start traffic
resulting from unlimited access to roads. The problems do
not always end when drivers turn off onto county or municipal roads.

The counties and municipalities are responsible for
maintaining about 90 percent of the state's center-line mileage, but their ability to fund such repairs has diminished
sharply in the past decade. Many of these roads are not eligible for federal funds, and state aid to counties and municipalities for streets and bridges disappeared between 1974
and 1979, a period during which most available state monies were used to match federal transportation assistance.

The general shortfall in transportation funding in New
Jersey necessitated a turn to new sources after 1945

—namely, the use of authorities to build three toll roads and participation in the federally funded interstate highway program.

New Jersey Toll Roads

Nearly all toll mileage (366 miles with part of the New Jersey Turnpike also being designated as an interstate highway) is accounted for by the New Jersey Turnpike (118 miles) and the Garden State parkway (174 miles). Each route was initiated by the state Highway Department immediately following World War II, and small sections were subsequently built. A shortage of funds prevented further construction by the state, however, and separate authorities were created by the legislature to complete the routes by means of private bond financing.

Each toll road authority is administered by a separate group of commissioners, appointed by the governor with senate consent, who serve without pay for five-year terms. The toll roads and all their additions and improvements have been financed through the sale of bonds to private investors. The authority pays off the bondholders from the tolls collected and through a percentage from the sale of food, gasoline, oil, and other products sold by concessionaires. All expenses are paid by the authority, including the salaries of the State Police who patrol the road.

An additional project undertaken by the authority which built the Garden State Parkway is the Garden State Arts Center. This 350-acre site is located at Telegraph Hill Park in Monmouth County, thirty miles south of Newark. The arts center has a large amphitheater, botanical gardens, an art exhibition mall, nature trails, large parking areas, and refreshment facilities. The authority operates the center with money earned by admissions for events plus the additional toll income from motorists traveling to and from the center via the parkway.

The Atlantic City Expressway (44 miles) connecting the Camden area with Atlantic City was built by an authority created by the legislature in 1962.

Federal Interstate Highway Program

The interstate highway system is the largest public works program in history. The 42,500 mile national system is an example of cooperation between federal and state governments. The federal government contributes 90 percent of the highway costs and exercises its right of approval and reasonable control. Individual states, paying the remaining 10 percent, determine the routes (subject to the approval of the federal Department of Transportation), design the highways, and award construction contracts to low bidders.

The roads are financed from the federal Highway Trust Fund which derives its funds from the following sources:

- Motor fuel tax—$0.09 per gallon
- Sales tax on trucks and trailers, tires, and truck and bus parts and accessories
- Lubricating oil tax—$0.06 per gallon
- Heavy-vehicle use tax

Four hundred and sixteen miles of interstate highway were planned for New Jersey, and much of that system was in place by the mid-1970s. By the mid-1980s, 340 miles of interstate were completed and an additional 40 miles were in final design and construction stages. But as the interstate building program progressed decade after decade, it became obvious that there were other unmet transportation needs: one was the need for maintenance and improvements on the existing roads, the other was for mass transit.

Changes in the federal highway funding acts expanded the scope of federal involvement in the state transportation systems. The federal Highway Act of 1973 not only authorized additional monies for interstate highways, it also permitted funds to be used for mass transit. Flexibility was added as this law allowed states to withdraw proposed sections of interstate highway from the state plan (with the approval of the Secretary of Transportation) and reallocate that funding to other transportation needs. This was one way New Jersey gained federal funds for capital improvements on federally aided highways, improvements such as widening or reconstructing sections of road.

The 1982 Federal Surface Transportation Act added additional funds for reconstruction and replacement of federally aided highways and bridges. Additional funds were raised by increasing the motor fuel tax from $0.04 per gallon to $0.09 per gallon. The resulting increase of federal funds to New Jersey dramatically improved the state's ability to maintain and upgrade the interstate and federal highway system.

Mass Transit

Mass transit to carry New Jersey residents to jobs in Philadelphia and New York City is essential, not only because of the volume of traffic but also because all traffic must funnel over or under rivers to reach these employment centers. New Jersey has internal mass transit needs as well to carry residents to jobs within the state's major cities. In addition to the needs of those traveling to jobs, mass transit continues to provide essential mobility to those who cannot afford an automobile, to the elderly, to students, and to some handicapped persons.

By the 1960s the federal and state governments were looking at mass transit as a partial solution to traffic congestion. In 1960, following a series of studies and the creation of the Division of Railroad Transportation, the Highway Department began subsidizing all major commuter rail lines to ensure continuation of essential passenger service in the state. Later, after prolonged negotiations, the Port Authority of New York and New Jersey acceded to New Jersey's demand that the Port Authority acquire, rehabilitate, and operate the Hudson and Manhattan Railroad as a quid pro quo for the state's consent to the authority building the World Trade Center in downtown Manhattan. Largely at the Highway Department's insistence, the program included provisions for transfer stations to link up with commuter railroads, a new bus terminal in Jersey City, and the Port Authority's commitment to spend a substantial amount each year on mass transit, even as a deficit operation. The latter provision was ruled unconstitutional when challenged by Port Authority bond holders.

The New Jersey Transit Corporation

In the face of a disintegrating private commuter bus system, the legislature chartered the New Jersey Transit Corporation (NJ Transit) in 1979. First serving as a conduit for the distribution of federal and state subsidies to contract operators, NJ Transit in 1980 took over direct operation of the nation's largest private bus company, Transport of New Jer-

Figure 8.1

NJ Transit Passenger Rail System Map

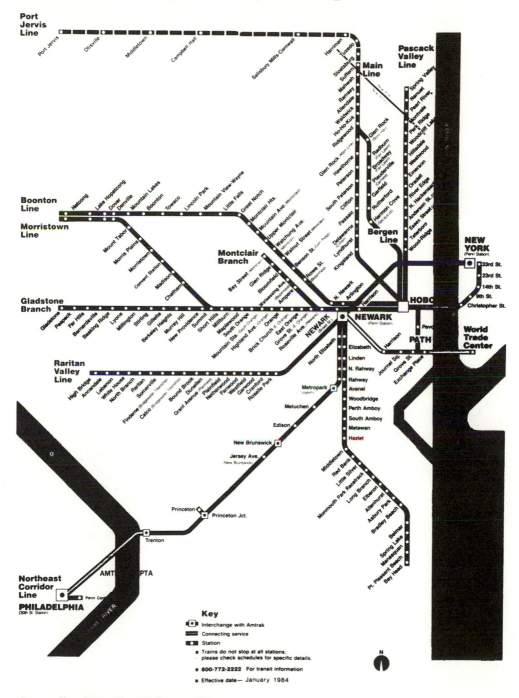

Source: New Jersey Transit Corporation.

sey. In 1981 congress passed legislation enabling NJ Transit to assume direct operation effective January 1, 1983 of commuter rail service in New Jersey from Conrail, which had operated the service under contract with the state since 1976. The bus and rail systems are operated by the NJ Transit subsidiaries, NJ Transit Bus Operations, Inc. and NJ Transit Rail Operations, Inc.

As a publicly funded corporation, NJ Transit essentially has the citizens of New Jersey as its shareholders. NJ Transit is governed by a seven-member board of directors, appointed by the governor with the consent of the senate. Four private citizens form the majority of the board; the commissioner of transportation chairs the board. Additional citizen representation is ensured by two fifteen-member Transit Advisory Committees, one in the northern part of the state, one in the south.

NJ Transit took over one of the oldest, more outdated mass transit systems in the country. Significant investment of capital funds was needed to transform it into a modern, efficient transit network which would not only serve existing riders but attract new ones. The money to finance this modernization came from a variety of sources.

New Jersey voters approved a $475 million transportation bond issue in 1979 which, when combined with federal funds, annual state appropriations, and funds from the Port Authority of New York and New Jersey, generated over $2 billion for public transportation. Of this sum, about 40 percent went to mass transit to be spent between 1981 to 1987. The mass transit portion of the federal funds came from the Urban Mass Transportation Administration (UMTA), and the Port Authority Funds came through the TRANSPAC program.

The sheer size of the NJ Transit system as well as the poor condition of much of the capital stock made the challenge of modernization expensive. NJ Transit Bus operates close to 2,250 buses on over one hundred routes in twenty of the state's twenty-one counties. Included in this system is the Newark City Subway, a 4.3 mile light rail system spanning the city's central business district. In addition, the corporation provides financial assistance and equipment or leases buses to a number of other private bus companies which in turn coordinate routes and service with NJ Transit Bus.

Modernization of the bus system has focused on replacing all buses more than twelve years old used in peak period service. Fifteen hundred new buses, many of them similar to those used by the major interstate bus companies, have been purchased. Other buses have been refurbished, and some of these have been allocated to private carriers. By eliminating expenditures for new buses, the private carriers are able to hold down fare increases. The modernization program also included installing over a thousand new bus shelters and upgrading the Newark City Subway.

The rail system consists of nine lines in sixteen counties and is the third largest system in the nation. NJ Transit Rail has concentrated on replacement of old coaches and locomotives, re-electrification of the Morristown Line and its two branches, and extension of electrification from South Amboy to Matawan on the North Jersey Coast Line. Rail stations are also being upgraded, and major rehabilitation was undertaken for both the Broad Street and Penn Stations in Newark and the Hoboken Terminal. A new transportation center, both rail and bus, is being built by the City of Camden and is scheduled for completion in 1986.

New maintenance facilities for rail and bus include a rail maintenance site and a bus facility in the Meadowlands and new bus garages serving the Route 9 Corridor and southern New Jersey.

While the upgrading of buses and trains is vital to the viability of NJ Transit, major initiatives have also been taken in the areas of service and marketing to better serve existing customers and to attract new ones. Bus routes have been reorganized, as has the information and ticket sales system. Project Access uses a fleet of over four hundred lift-equipped buses to help meet the needs of physically handicapped bus riders.

In those areas where both housing and employment is dispersed, for example, along Interstate 287 in Morris County, grants are made available for companies to purchase vans for employee van pooling. There are also private van programs in some places that compete with the bus systems and provide door-to-door service for commuters.

NJ Transit is creating a mass transit system to meet commuter needs, but it remains to be seen if commuters will choose to leave their automobiles at home and take advantage of mass transit. As waiting time at the Hudson River tunnels and bridges increases, automobile travel to New York City may become less and less desirable. However, the growth of dispersed job sites in New Jersey, not easily accessible by mass transit, increases dependence on the automobile. Renovation of Penn Station in Newark, if not accompanied with development to locate a large number of jobs close to the station, will not achieve the goal of attracting people back to mass transit. Essentially, a number of the factors necessary for the success of mass transit are beyond the control of NJ Transit—they lie in the realm of land-use planning and coordination between economic development and the transportation system. (See figure 8.2.) The Department of Transportation Master Plan released in 1984 following the creation of the Transportation Trust Fund includes a number of long-range planning guidelines that foster a complementary relationship between mass transit and the highway system.

Authority-Operated Transportation Facilities

Corporate public authorities, chartered by the legislature and able to sell revenue bonds backed by user fees, offer another solution to funding New Jersey's transportation needs. (See chapter 6, Long-term Capital Financing.) Authorities both ensure funding continuity for projects and remove the necessity for annually winning major capital improvement appropriations from the legislature.

The Port Authority of New York and New Jesery

The Port Authority of New York and New Jersey was created in 1921 by compact between the two states and with the consent of the Congress of the United States as required under the compact clause of the United States Constitution. The authority is administered by a board of commissioners, six from each state appointed by their own governor and subject to confirmation by the respective state senate. The commissioners serve without pay for overlapping six-

Figure 8.2

Transportation Planning and Land-Use Decision Making in New Jersey

The Council on New Jersey Affairs, a citizens' group composed of former governors, business, labor, and civic leaders and working with the Woodrow Wilson School of Public and International Affairs at Princeton University, studied the relationship between transportation and land-use decision making in New Jersey. The research paper prepared for this study includes the following:

> Land-use decisions are made primarily at municipal and county levels, while transportation policies are generally set by the state. Better integration of transportation planning with land-use decision making could lead to greater efficiency by coordinating development locations with available or planned transportation facilities. This, in turn, would bring about better utilization of existing transport facilities, more precise targeting of new construction, increased use of mass transit, and better use of limited public funds. These changes need not require total state or regional control over local land use and zoning, but could range from simple advisory reports to regional cooperative efforts to state veto power.
>
> Land-use patterns could be shaped to reduce demands placed on New Jersey's transportation system. High-density land uses supported by mass transit could be encouraged with land controls that cluster development, preserve open space, and contribute energy savings.

The study goes on to describe what Florida and Colorado have done to coordinate transportation and land-use decision making.

> Florida has a state comprehensive plan that provides long-range guidelines for orderly social, economic, and physical growth. The plan serves as an advisory document, and includes economic, environmental, and transportation components. Colorado has taken steps to increase land-use control over areas near highways. Virtually all state routes have been designated as "controlled access," limiting the number of access points to them. Developers do not have a legal right to curb cuts and may be required to use secondary roads to gain access to state highways. The Colorado DOT is also involved in setting development standards and reviewing proposals for construction on lands near state highways. This gives the state the authority to regulate strip development along major highways.

Source: Dwight Dively and John Lago *Transportation Planning and Land-Use Decision Making in New Jersey* (Program for New Jersey Affairs, Princeton Urban and Regional Research Center, Woodrow Wilson School of Public and International Affairs, Princeton University, 1982).

year terms and report directly to the governor of their state. The actions of the commissioners taken at Port Authority meetings are subject to gubernatorial review for a period of ten working days and may be vetoed by the governor of their respective states. This veto has been exercised from time to time.

The authority is a public corporate agency of both states, with the power to issue revenue bonds and notes. The revenues of the authority are derived principally from the toll, fare, rental, landing, dockage, and other charges for the use and privileges at its various facilities. The two states empowered the authority to buy, build, lease, and operate any transportation or terminal facility within the Port District (approximately the area within a twenty-five mile radius of the Statue of Liberty) and to charge for its use. The authority also has the power to acquire real and personal property by condemnation or the exercise of the right of eminent domain. The original mandate of the authority was to provide transportation, terminal, and other facilities of commerce within the Port District. This charge was expanded several times. (See figure 8.3.)

Delaware River and Bay Authorities

The Delaware River Port Authority (DRPA) was created in 1951 by compact legislation between New Jersey and Pennsylvania, to which the United States Congress assented in 1952.

The DRPA owns and operates:
■ the Benjamin Franklin Bridge (linking center-city Philadephia to Camden),
■ the Walt Whitman Bridge (linking South Philadelphia and Gloucester),
■ the Commodore John Barry Bridge (linking Bridgeport, New Jersey and Chester, Pennsylvania),
■ the Betsy Ross Bridge (linking northeast Philadelphia and Pennsauken).

Through the DRPA's Port Authority Transit Company, the 14.5 mile Lindenwold High Speed Line was constructed, connecting suburban and center-city Philadelphia by rail.

The Delaware River Joint Toll Bridge Commission was

The Port Authority's Expanding Role

1947 Encouragement of the integration of air terminals into a unified system

1962 Acquisition, rehabilitation, and operation of the Hudson Tubes (the PATH)

1971–1973 Provision of mass transportation facilities connecting with John F. Kennedy and Newark International Airports

1978 Participation in highway projects in the vicinity of an air or marine terminal, providing those projects improved access to such terminals

1979 Encouragement and development of economically sound commerce and industry through government action, especially with the development of industrial development projects, including resource recovery and industrial pollution control facilities

1979 and **1982** Purchase of buses to be leased (in exchange for an agreement to use the buses in accordance with Port Authority mass transit goals) to both public and private bus companies serving the Port District

1980 Participation in port-related railroad freight projects (freight yards)

1984 Provision of site development for the Hoboken waterfront (and Hunters Point in Queens) in preparation for private development of the area

Figure 8.3

Figure 8.4

Port Authority Facilities in New Jersey

Port Authority facilities in or connecting with New Jersey are an important part of the region's infrastructure.

Newark International Airport. Officially opened by the City of Newark in 1928, the airport's operation was turned over to the Port Authority in 1948 under a long-term lease. In its development program the authority increased the airport's total area to about 2,100 acres. Three new terminal buildings were constructed (two completed in 1973 and the third shell to be completed in 1986). By the mid-1980s Newark surpassed LaGuardia in volume of business.

Teterboro Airport. Located in Bergen County, this airport is devoted primarily to training, business, and private aircraft operations.

Holland Tunnel. Two two-lane tubes connect lower Manhattan in the vicinity of Canal Street with the New Jersey Turnpike Extension and other highways in Jersey City.

Lincoln Tunnel. Three two-lane tubes connect midtown Manhattan in the vicinity of West 39th Street to the New Jersey Turnpike (I-95) and other highways at Weehawken.

George Washington Bridge. This fourteen-lane, two-level suspension bridge joins upper Manhattan and Fort Lee, New Jersey.

Other Bridges. In addition, the Port Authority maintains the three bridges linking Staten Island in New York with New Jersey points: the Bayonne Bridge to Bayonne, the Goethals Bridge to Elizabeth, and the Outerbridge Crossing to Perth Amboy.

Port Authority Trans-Hudson system. PATH is an interurban electric railroad connecting Manhattan with Newark and Hoboken.

Port Authority Bus Programs. Along with the Port Authority Bus Terminal at the Manhattan end of the Lincoln Tunnel, the Port Authority purchases buses (and matches federal Urban Mass Transportation Administration funds for such purchases) for bus companies, both public and private, serving the Port District. This aid allows the bus companies to maintain lower fares and helps to form a more integrated bus system essential to meet the mass transit objectives of the Port Authority.

Port Newark. Port Newark is a waterfront terminal development located on Newark Bay adjacent to the Newark International Airport. The marine terminal now contains about 930 acres and includes wharves, deep water ship berths, transit sheds, open storage areas, buildings, roadways, and railroad trackage. Direct ship-to-rail transfer is offered at Port Newark.

Port Elizabeth. The south side of Port Newark and Port Elizabeth are served by a channel along the boundary between the two facilities. Twenty-three container cranes serve fully-equipped container ship berths.

Elizabeth Industrial Park. Located adjacent to Port Elizabeth, this industrial park is being constructed and operated by the Port Authority to aid industrial development. An unexpected problem in this project was the discovery of waste oil containing PCBs on the site, formerly a landfill. The Port Authority, working with the New Jersey Department of Environmental Protection, is conducting a cleanup.

Resource Recovery Plant. In addition, the Port Authority is participating in construction of a resource recovery plant in Newark. The Port Authority will act as project developer and will invest a major portion of the capital.

created in 1934 to purchase and make free the privately owned toll bridges crossing the Delaware River on its course from the New York state line to Trenton. The commission not only maintains more than a dozen free bridges, it also has built six toll bridges, financed by revenue bonds. When the bonds are retired, the bridges will become free and be maintained by the commission with expenses being shared equally by the states, as it is for the other bridges.

The Delaware River and Bay Authority was created in 1961 by the legislatures of New Jersey and Delaware for the purpose of planning, financing, constructing, and operating Delaware River or Bay crossings. The authority operates two facilities: the Delaware Memorial Bridge from New Castle, Delaware, to Pennsville, New Jersey; and the Cape May–Lewes Ferry, a year-round service. All of the authority's operations are financed by tolls.

LABOR

New Jersey's location as a pivotal state within a populous and prosperous area attracted business and industry. The legislature was generally cooperative and encouraged these companies. However, when conditions deteriorated sufficiently to arouse citizen concern, the public exerted pressures on the government for business reform and extension of certain protections to the workers.

The formation of the Bureau of Statistics of Labor and Industries in 1878 was a response to the growing demands of the labor force, which required a means to substantiate its claims of the need for better treatment at the hands of business. As organized labor gained significance in the state, safety standards were established, utilities came under state regulation, restrictions were placed on weights and measures, taxes on railroads were increased, and more stringent labor laws were enacted. During the legislative reorganization of the administrative branch in 1948 some of these varied programs were gathered into a Department of Labor and Industry. Recent years have seen a continuation of legislative concern for protecting the public interest and workers from exploitation by business and industry, most recently evidenced by passage of the Worker and Community Right to Know Act. (See chapter 10, The Worker and Community Right to Know Act.)

In 1981, in response to repeated cycles of depressed economic activity, the New Jersey Legislature decided the interests of industry and labor should not both be represented by one cabinet-level department. The Department of Labor and Industry was split into the new departments of Labor and of Commerce and Economic Development. (See chapter 9, Commerce and Economic Development.)

The department is headed by a commissioner appointed by the governor with senate consent. Included in the department are a multitude of programs, some in existence unchanged for many decades, some reformed and updated by current legislation. For purposes of discussion (although it does not exactly match the department organizational chart) these programs are grouped under Job Training and Employment Services, Workplace Standards, Labor Relations, and Income Security.

The Department of Labor

Job Training and Employment Services

Job Training
In 1983 the Comprehensive Employment and Training Act (CETA) was replaced by the Job Training Partnership Act (JTPA) as the major federal job training program. JTPA focuses on job training directly related to the available jobs in private industry. The design of the program is oriented to grass-roots decision-making in each Service Delivery Area (SDA). In each of the nineteen SDAs in New Jersey, a Private Industry Council composed of representatives from labor, industry, government, education, and veterans groups identifies both local unemployed and target industries where jobs are or will be available. Then, customized job training programs are developed to train the unemployed for those specific jobs. The Division of Employment and Training is the state agency coordinating this federal jobs program.

Employment Services
Separate from but closely related to the JTPA job training program are the services of the Division of Employment Services which has as its primary goal providing job placement services to unemployment insurance claimants.

The New Jersey Job Service provides no-fee placement services for job seekers and recruitment services for employers. Anyone looking for work or job-related information can receive help in areas such as employment counseling, training opportunities, and job development. Related services available to employers include labor market information, testing programs, alien labor certification, tax credits, and on-site recruitment.

The New Jersey Job Service continues to be heavily involved in recruiting replacements for vacancies in the casino hotel industry. The Atlantic City Job Service office maintains the Casino Career Information Center which serves as a central information resource on jobs in the casino hotels and also on employment-related services from government agencies.

Special programs to develop employability are targeted for welfare recipients, disadvantaged youth and adults, unemployment insurance claimants, and displaced workers. The Work Incentive program (WIN) is designed to provide welfare recipients of Aid to Families with Dependent Children (AFDC) with the opportunity to become gainfully employed and skilled members of the working population, while at the same time reducing the rise in welfare costs. The Job Corps is a residential vocational training program for disadvantaged youth. This program is federally funded. The General Assistance Employability Program (GAEP) began in response to legislation requiring general assistance recipients, except when good cause exists, to perform public work in return for their welfare grants.

The Office of Customized Training designs training programs for new, relocating, and expanding businesses and industries and for industries having difficulty obtaining skilled workers. For example, a program operated through a joint agreement between the Department of Labor and the Meadowlands Chamber of Commerce provided training opportunities in Meadowlands businesses and industry for disadvantaged, unemployed individuals living in the urban areas surrounding the Meadowlands.

Vocational Rehabilitation

The Division of Vocational Rehabilitation is charged with providing vocational rehabilitation services, Extended Employment Services, and Work Activity Training Center services to eligible disabled persons in need of assistance in preparing for, securing, and maintaining employment. Much of the division's activity is supported with 80 percent federal 20 percent state funding arrangements.

Services are available to any man or woman with a physical or mental disability meeting the following requirements: there must be limitations that constitute a substantial handicap to employment and a reasonable expectation that rehabilitation services may render the individual fit to engage in gainful occupation. The populations served by these programs include those with physical disabilities (including cardiac and back problems), hearing and speech disabilities, emotional disabilities, mental retardation, alcoholism, and developmental disabilities.

The division also funds an extended employment program for severely disabled, mentally retarded, and mentally ill persons. Close to four thousand clients were in this program in 1983.

Clearinghouse for Services for the Deaf
The Division of the Deaf is an information and referral agency that acts as a clearinghouse for information on programs and services for the deaf in New Jersey. Included is an interpreter referral service and public education of employers and government agencies about the needs and abilities of the deaf.

Safety
Industrial New Jersey has its share of potentially dangerous or unhealthy working places: construction projects, high voltage lines, mines and quarries, foundries, chemical processing and other manufacturing plants, and home industries. The inspection of these places of employment was previously the work of the Bureau of Engineering and Safety. For many years the state was a leader in safety standards for the country. In 1971, however, a major change occurred with the passage of the federal Occupational Safety and Health Act (OSHA) which pre-empted all matters of occupational safety and health from the state. (See chapter 10 for the Right to Know Act, which has been tied up

Workplace Standards

in court on the issue of OSHA regulations pre-empting state regulations.)

Under the OSHA law several options were offered each state. If the state had safety regulations already, the federal government would assume approximately 70 percent of the costs necessary to update the present laws or to create a new program; or, the state could bow out completely and permit the federal government to run its own program. In 1975 New Jersey selected the second option, and department responsibility in safety standards was curtailed.

Although a major part of the department's safety activities was diminished, the Division of Workplace Standards still is concerned with the establishment and enforcement of safety standards to protect the public in matters concerning carnival and amusement rides, ski lifts, fireworks, boiler and pressure vessel construction and operation, and the distribution and use of liquified petroleum. Under the Mine Safety Act the division inspects approximately 250 mines, quarries, and pits to assure safe and healthful working conditions and operating practices that will protect employees, the public, and property. As part of this responsibility, the division regulates the storage, transportation, and use of millions of pounds of explosives in the state's mining and construction industries. Under a grant from the United States Department of Labor the office has conducted mine safety training in a number of locations.

In addition to safety concerns, the Division of Workplace Standards administers and enforces a number of laws dealing with minimum wages, child labor, the licensing and regulation of migrant and seasonal farm labor crew chiefs, and the establishment and enforcement of wage rates to be paid on all public works contracts of more than two thousand dollars let by public agencies in New Jersey.

Wages and Child Labor

Since 1976 New Jersey has had a minimum wage ($3.35 per hour in 1984). The Office of Wage and Hour Compliance staff enforces provisions of this law, with inspection of industrial homework facilities (piecework done at home) receiving special attention in the effort to eliminate sweatshop working conditions.

A wage collection court hears well over a thousand cases each year. This court has the same authority as a superior court to adjudicate claims of workers against employers for wages not in excess of three hundred dollars.

Child labor is another concern. Minors under eighteen years of age are prohibited from working in specified hazardous occupations or for extended hours. To reinforce the compulsory school attendance law, the employment of minors under sixteen years old is permitted only after school hours and during school vacations except under certain conditions (such as school sponsored work-study programs). Minors between fourteen and sixteen years of age may be employed if their jobs will not interfere with their health or standing in school but are prohibited from working in factories, near power-driven machines, or in dangerous occupations.

Special restrictions on working conditions for women were repealed in 1971 as a result of the equal rights movement.

Migrant Workers

Supervision of migrant worker concerns is a responsibility of the Division of Workplace Standards. Migrants working on farms that employ more than ten workers come under OSHA regulation protection as well. Enforcement of the New Jersey Crew Leader Act ensures that crew leaders and farm labor contractors are property registered, possess required documentation and insurance for vehicles which have been inspected, maintain adequate records of wages paid to workers, and are providing required information to the workers. In 1984 there were approximately four hundred crew leaders and farm contractors whose activities involved some thirteen thousand seasonal farm workers. Additional checks are made on vehicles transporting seasonal farm workers to make sure the vehicles and drivers are in compliance with the law. Also inspections are made to ensure compliance with the Drinking Water and Toilet Facilities Act which provides that access to toilet facilities and drinking water be available to seasonal farm workers in the field where the work takes place. Farm labor camps are inspected for those workers recruited through the State

Employment Service, those owned or controlled by crew leaders or farm labor contractors, or those coming under OSHA regulations.

Labor Relations

State Board of Mediation

The New Jersey State Board of Mediation was established in 1941 to promote the mediation, conciliation, and arbitration of labor disputes. The board is an autonomous agency technically in, but effectively not of, the Department of Labor. Board members appointed by the governor with the consent of the senate represent the public (three members), labor (two members), and management (two members).

The board provides mediation and arbitration services to private employers and employees throughout the state. Mediation includes assisting in contract negotiation, conducting consent elections, and mediation under contract. Arbitration includes facilitating hearings that result in final and binding awards. The board handles well over four thousand cases a year, entering a case at the request of either party or on its own initiative.

Public Employment Relations Commission

The Public Employment Relations Commission (PERC), created in 1968, is responsible for the administration of the New Jersey Employer–Employee Relations Act as it applies to the public sector. This act guarantees the right of public employees to organize and negotiate collectively concerning grievances and terms and conditions of employment. It also grants the commission exclusive responsibility for the prevention of specified unfair practices and provides that the commission determine whether matters in dispute between public employers and employees are within the scope of collective negotiations. The seven-member commission has two representatives from public employers, two from employee organizations, and three from the general public, one of whom is designated chairman and serves as a full-time chief executive officer and administrator. Commission members are appointed by the governor with senate consent.

Like all states, New Jersey operates programs to ease the hardship of unemployment brought about either by lack of work or by job-connected disabilities. New Jersey's income security program is an extension of the unemployment compensation program created in 1935 with the Social Security Act.

Under Social Security the federal government collects contributions from both employers and employees and pays retirement, survivor, and disability benefits as well as medical benefits for the aged (Medicare).

Social Security laws provide not only for the nation-wide system but also for state-operated unemployment compensation systems. Because of these laws' built-in financial incentives, each state quickly adopted a program meeting minimum federal standards. Since each state can adopt its own policies on such matters as coverage, eligibility, and benefit amounts, the programs vary from state to state.

The state's income security program is administered through three divisions: Division of Unemployment and Disability Insurance, Division of Workers' Compensation, and Division of Disability Determinations.

Unemployment Compensation

New Jersey's unemployment compensation program is an insurance system providing cash benefits for unemployed workers. A companion program, the temporary disability benefits system, provides cash payments for workers who are injured or become ill off the job and are unable to perform their duties. (New Jersey is one of a very few states that has a program for those whose unemployment is caused by disabilities that occur off the job.) Both programs are administered by the Division of Unemployment and Disability Insurance.

Benefit payments are financed by a tax on both employers and employees. However, during the years of depressed economic activity during the mid- and late 1970s, extended benefits, emergency compensation, and extended emergency compensation benefits were paid out. The cost of these extended benefits was shared by New Jersey and the federal government. The emergency compensation payments were funded wholly by the federal government. In

Income Security

addition, federal legislation set up a temporary program in 1975 known as special unemployment assistance which provided for payment of benefits to qualified unemployed workers not eligible under any other unemployment insurance programs.

As a direct result of the heavy cost of state benefits paid during this period, the New Jersey unemployment compensation fund ran dry, and the state was forced to borrow $735 million from the federal government. By 1984 $422 million of that debt still remained. As a result, employers in New Jersey were assessed a higher federal unemployment compensation tax on payroll, a factor making New Jersey a less attractive business location.

In 1984 Governor Kean signed legislation reforming the unemployment compensation system. The legislation represented a compromise developed by a five-member gubernatorial commission comprised of business and organized labor representatives. Included in the law is a two-year plan to pay off the debt to the federal government by imposing a 10 percent surtax on employers, raising the tax on employees an eighth of a percentage point. The law also transferred $50 million from the Temporary Disability Benefits Fund.

Eligibility for benefits has been tightened; for example, full-time students are now disqualified unless they have earned the major portion of base year wages while attending school. An individual who leaves work without good cause has a longer waiting period before qualifying for benefits, and an individual discharged for a criminal act in connection with work loses all benefit rights accruing from employment with that employer and is disqualified from receiving benefits. For those who receive benefits illegally (for example, if they are employed at the time) a fine of 25 percent of the total amount illegally received is levied, and the individual is disqualified from receiving benefits for one year from the date of discovery.

The change in New Jersey to a "wage record" system, which relies on an ongoing and continuous accumulation of individual wage records on a quarterly basis, has made determining benefits more accurate. When an individual files a claim, the computer can instantly determine eligibility. The old system required writing to the employer and requesting wage and separation information—a time-consuming and all too often inaccurate system.

Temporary Disability Benefits

New Jersey's temporary disability program, initiated in 1948, pays weekly cash benefits for nonwork-related illnesses or accidents (those not covered by workers' compensation.) This state program is financed independently of the federal government and is one of the few such programs in the nation. Employers subject to the law may provide coverage under either a private plan or the state-operated plan. The division administers the state plan, collects the funds, and pays benefits. The division also examines the private plans to ensure that they meet state requirements.

Workers' Compensation

The Workmen's Compensation Law of New Jersey (now called Workers' Compensation) preceded all other forms of social insurance in the United States. It superseded the common-law doctrine that an employer was liable for job-connected injuries only if the employer was at fault and the worker or a coworker had not contributed to the injury in any way. The employer's liability had to be proved in court. The Workmen's Compensation legislation adopted in 1917 compelled all employers to provide payments to injured workers and set up a separate administrative agency—now the Division of Workers' Compensation—to administer the law and to adjudicate disputed claims. The division's purpose is to have the employer or his insurance carrier furnish or pay for the medical, surgical, and hospital services made necessary by occupational accidents or diseases and to pay weekly cash benefits for temporary or permanent disability caused by such accidents or illnesses.

Major reform of the Workers' Compensation Law was signed into law in 1980. The major goal of the new law was to eliminate from compensability the less severe permanent partial disabilities and to divert the money awards for those injuries to the more seriously disabled workers.

Under Workers' Compensation an employee loses the right to sue the employer in court for negligence. In return the employer accepts absolute liability for accidents arising "out of and in the course of employment," and the employer's insurer must compensate the employee according to a statutory formula. Benefits depend on how long the worker has to stay away from the job and the extent of any permanent disability.

Special Compensation Funds

Although payments under Workers' Compensation are normally made directly by the employer's insurer (or by the employer if self-insured), the division administers the Office of Special Compensation Funds, formerly known as the second injury fund. The purpose of the fund is to aid a partially disabled worker who sustains a second and permanently disabling injury. Rather than burden the employer with the cost of the employee's total disability, the fund pays the difference between the award against the employer and compensation for permanent total disability. The fund's income is derived from assessments on compensation insurers and self-insurers.

Disability Determinations

In 1956 federal legislation on disability insurance (DI) provided for Social Security benefits to be paid to disabled workers under the age of sixty-five who met certain earning requirements. Subsequent DI legislation has reduced the age requirement and increased the scope of eligibility to include disabled widows, widowers, divorced wives, and some persons disabled before the age of eleven. In 1984 Supplemental Security Income (SSI) was approved as a federally administered assistance program for the aged, blind, and disabled with limited incomes and resources.

It is the responsibility of the Division of Disability Determinations to assess such disability claims. The division's primary activities include documenting, evaluating, and adjudicating disability claims filed in accordance with Titles II and XVI of the Social Security Act. Staff processes initial claims, reconsideration (first level of appeal) claims, and Continuing Disability Reviews (periodic reassessments of disability beneficiaries' continuing eligibility).

In the face of a federal practice of terminating disability cases based on questionable evidence, and with the support of a Third Circuit Court decision mandating that all present benefits be preserved until the Social Security agency can show a distinct improvement in a recipient's medical condition, Governor Kean imposed a temporary moratorium on all Continuing Disability Review cessations in 1983 to remain in effect until a uniform national policy is established.

The New Jersey Division of Disability Determinations conducts face-to-face evidentiary hearings, presided over by a hearing officer, for individuals whose benefits were terminated. This policy is intended to afford the individual a better understanding of the program and a personal explanation of how the determination was reached in his or her case.

9.
Regulating and
Promoting Business

The fine line between promoting a healthy business climate and regulating business in order to protect the rights of workers and consumers has caused much debate in New Jersey. The interplay between jobs and labor, between jobs and the environment, between protecting the consumer and protecting the interests of investors in public utilities, is an important part of the fabric of New Jersey political life.

In 1981 the New Jersey Legislature decided that the interests of industry and labor did not go hand-in-hand. It severed the relationship by forming two separate departments—the Department of Labor and the Department of Commerce and Economic Development—from the existing Department of Labor and Industry. As a result, each department had a clearly identified clientele and mission. Conflicts between these missions could be resolved at the highest level as the governor practiced the fine art of politics, seeking compromises which would best serve the citizens of New Jersey as a whole.

The stated purpose of the Department of Commerce and Economic Development (Department of Commerce for short) is to secure jobs already here, to expand existing job opportunities, and to attract new jobs. In its efforts to court industry and the accompanying jobs, the department faces many challenges. Environmental issues, building codes, transportation priorities, and a variety of permit require-

COMMERCE AND ECONOMIC DEVELOPMENT

ments—can all pose obstacles to securing those desired jobs. One can imagine the lively discussions that must go on at cabinet meetings as these various interests are advocated and as eventually the conflicts are resolved.

While the United States Constitution reserves the right to regulate interstate commerce, the states are given the right to regulate intrastate business. With this broad power the state may prohibit or encourage the conduct of business and may, if it chooses, protect the public interest against the interests of the few. The interests that the state of New Jersey has chosen to champion have varied over the years.

Initially, New Jersey's location as a thoroughfare state within the most populous and prosperous corridor of the nation brought business and industry eager to settle in the state. The legislature has traditionally responded in a cooperative fashion, even to the point of aiding single companies with exclusive franchises. New Jersey's lax corporation laws, particularly the holding company legislation adopted at the close of the nineteenth century, earned the state the pejorative title, "Mother of Trusts."

However, eventually conditions deteriorated sufficiently to arouse citizen disapproval. Public opinion exerted pressure on the government for business reform. Various programs were initiated to protect both labor and the consumer. (See chapter 8, Labor.) In the legislative reorganization of the executive branch in 1948, a number of these programs were collected within the Department of Labor and Industry.

However, by the 1960s the economic climate again altered. Business and industry called out for government attention as New Jersey's economy went into a long-term decline. Cyclical economic pressures led to a push for a shift in state priorities. Securing jobs came to the forefront. It was against this background that the Department of Commerce was formed as a separate cabinet-level entity in 1982. Rather than a move away from advocating the interests of the working man, the new department was envisioned as a mechanism for fulfilling the prime need of New Jersey's workers—the need for jobs, preferably permanent jobs that pay decent wages.

The Department of Commerce and Economic Development is headed by a commissioner chosen by the governor with the consent of the senate. The three major divisions charged with providing a comprehensive program of economic development and promotional services are industrial development, international trade, and travel and tourism. The New Jersey Motion Picture and Television Commission, the South Jersey Port Corporation, and the Atlantic City Convention Center Authority are also associated with the department. Providing advice and research to the executive and legislative branches of government are the Office of Economic Policy, the Economic Policy Council, and the Office of Economic Research. Finally, attached to the department is the important funding mechanism—the Economic Development Authority.

During the early 1980s New Jersey's economic picture had been more rosy than that of the nation as a whole and much better than that of several neighboring states. New Jersey has always been a very prosperous state, ranking among the top six in per-capita personal income for almost fifty years. New Jersey's high personal income has resulted not only from a highly skilled labor force but also from a larger portion of labor employed in highly paid industries, such as chemicals and drugs. Another factor previously contributing to our top economic rank has been a relatively high concentration of employment in the higher paid professional and technical occupations because of New Jersey's large numbers of corporate headquarters and research and development centers.

Over a ten-year period New Jersey saw a 15 percent decline in manufacturing jobs, but that appeared to bottom out in 1983. Increases have been registered in service industries, and the current administration has high hopes to attract many more jobs in high technology fields. To promote this, a number of state departments, including the department of Education and Higher Education, are seeking to improve education and enhance the business climate for high technology companies. A bond issue to finance

The Department of Commerce and Economic Development

Departmental Activities

Figure 9.1

Methods for Securing and Increasing New Jersey Jobs
Used by the Division of Economic Development

Economic Development Authority: Provides direct loans, loan guarantees, and industrial development bonds.

New Jersey Local Development Financing Fund (the "701" Program): A $45 million revolving loan and grant program to create permanent private sector jobs for low- and moderate-income families, broaden the tax base of the community, and leverage private sector investment. (Modeled after the Federal Urban Development Action Grant Program, it is estimated the fund could generate $270 million in first-round investments and create 6,500–8,000 permanent jobs.)

Urban Enterprise Zones: The 1983 law provides for the establishment of enterprise zones in urban areas. Two such zones will be established each year, starting with large sections of Newark and Camden, to revitalize inner-city areas. Relocation assistance to new commerce and industry will be supplemented with tax incentives, including exemption of half the state sales tax for commerce and business located inside the enterprise zones, and the relaxation of certain government regulations. The success of this approach depends on coordination with state and local government to stimulate private investment.

The Employee Stock Ownership Program: A business retention tool to keep viable businesses running under employee ownership.

The Site Finder. A statewide computerized listing of available land and buildings.

The Office of Business Advocacy: Functions as an industry ombudsman and works for regulatory reform to improve New Jersey's business climate. Especially important is the office's work in permit coordination for businesses seeking to expand or locate in New Jersey. A "One Stop" permit identification system lets an industry know just what regulatory permits are needed and how to obtain them.

The Small Business Revitalization Program: New Jersey is one of twenty-one states participating in this program sponsored by the U.S. Department of Housing and Urban Development (HUD) in cooperation with the U.S. Small Business Administration. The multi-faceted program includes grants, loans, and tax incentives to provide investment capital for small businesses.

The Corporation for Business Assistance: A program to aid viable small businesses in attracting long-term capital for expansion.

The Office of Minority Business Enterprise: A joint project of the Department of Commerce and the Federal Minority Business Development Agency.

The Casino Reinvestment Development Authority: Every casino is required to invest 1.25 percent of its winnings each year for 25 years or pay an additional tax of 3 percent in each year the investment obligation is not met. In the first three years, all investments must be for housing and community redevelopment projects in Atlantic City. In the forth and fifth years, 90 percent of the investments would go to Atlantic City, 8 percent to the nine South Jersey counties of Atlantic, Burlington, Camden, Cape May, Cumberland, Gloucester, Mercer, Ocean, and Salem, and 2 percent to the remaining 12 counties in North Jersey. In later years those percentages would shift to divert more of the investments to New Jersey areas outside of Atlantic City. For the last five years, Atlantic City would receive 20 percent, South Jersey 45 percent, and North Jersey 35 percent. Other provisions of the law require 20 percent of authority contracts to be awarded to businesses owned by nonwhites and women. The Casino Reinvestment Development Authority, created by law to control the casino investments, also has the power to take land in Atlantic City by condemnation, to facilitate the renewal of the deteriorated resort city.

several high technology research centers connected with New Jersey institutions of higher education was approved by voters in 1984.

Students of business climates in the United States are currently ranking New Jersey much higher both for general manufacturing business climate and for small business climate than they did five years ago. The creative efforts of the Division of Economic Development (see figure 9.1) are in part responsible for this improvement.

The image of New Jersey as a desirable place to do business, to live, and to visit has also been enhanced by an active state advertising campaign—that of the Division of Economic Development aimed at the business community and that of the Division of Travel and Tourism focusing on Americans and Canadians living within a day's drive of New Jersey. An important byproduct has been the pride that the advertising campaign has inspired in New Jersey's own citizens.

Looking farther afield, the New Jersey Motion Picture and Television Development Commission has actively promoted New Jersey as a location to film productions. The commission offers, among other things, location scouting services, a complete slide and photograph location library, and a liaison with all county and municipal offices and agencies. Currently negotiations are underway to establish a film studio in Jersey City, an effort to establish a full-fledged film industry in New Jersey.

The export of New Jersey goods and the attraction of foreign investment and industry are the responsibility of the Division of International Trade. Working largely with small companies (large and multi-national companies have their own international offices), the division assists New Jersey firms in entering the export market and in displaying their products in foreign trade shows.

The shipping of products to and from New Jersey from the Camden area is also a department responsibility. The South Jersey Port Corporation, attached to the Department of Commerce, operates two marine terminals in the Camden area for the import and export of goods and materials and for cargo handling. The corporation has the authority to lease, construct, purchase, operate, equip, and maintain the port facilities, and may issue bonds in the name of the corporation to achieve these ends. The Atlantic City Convention Center Authority is a similar agency with its mission limited to promoting, operating, and maintaining a convention center in Atlantic City.

The Economic Development Authority (EDA) was created in 1974 to maintain and expand job opportunities and to enlarge the tax base of state and local governments in New Jersey by arranging low-interest financing for firms wishing to expand or locate within the state. The authority is directed by a board consisting of the commissioners of Commerce and Economic Development, Environmental Protection, Community Affairs, and Labor; the State Treasurer; and four members nominated by the governor with the consent of the senate.

To accomplish its objectives, the authority has several funding vehicles. Through state appropriations, federal grants, and loan repayments, the EDA obtains money to provide low-interest loans to industry. Another option is to provide guarantees for industrial loans from the private sector. A third avenue for helping industry finance capital expenditures is to arrange for the sale of industrial development bonds. These bonds, while not in any way backed by the state, are tax-exempt, and thus offer industry a lower interest rate for financing the purchase of land, equipment, machinery, and buildings.

The authority's bonds differ from other revenue bonds in that the authority is under no legal obligation to repay the debt, nor is the state. The bonds are secured by pledges of repayment, mortgages, or other collateral of the firms receiving assistance. Repayment is made directly to the bond purchaser.

The banks and other private investors that purchase these bonds, then, have a direct investment in the success of the industry for whom the bonds were sold. In each case these aids to industry are predicated on the prospect that such expansion will provide new jobs for the state work force, retain existing jobs, and/or add tax ratables.

Guidelines for assistance by the EDA have been revised a

The Economic Development Authority

number of times. Loans are now permitted to a broad spectrum of commerce and industry. The authority assists manufacturing, distribution, warehousing, research, agriculture, and certain service, nursing home, and residential health care activities. The EDA also aids the construction of certain types of office buildings anywhere in the state. Other projects it will assist, regardless of location, include airports, docks, wharves, mass commuting facilities, parking facilities, storage facilities, convention or trade show centers, industrial pollution control facilities, water and sewer facilities, industrial parks, and solid waste disposal facilities. The authority also considers financing for commercial and retail facilities if they are located in communities that have been targeted for special economic development attention. Hotels are financed under certain circumstances.

The authority also operates an industrial park development program. It buys, improves, and sells land and buildings in urban areas for private business use.

The authority is empowered to enter into contracts and conduct necessary studies relative to its legislative mandate to stimulate employment and investment in New Jersey. It derives its operating costs from financing fees charged to companies receiving assistance.

While the EDA is by far the heaviest issuer of tax-exempt financing among the New Jersey authorities ($5 billion of revenue bonds during the last ten years), these bonds are repaid when industrial loans are, in turn, repaid. Furthermore, definite results can be shown. As of 1984 the EDA had approved over three thousand projects creating eighty-nine thousand permanent jobs for New Jersey workers.

AGRICULTURE

Despite growing urban encroachment, New Jersey is still called the Garden State, and agriculture plays an important role in New Jersey's economy. Urbanization has taken its toll on our agricultural Eden. Thirty years ago New Jersey had over 1.7 million acres of farmland; by the mid-1980s this has been reduced to 970,000 acres. In just the last twenty years farmland has declined 30 percent in the state. The number of farms has dropped from 24,000 in 1953 to 9,400 in 1983 with the average farm size remaining

at about one hundred acres. Production totals have been
relatively stable, however, because mechanization and innovative techniques have produced higher yields.

Skyrocketing land values in the metropolitan areas
(now all of New Jersey is included in a metropolitan statis-
tical area according to federal reckoning), growth pressures,
and some of the nation's highest per acre property taxes,
have forced farmers to sell to developers. As population has
grown, the value of land for development has outpaced the
value of land kept in agriculture.

Although New Jersey is the most densely populated
state in the nation, Garden State farms still produce a great
variety of vegetables and fruits, both for market and for processing, as well as substantial quantities of milk and eggs.
Growing ornamental trees and shrubs is an expanding industry as is horsebreeding. Production of hay, grains, meat
animals, and wool are other segments of the agricultural
complex. Moreover, despite its small size, New Jersey is a
national leader in cultivated blueberries and cranberries.
New Jersey's farmers and consumers of farm products are
served by the state Department of Agriculture.

The organization of the Department of Agriculture is
unique in New Jersey state government. Policy is set by the
New Jersey Board of Agriculture. This unsalaried board is
composed of eight working farmers who serve staggered
four-year terms and represent a variety of agricultural speci-
alities. Two members are chosen each January by the delegates to the New Jersey Agricultural Convention and are
then appointed by the governor with the consent of the senate. This board, with the approval of the governor, selects
the secretary of agriculture to serve an indefinite term as the
department's chief executive officer.

The department provides a wide array of programs
and services in support of the state's agricultural industry, its
rural areas and natural resources, and consumers of agricultural products.

The division of Plant Industry and Animal Health focus on the detection, control, and eradication of animal
and plant pests and diseases. The Division of Plant Industry

The Department of Agriculture

works to limit pest damage while providing farmers with alternative methods of treating pest problems (such as using parasites of the gypsy moth). The division also enforces quarantines and regulations governing insect pests; it also has a seed certification and inspection program that helps guarantee the quality of packaged vegetables, sod, field crops, and lawn seed. The Division of Animal Health offers inspection, regulation, and diagnostic services for the prevention, control, and eradication of livestock and poultry disease. By routine testing, state and federal veterinarians carry on an intensive cooperative program for the control of tuberculosis and brucellosis in dairy herds, for pullorum in poultry, and for equine and hog diseases.

The Division of Dairy Industry regulates prices of milk at both the producers' and retailers' level. State control of milk prices dates from the depression of the 1930s when out-of-state milk dealers, with lower labor and feed costs, were able to flood New Jersey with cheaper milk. At the request of the threatened dairy business, the legislature established the mechanism for licensing dealers and setting minimum prices for milk.

The Division of Regulatory Services helps guarantee New Jersey's farmers and consumers of truth-in-labeling and the integrity of agricultural products. Through inspection, certification, grading and licensing programs, such agricultural products as eggs, egg products, poultry, fresh fruits and vegetables, animal feeds, and fertilizers are checked for purity, quality, and size.

The joy of eating Garden State produce is promoted by the Division of Markets. Through an intensive program of promotion, merchandising, and information, the fruits, vegetables, eggs, dairy products, and non-food agricultural industries, such as horses and ornamental horticulture, garner attention and consumer dollars. In the mid-1980s exports of New Jersey agricultural products totaled an estimated $15 million annually, and the combined value of sales of farm commodities, farm equipment, transportation refrigeration, and other agriculturally-related products and services brought the value of New Jersey agribusiness to around $3 billion. Employment in New Jersey agribusiness is estimated at over 81,000 people in on and off-the-farm occupations in both seasonal and year-round employment. Thus, agribusiness is an important part of the New Jersey economy.

The Division of Markets coordinates with federal marketing programs and also handles the distribution of millions of pounds of federal surplus commodities for school and institutional lunches and for needy residents.

The Division of Rural Resources is concerned with both conservation of rural resources and the betterment of rural areas. A program for the conservation and development of the state's soil, water, and related natural resources is administered by the State Soil Conservation Committee, housed in the Division of Rural Resources. The committee oversees local soil conservation district offices which provide technical assistance to landowners in order to alleviate soil and water management problems. The monitoring and regulation of construction and other land disturbance activities help prevent soil erosion and damage from sedimentation and pollution of water resources.

Farmland Retention and Protection

New Jersey's farmland offers its citizens the beauty of miles of taxed open space, an efficient groundwater recharge system that replenishes our drinking water supply, and economic opportunity for those who choose to farm. New Jersey voters have demonstrated their commitment to preserving this agricultural heritage. In 1964 voters approved a farmland assessment program permitting taxation of farmland based on its production value rather than on its development value. In 1981 voters again affirmed their interest in preserving farmland by approving a $50 million bond issue.

The Agricultural Retention and Development Act of 1983 established the framework for utilizing the bond monies—part to be used as matching funds for local programs purchasing the development rights on prime agricultural land and part to match farmers' investment in soil and water conservation projects. The New Jersey Agricultural Development Committee was formed to establish the guidelines for these programs which will be implemented on the county levels by agricultural development boards.

Also in 1983 the Right to Farm Act became law.

Commercial farming operations using agricultural management practices are protected from harassment and nuisance complaints from non-farmers in the area. Agricultural management practices are defined as those practices recommended by the agricultural experiment station or those practices which represent the best collective judgement of the faculty of the experiment station. (See below.)

In 1984 additional legislation was enacted protecting farmers from malicious trespassers and vandals. Not only are fines increased, but restitution may be demanded for convicted vandals. Additional legislation now pending would hold parents and guardians of vandals responsible for up to five thousand dollars in damages and would limit the liability of farmers who give permission to sportsmen and women to use their land for recreational activities.

Rutgers' Role in New Jersey Agriculture

Under the federal Morrill Act Rutgers in 1864 became New Jersey's land-grant college, receiving public lands and funds for the purpose of agricultural education. Since that time Rutgers has actively promoted scientific farming through what is now know as Cook College (formerly the College of Agriculture and Environmental Science) in New Brunswick. The Agricultural Experiment Station is the college's research arm, and the Cooperative Extension Service is its off-campus information arm.

From its origin in 1880, the experiment station has worked on a wide variety of agricultural problems ranging from pest control, plant diseases, soil conservation, and fertilization to farm management techniques. The staff also works to develop new varieties of fruits and vegetables and improved animal breeds. More recently, some of its many research projects have probed such environmental questions as the effects of air pollution on plants, methods of purifying industrial wastes, the safe use of pesticides, and channeling solar energy.

The task of disseminating information gained through agricultural research is carried out by the extension service's specialists, county agents, and home economics agents. The work of the extension service falls into three categories: agricultural education for farmers and other adults; home economics education for adults; and agricultural and home economics education for youth through the 4-H clubs. The nonfarmer too may turn to the county agent for aid with a variety of problems—including advice on lawn care.

When you turn on a light, draw water, pick up a phone, or turn on an oven, you are using a service that, if privately owned, is regulated by the Board of Public Utilities (BPU). The BPU regulates over 1,000 investor-owned companies that provide New Jersey customers with electricity, gas, cable television, telephone, water, sewer, and garbage collection and disposal services. However, the BPU has no jurisdiction over the public utilities operated by municipalities or over county utility authorities, except for rates charged by such a utility for service provided outside its borders.

The Board of Public Utilities is the oldest consumer protection agency in New Jersey. It was established in 1911 during the administration of Woodrow Wilson (governor from 1911–1913) with bipartisan support. Its three members or commissioners are also bipartisan by law—not more than two of the three can hold affiliations with the same political party. Commissioners are appointed by the governor, with the consent of the senate, for overlapping six-year terms. One member is designated board president by the governor, a position that requires its holder to serve as the chief executive officer of the board, in addition to presiding over meetings. Except for the commissioners and their immediate aides, all board employees are under civil service. An independent agency, the BPU is technically in, but effectively not of, the Department of Energy.

As an administrative agency, the BPU promulgates rules that the regulated utilities must follow, investigates services, and grants or denies applications for rate or service changes. The BPU can order an agency to improve services under penalty of losing its franchise. In support of such an order, the BPU can order a utility to purchase new equipment and can authorize it to float bonds and raise rates. The board can also seek court appointment of a custodial receiver for a company it determines is not fulfilling its obligations to provide good service. The board cannot, however, compel a company to stay in business, once the services it provides

PUBLIC UTILITIES

are no longer essential or are assumed by the government or by another company.

State control over public utilities arises from the fact that these companies, because of their lack of effective competition, would enjoy the possibility of monopoly profits if unregulated. Monopoly profits occur when a company is able to raise its prices above its costs and a reasonable return on its investment, because of the lack of other companies willing to come into the market and sell at a lower price. Since utilities provide what are regarded as essential services, the state employs regulation to prevent these services from being over-priced.

Most utilities also hold state franchises giving them official monopoly rights in their service area. The franchises require the company to provide good service and can be lifted (or placed under control of a court-appointed receiver) if they fail to do so. Garbage companies, while lacking formal monopoly rights, are also subject to loss of their BPU operating certificate allowing them to do business in New Jersey if they fail to provide satisfactory service. (See chapter 10, Solid Waste.)

In setting rates the BPU considers the investment of a company in plant and equipment used and useful for customers; the return necessary on that investment (for interest and profits) in order for the company to continue to attract investors; and reasonable expenses, including a depreciation expense. The board's practice has been to base these expenses on a company's needs at some point in the recent past (employing, in accounting terminology, a historical test year) without adjustment for anticipated continued inflation. The lack of an inflation adjustment puts pressure on the company to stay within these levels of expenses. An exception to this expense rule is employed for fuel and purchased power expenses for electric utilities and wholesale gas expenses for gas utilities. Because of the volatility of these expenses, frequent rate adjustments are made.

The public is most aware of BPU activities when utility rate cases come before the board. These utility rate request cases involve not only the BPU, but also the Office of Administrative Law (OAL) (see chapter 2, Office of Administrative Law), which generally conducts hearings on utility rate requests, and the Division of Rate Counsel in the Department of the Public Advocate, which participates in all rate cases as an attorney on behalf of the company's customers.

Each hearing for a utility rate request includes at least one field hearing, held in the service territory at a time convenient to customers, to receive comments from the general public on the proposal. Additional hearings to take company evidence and cross-examine company witnesses may be required by board staff and/or the Public Advocate's Division of Rate Counsel. These hearings are generally held at Office of Administrative Law offices in Newark or Trenton.

In these hearings BPU staff, as a rule, does not present testimony but takes a position at the conclusion of the hearings, applying its accumulated expertise to the proceedings. The official Public Advocate's Division of Rate Counsel, as attorney participating on behalf of the company's customers, employs consultants to analyze rate filings and present testimony. The company seeking the rate hike often cross-examines the Public Advocate's witnesses. At times other parties intervene in rate cases and take on an active role. These outside intervenors may be representatives of local governments, individual citizens, or organizations representing specific customer groups such as senior citizens or various industries.

The administrative law judge who serves as hearing officer reviews all the documents and testimony submitted in the case, reads the briefs summarizing the positions of the parties at the conclusion of the hearing, and recommends a decision to the Board of Public Utilities. The board then reviews both the record of the case and the recommended decision of the hearing judge and makes its decision. The board's decision is final, but is reviewable in the state courts.

This procedure is generally followed in cases other than rate increases, although not necessarily in so elaborate a form. Customers, for instance, can obtain less formal hearings on complaints against a utility and need not employ lawyers to have their cases heard, although often they do. Board staff works to investigate complaints and settle disputes without the need for a formal hearing; however, if a hearing is sought, the board staff, and at times the Public Advocate, work within the process to assure a fair proceeding.

The cost of the Public Advocate's review is supported by customers and is included as an approved expense, within reason, in rate cases. Generally, the company's own costs for prosecuting the case are also included in customer rates. For large utilities, however, the board has also recently been requiring that these company costs be split between customers and stockholders.

The BPU itself sits on hearings in issues involving major policy questions or requiring rapid action to prevent costly consequences. Recent examples of such full board involvement have been the Jersey Central fault-finding case on the Three Mile Island nuclear accident and cases involving requests by telecommunication companies to enter the long-distance telephone business within the state.

The board has broad responsibilities going beyond the setting of rates and the investigation of customer complaints. Board approval is also necessary before a utility company can issue stocks or bonds or sell property above a certain value. Board auditors review company books to assure the proper accounting treatment of expenditures and also to investigate allegations of misapplications of funds. Board engineers also investigate accidents and complaints of inferior service. The board has the power to order safety improvements if needed. The federal Nuclear Regulatory Commission (NRC), however, pre-empts state jurisdiction in setting safety standards for nuclear power plants.

In recent years the BPU has been wrestling with the issues of reasonable and fair ways to charge customers for the costs of nuclear construction, the breakup of the AT&T telephone system, the supply of natural gas, and the closing of garbage landfills. The cost of water supply, to meet increasingly stringent treatment requirements, also looms as an issue.

In a major departure from past policies, the board recently ordered the gas and electric utilities of New Jersey to embark on a comprehensive and aggressive program for the delivery of conservation services. These programs, which range from no-cost or low-cost loans for household energy conservation improvements to rebates on the sales of high-efficiency air conditioners, are now in place statewide. They

are viewed as an important means for holding down electricity and natural gas prices by reducing demands for new
generating plants and new gas wells.

ENERGY

While the Board of Public Utilities (BPU) is now administratively of the Department of Energy, originally the roles
were reversed. An energy office was created in response to
the energy crisis of 1973–1974 and attached to the Department of Public Utilities (containing the Board of Public
Utilities). Charged with responsibility for developing contingency plans to meet fuel shortages in New Jersey, the
energy office was also established to administer federally
funded energy conservation programs. In 1977 the Department of Energy was created, combining the energy office
with the BPU into a single cabinet-level department. Since
that time the New Jersey Public Broadcasting Authority was
created and attached administratively to the Department
of Energy.

The Department of Energy is headed by a commissioner
appointed by the governor with the consent of the senate.
Department offices are located in Newark. Various programs of the department are aided by citizen and industry
advisory councils.

A major effort of the New Jersey Department of Energy
(NJDOE) has been development of the Ten Year Master
Plan for the production, processing, storage, transmis-
sion, consumption, and conservation of all forms of energy
within the state. Other duties of the department include establishment of a central information bank for energy information and data and intervention in any proceedings before
state, regional, or federal agencies in order to represent the
energy interests of New Jersey. The department has been
particularly active before the Federal Energy Regulatory
Commission in natural gas rate cases. Its intervention in
several major cases resulted in sizeable savings to New Jersey gas consumers.

The department administers a number of conservation
programs. These include the Home Energy Savings Program which offers low-cost home energy audits to residential customers; the Commercial and Apartment Conservation Service which offers the same to multi-family buildings

and commercial establishments; the Business Energy Improvement Loan Subsidy program which subsidizes up to half the interest rate on loans to businesses for energy-efficient renovations; the Institutional Conservation Program which provides matching grants to schools, hospitals, and other institutions for energy conservation improvements; and the Energy Conservation Bond Issue, a $50 million program to improve the energy efficiency of state-owned facilities.

Many of these conservation programs are financed in whole or in part by oil overcharge funds (i.e., revenues paid by the major oil companies that violated the federal price controls of the 1970s). The department was party to the federal suits that sought the recovery of these overcharges to assure that New Jersey received its fair share of the revenues.

In addition the NJDOE participates in a number of cooperative efforts with other state agencies. The Office of Recycling is jointly administered by the NJDOE and the Department of Environmental Protection. Financed by a surcharge on use of landfills, the recycling effort includes a program of grants to municipalities to encourage their recycling programs. The legislature is expected to consider the administration's proposal to make recycling mandatory. The recycling program also includes an educational component on recycling and litter abatement and a program for low-interest loans and loan guarantees to recycling businesses.

NJDOE is also involved with other agencies in the siting of resource recovery plants, in the promotion of ridesharing, and in establishing specifications for energy conservation and savings in state purchasing. In addition, the office of energy was instrumental in lobbying for the passage of the "right turn on red" legislation in 1977—legislation which has not only saved gasoline but has also reduced air pollution emissions caused by idling engines.

The New Jersey Public Broadcasting Authority

This authority was established in 1969 to serve the non-commercial, educational broadcasting needs of the state. The authority operates the New Jersey Network, a system of four UHF television stations: WNJS Channel 23 in Camden,

WNJT Channel 52 in Trenton, WNJB Channel 58 in New Brunswick, and WNJM Channel 50 in Montclair. The network produces a wide variety of state-oriented programs including the *New Jersey Nightly News* which makes possible expanded news coverage concerning New Jersey in an area dominated by New York City and Philadelphia commercial news broadcasts. In addition to news and public affairs programming, the network also produces programs of special interest to the black and Hispanic communities, arts and sports programming, and the New Jersey Lottery drawing. The New Jersey Network signals are carried by all New Jersey cable systems. Funding for these activities comes from state and federal grants as well as grants from corporations, foundations, and individuals. The authority is technically in, but effectively not of, the Department of Energy.

BANKING

States impose more stringent regulations on financial institutions than on most other corporations in order to safeguard the money—often a substantial part of many people's savings—entrusted to them.

The regulation of banks and savings and loan institutions doing business in New Jersey is the work of the Department of Banking, headed by a commissioner appointed by the governor with the consent of the senate. Among the institutions regulated are state-chartered commercial banks, savings and loan associations, home improvement financing companies, pawnbrokers, and consumer credit companies. Also regulated by the department are mortgage bankers, mortgage brokers, check-cashing and check-selling companies, and non-denominational cemeteries (because state law requires that they place a portion of their income in particular types of interest-bearing investments to insure permanent maintenance of the property).

New Jersey also has national banks supervised by the United States Comptroller of the Currency, federally chartered savings and loan associations regulated by the Federal Home Loan Bank Board, and federal credit unions supervised by the National Credit Union Administration.

By law the department staff examines state-chartered banks "to determine whether the bank is conducting its business in conformity with the laws of this State . . . and with safety to its depositors, other creditors and the public." Similar examinations are required of the other financial institutions. The department also has the power to grant or deny applications, after public hearings, for new bank charters, branches for existing banks, bank mergers, and bank holding companies. Investigation of consumer complaints is another important function of the department.

Apart from conducting examinations, the department is a source of new legislation and administrative regulations enacted from time to time in response to emerging needs of the consuming public or the financial industry. In the past twenty years legislation has brought extensive and important changes to banking practices in New Jersey. By lifting a number of restrictions, these laws attracted business previously diverted to other states. In particular, restrictions on mergers, branch banking, and bank holding companies were eased. In recent years many banks have formed or joined holding companies in order to attract capital, to diversify into bank-related fields, and to protect against unfriendly take-overs. The department predicts that, in time, virtually all banks will be holding-company owned. Currently New Jersey bank holding companies hold 78 percent of the total New Jersey bank assets and own about half of the state's banks.

INSURANCE

The hundreds of insurance companies doing business in New Jersey are regulated by the Department of Insurance. Becoming a separate department in 1970 when the Department of Banking and Insurance was split into two entities, the Department of Insurance is headed by a commissioner appointed by the governor with senate consent. Included in the department is the New Jersey Real Estate Commission which regulates the real estate industry.

The department authorizes the formation of new companies and the types of insurance they may sell; it also grants or denies changes in insurance rates. Under the prior approval law effective in New Jersey, rates must be approved by the commissioner before they can be adopted by insurance companies.

A major challenge for the department is computerizing their financial information about each insurance company. Effective regulation of the highly sophisticated insurance industry depends on the ability of the commissioner and staff to have access to the information necessary to make informed judgments on issues such as rate increases.

In its regulatory function, the department examines not only insurance companies but also examines and licenses all insurance agents and brokers. The department is responsible for investigating complaints against companies, agents, and brokers as well. The department also examines rating companies (companies engaged in setting insurance rates) and advisory organizations and insurance company underwriters.

In recent years the department has taken a more active role in regulating the industry and devising ways to meet the insurance needs of the public. For example, tremendous losses resulting from rioting and civil disorders in 1967 caused widespread cancellation of policies covering properties in ghetto areas. To meet this problem the state devised a pool arrangement enabling qualifying businessmen to obtain fire insurance at reasonable rates. The coverage was later extended to include losses from vandalism and malicious mischief.

In 1973 New Jersey initiated a no-fault automobile insurance program. Under this concept auto insurance is compulsory, and accident victims are reimbursed for their medical expenses and other out-of-pocket losses by their own insurance companies regardless of fault. The original law permitted suits for pain and suffering damages if an injured person's medical expenses were two hundred dollars or more. Because this two hundred dollar threshold is easily met in this age of expensive health care, many people sue. The no-fault system by the early 1980s was neither preventing a heavy load of personal injury litigation in the state courts nor providing low-cost insurance for New Jersey residents. Some legislative reform of the system was enacted in 1983, but critics say real reform is yet to be legislated.

10.
Environmental
Protection

The dual goal of having both a healthy economy and a healthy environment has raised complex problems in New Jersey. This state, the most densely populated in the union, must somehow balance the pressure to produce goods and employment opportunities with the challenge to conserve and protect natural resources. Typical New Jersey industries such as chemicals, pharmaceuticals, and petroleum products have brought many jobs to the state, but they have also contributed to damage of the environment. Moreover, booming development has meant fewer acres for agriculture and open space.

As the state's politicians try to resolve these conflicting interests, it is the task of the Department of Environmental Protection (DEP) to advocate environmental interests and to administer and enforce legislated protection programs.

The New Jersey Department of Environmental Protection was established in 1970 to unite all state governmental agencies involved in the protection, conservation, restoration, or enhancement of the environment. Departmental responsibilities include the protection of human health and welfare through management of water, air, land, forests, shore, fish and game, and shellfish resources, and the provision of outdoor recreational opportunities.

The DEP regulates air, water, and noise pollution, pesticide use, and the disposal of solid, hazardous, and low-level radioactive wastes. It also protects the Pinelands, wetlands,

The Department of Environmental Protection

and the coastal zone. Major capital improvement projects include sewage facility and reservoir construction, loans to municipalities to repair aging water supply systems and to control flooding, dam reconstruction, shore protection, and dredging. DEP is also responsible for the preservation of lands for recreation and for conservation at both the state and local levels.

The DEP is headed by a commissioner appointed by the governor with the consent of the senate. The major DEP divisions include Water Resources; Environmental Quality; Parks and Forestry; Fish, Game and Wildlife; and Waste Management. The units of the department are assisted in their work by a number of councils and commissions which bring expertise from other governmental departments, industry, academia, environmental groups, and citizens. Close communication is maintained both with these boards and with other governmental departments and agencies that are affected by DEP decisions—such as the departments of Health, Labor, Economic Development, Community Affairs, Agriculture, Transportation, and the Board of Public Utilities.

The discussions that follow are brief descriptions of the legislation on the books and the administrative and enforcement machinery currently in place. The frequent headlines given environmental concerns indicate the range and severity of the problems. They also point up the need for continuing efforts by state and local governmental agencies, by concerned citizens, and by national, state, and local environmental groups to ensure that those regulations currently on the books are enforced. For those problems that have not yet been adequately addressed, these efforts need to focus on wise legislative solutions.

Water Resources

New Jersey, like other states in the Northeast, is blessed with abundant natural water supplies. Yet its dense population and many industries make heavy demands. Maintaining the quality and adequacy of water is a major function of state government.

Managing the Water Supply
State regulation of the water supply began with a 1905 law prohibiting the export of New Jersey surface water. In 1929

responsibility for water allocation was given to the New Jersey Water Policy and Supply Commission, a citizen board. Not until the droughts of the 1960s and the early 1980s, however, did the state gain any real control over the water supply and its distribution.

A bond issue approved in 1958 provided funds for New Jersey's largest reservoir system—Round Valley (55 billion gallons) and Spruce Run (11 billion gallons), both in the Raritan River basin. The reservoirs were of little help, however, during the drought in the 1960s because the mechanism to transfer water from these reservoirs to the Raritan and Passaic Rivers had not been funded. In the 1970s a statewide Water Supply Master Plan was prepared. The 1980–1982 drought, hitting just as the master plan was in the final stage of development, became the impetus both for the adoption of the master plan and for additional water management legislation.

Recent Legislation

The water management legislation of the early 1980s gave DEP's Division of Water Resources broad powers over various aspects of water management including responsibility for water supply and quality, flood control, drainage, discharges into ground and surface waters, and dams. The laws, (see figure 10.1) provide for, among other things, adoption of the Statewide Water Supply Master Plan, creation of a Water Supply Advisory Council, funding for new water projects and rehabilitation of existing systems through a $350 million bond issue, and takeover of small water companies unable to meet the needs of their customers.

Under the amended New Jersey Safe Drinking Water Act, DEP will set standards for currently unregulated water contaminants. The Division of Water Resources will also have the authority to specify treatment techniques needed to reduce any contamination to acceptable levels.

Distribution of the Water Supply

There are over six hundred water companies in New Jersey of which the twenty-five largest—in the trade called purveyors—distribute 75 percent of the water. Almost half of them are private, the rest are publicly owned. Private com-

Figure 10.1

New Jersey Water Supply Management Legislation

WATER SUPPLY MANAGEMENT ACT OF 1981

A. The Division of Water Resources in DEP is given authority to administer a uniform permit system for anyone wishing to divert (withdraw) more than 100,000 gallons per day from surface or ground water. Each permit is for a period ranging from five to fifteen years, and the permit holder must show that:

- the water use is in the public interest,
- it will not exceed the safe yield of the source,
- it will not significantly affect other water users,
- it will not cause groundwater depletion, pollution, or saltwater intrusion.

The permit system is self-supporting through imposition of substantial fees, both initial and annual. Public imput is provided through provisions for public hearings on new permits and on renewal permits involving increases in the rate of diversion. Agricultural and horticultural water withdrawals are not subject to formal diversion permits; rather, they are covered under a separate water usage certification issued by county agricultural agents upon approval of the Division of Water Resources.

B. A Water Supply Advisory Council, composed of seven citizens appointed by the governor with senate consent, is established to advise the Division of Water Resources on the preparation, adoption, and revision of the master plan and to advise the New Jersey Water Supply Authority on all matters pertaining to water supply, including approval of new water projects.

C. A 1980 amendment also provides for low-interest loans to municipalities for development of alternate water supplies to replace contaminated wells.

D. Other provisions of the law include:

- Adoption of the New Jersey Statewide Water Supply Plan is mandated.
- Updating of the Water Supply Plan is required at least every five years.
- DEP is given emergency powers during drought to regulate water use in affected areas and to impose surcharges.
- DEP is given enforcement authority to require utilities to maintain their systems in good repair, thus reducing waste, and also to provide sufficient reserves to maintain the safe yield needed for their customer commitment.

WATER SUPPLY BOND ACT OF 1981 (approved by the voters in a referendum)

A. This $350 million bond act provided funding essential to the implementation of the Water Supply Management Act of 1981. Money was provided both for construction of the new water projects and for rehabilitation of existing distribution systems.

B. A unique feature of the Water Supply Bond Act is provision for studies to provide basic information on watershed and acquifer protection and evaluation of contaminated well fields and groundwater to guide DEP in making water management decisions.

C. Other provisions of the Water Supply Bond Act include:

 ■ the stipulation that any project or study undertaken must be included in the Water Supply Master Plan and be funded by a specific appropriation by the legislature,

 ■ and the award of low-interest loans rather than outright grants of funds for water system rehabilitation or interconnections.

THE WATER SUPPLY MASTER PLAN

A. Adopted in spring of 1982 after almost five years of study, the Water Supply Master Plan is a comprehensive document identifying water needs, resource capabilities, areas needing further study, management options, and requirements for public involvement in water resource planning. Periodic updates are required, with a complete review mandated every five years. (An update was published in 1983 and another is planned for 1985.)

B. The action program for 1983–1986 lists both projects and studies feasible for implementation by the state and other agencies. Most are dependent on funding from the Water Supply Bond Act of 1981.

C. The plan emphasizes the importance of public participation in development of the plan and in future planning. Public meetings and hearings are held on amendments to the plan. Advisory committees work with staff and consultants on feasibility studies. On project construction there is extensive input, not only from citizens, but also from the legislature which must appropriate funds from the Water Supply Bond Act. In addition, DEP's Division of Water Resources has a coordinator of public participation responsible for keeping the public informed on progress in water resources management and for encouraging two-way communication.

Figure 10.1
(continued)

NEW JERSEY WATER SUPPLY AUTHORITY ACT OF 1981

A. The authority was established to operate the state-owned water facilities—the Round Valley and Spruce Run reservoirs and the Delaware and Raritan Canal—and to acquire, finance, construct, and operate wholesale water facilities needed, but not able to be constructed by any other public or private entity.

B. The authority is technically in, but functionally not of, DEP. The commissioner of DEP chairs the authority. Six public members, appointed by the governor with senate consent, serve three-year terms without compensation. The six members must include recognized experts in water resource management and distribution, and public finance. They must also represent the following interests: agriculture, industry, residential water users, and private watershed associations.

C. The authority finances projects through the issuance of general obligation bonds. Authority expenses for bonded indebtedness plus operations and maintenance are covered by wholesale water sales to public and private purveyors.

D. The authority has the right of eminent domain. Authority minutes must be signed by the governor, which gives the governor a degree of control.

E. The first authority project, started in 1984, is dredging the silt from a thirty-two mile stretch of the Delaware and Raritan Canal, an important channel for carrying water from the Delaware River to the Raritan River and thus to central New Jersey. Upon completion of the major dredging program in 1985, the canal will be restored to its full 100 million gallons per day carrying capacity.

F. The authority, along with the Division of Water Resources, is conducting a major feasibility study to determine whether to proceed with construction of Manasquan Reservoir in Monmouth County. It would provide surface water for conjunctive (supplemental) use with overdrawn ground water in that region.

STATUTE PERMITTING TAKEOVER OF SMALL WATER COMPANIES

This law established a procedure for private or public purveyors to takeover small water companies serving under 1000 customers when such action is justified to protect the water user or the water supply.

226

panies are subject to rate regulation by the Board of Public Utilities; public companies are subject, in some instances, to oversight by the Department of Community Affairs. Under the Water Supply Management Act of 1981 DEP has control over a number of other distribution elements: water diversions, system maintenance, adherence to safe yield of the system, source of water, and interconnections among purveyors.

Flood Control

Flooding along New Jersey's major rivers is a natural phenomenon. Industrial and residential development on flood plains is a result of governmental failure to take action on land-use issues and flood control.

Flood control has two components—alleviation of existing flooding situations (usually a structural solution) and flood plain management to reduce future flood damage (often a zoning solution). Despite serious flooding once or twice each decade in this century, flood control has been haphazard and divided among many levels of government.

On the federal level, structural solutions are provided by two agencies. The Army Corps of Engineers assists in planning and also issues permits for development of wetlands and for construction of projects such as reservoirs or dredging. The Soil Conservation Service, part of the United States Department of Agriculture, provides guidance on agricultural pollution control and on watershed management. The service also provides assistance in flood prevention.

The federal Stream Encroachment Act of 1929 empowered the state to review and approve all plans for construction within or along a natural water course in order to ensure that the integrity of the stream was maintained. This law was strengthened in 1962 by a statute establishing the Statewide Program of Flood Hazard Delineation. Ten years later the federal government gave the state extensive powers to regulate land use in flood-prone areas.

The Emergency Flood Control Bond Act of 1978 authorized $25 million in state bonds for flood control planning and matching grants-in-aid for local flood control projects. The state Flood Control Facilities Act of 1980 empowered DEP to acquire, control, and operate flood control

facilities in conjunction with either federal or local governments. The state's stream encroachment program became
more effective in 1984 with adoption of the Flood Hazard
Area Regulations which limit the amount of fill allowed in
flood plains.

Local governments have powers affecting flood control as
well. Municipalities may zone to prevent development on
the flood plains and wetlands or development that increases
the risk of flooding. Counties may prepare stormwater control and drainage plans to prevent flooding and coordinate
local flood control programs.

Dam Safety

Dams are an important component both in flood prevention and water supply. The Safe Dam Act of 1981, providing for periodic dam safety inspections by a professional en-
gineer, supplements a 1912 law giving the state responsibility for the safety of dam construction, including review
of initial plans and the right to order repairs. The legislation
applies to New Jersey's approximately sixteen-hundred
dams, including those on thirty major reservoirs, both private and public.

The Delaware River Basin Commission

Water concerns do not stop at political boundaries. In 1961
the states of New Jersey, New York, Pennsylvania, and Delaware and the federal government formed the Delaware
River Basin Commission to manage the water resources of
that geographic area. The first compact of its kind, the Delaware River Basin Commission controls water supply and
quality, water withdrawals and sewage treatment plant discharges, watershed management, flood prevention, pollution control, hydroelectric power, and recreation within the
basin. All commission actions must be in accordance with
the comprehensive plan, a document that is constantly being updated and amended. The commission may build and
operate its own projects as called for in the plan, financing
them through loans, grants, or bond issues. The commission may also veto the projects of other agencies in the basin
if those projects do not conform to the plan.

The governors of the signatory states and the secretary of

the interior, representing the federal government, are the commissioners. However, these commissioners generally act through designated alternates. The commission staff, headed by an executive director, is headquartered in Trenton. The commission is funded by annual appropriations from the four signatory states and the federal government. Proceeds from sales of surface water are returned to the federal government as reimbursement for the water supply portion of several Army Corps of Engineers' dams in the basin.

The United States Geological Survey

This federal agency, working closely with DEP, provides hydrological data on stream flows and groundwater levels and the geology and hydrogeology of the aquifers. Thus, it supplies basic data for much of New Jersey's water management program. The state has currently entered into a five-year agreement with the survey to study groundwater in Atlantic City, Camden, and South River in Middlesex County. These studies will determine potential new water supply projects and outline the optimal solutions to contaminated well field problems.

Water Quality

Industrial and domestic waste waters are the largest identifiable (or "point source") contributors to New Jersey's water pollution problems. "Non-point sources" of pollution include uncontrolled rainwater runoff from roads, parking lots, and farmland. These non-point sources now are believed to be substantial contributors to water pollution.

The Water Quality Management Element of DEP is responsible for state implementation of the federal Clean Water Act program to eliminate point source pollutant discharge. The New Jersey Pollution Discharge Elimination System (NJPDES) permits provide a mechanism for imposing effluent limitations on dischargers. The program aims to maintain the water quality of the receiving stream even after the introduction of treated waste water. Where appropriate, DEP develops "water quality based effluent limitations" for inclusion in the NJPDES permit. A point source is required to meet these standards.

The state permit program, unlike the federal, also attempts to regulate the discharge of pollutants into the groundwater from such sources as unauthorized disposal of hazardous and toxic materials, leaks from underground storage tanks, and septage from inadequate or malfunctioning septic systems.

New Jersey has also passed significant water quality legislation. The Water Quality Planning Act of 1977 requires the development and maintenance of the Statewide Water Quality Management Plan to identify strategies, policies, and implementation activities for the control of point and non-point sources of pollution. This document is used in planning for county and local water quality-related issues such as sewer service, waste water treatment, and non-point pollution Best Management Practices (standards).

The 1976 State Clean Waters Bond Act provided $120 million, some of which was available to municipalities for matching federal grants for construction of municipal waste water treatment plants. In addition, much federal money has been made available (prior to the Budget Reconciliation Act of 1981 which drastically cut federal funding in this and other areas) as capital for sewage treatment plants as part of the federal effort to improve water quality in public waters. The Construction Grants Administration in DEP handles these funds. New Jersey currently has over two hundred applications for assistance which DEP ranks on a priority list. These applications represent $2.9 billion of need for construction and management of municipal waste water treatment plants in New Jersey. In a number of communities sewer connection bans are in effect while construction of adequate sewage treatment facilities is awaited.

The New Jersey Spill Compensation and Control Act provides funds for the cleanup of hazardous substances in the event of a spill. The fund is supported by a tax on transfers of hazardous substances.

Enforcement

New Jersey's environmental laws are among the nation's strictest. These laws, however, must be enforced, and that raises budgetary issues each year. Because DEP lacks sufficient staff to ensure compliance, there is some movement toward turning certain enforcement responsibilities over to the local and county level.

The Division of Water Resources reorganized its Enforcement Element into four Bureaus of Regional Enforcement. Each bureau's responsibilities include monitoring compliance with all permits imposed by the various water resources programs such as water allocations, stream encroachment, the New Jersey Pollutant Discharge Elimination System (NJPDES) permits, groundwater permits, and sludge permits. The bureaus also initiate actions as necessary to abate violations with the primary emphasis being on cleanup of hazardous waste sites by responsible parties.

Environmental Quality

Air quality, pesticide control, radiation protection, emergency response to nuclear and chemical accidents, noise control, and the environmental laboratory are all important components of the Division of Environmental Quality.

Air Quality
In 1954 New Jersey passed the Air Pollution Control Act, the first state air pollution legislation in the nation. Enforcement responsibility rested with the Department of Health and a commission drawn from private citizens, industry, and government. The commission promulgated regulations dealing with the most obvious and annoying air pollution problems—open burning, smoke and particulates from fuel burning, general odor and dust nuisances, and particulates and sulfur compounds from industrial processes.

Later amendments strengthened this law. In 1962 the act was amended, primarily to strengthen and expedite enforcement. DEP was authorized to issue administrative orders and assess penalties promptly upon discovery of violations.

Amendments added in 1967 abolished the earlier policy-making commission, replacing it with the Clean Air Council, a broadly representative body that serves in an advisory capacity to the commissioner of health. Under this arrangement rule-making power was vested in the Department of Health. The amendments also set up a system of permitting for facilities with the potential for air pollution. "State of the art" pollution controls were required for these facilities. A third provision of the amendment was a vehicle inspection program (administered by the Division of Motor Vehicles, see chapter 14) to ensure that all vehicles meet emission standards.

In 1970 the Department of Environmental Protection was formed and air quality concerns were transferred from the Department of Health to DEP.

Also in 1970 the federal Clean Air Act Amendments passed. These called for the development and attainment of national ambient (in the atmosphere) air quality standards. The act required the federal Environmental Protection Agency (EPA) to set standards for different pollutants and the states to develop strategies to achieve and maintain those standards. These state compliance strategies, called State Implementation Plans, are subject to federal approval.

EPA set standards for six pollutants: carbon monoxide, sulfur dioxide, nitrogen dioxide, total suspended particulates, lead, and photochemical oxidants (now regulated as ozone and commonly called smog). Deadlines for attainment of standards were set with five-year extensions available for areas with extreme ozone and carbon monoxide problems. Penalties for non-compliance included withholding grants for certain federal highway projects, sewage treatment plants, and state air control programs. Permits for construction could be denied to new emissions sources in areas not meeting air quality standards. Along with the standards and deadlines came technical assistance and financial aid from EPA.

New Jersey has been successful in complying with standards for four of the six critical air pollutants; the EPA extended New Jersey's deadline for meeting standards on ozone and carbon monoxide to 1987. Since almost all carbon monoxide and much of the ozone comes from automobile emissions, the state has worked on programs such as the automobile emission testing program to reduce the amount of pollutants from vehicle exhausts and the promotion of mass transit and ride-sharing to reduce vehicle use.

Standards for industrial and other stationary pollution sources are also being implemented by DEP through a comprehensive set of regulations dealing with open burning, smoke, particulates, sulfur compounds, fuel burning, incineration, volatile organic substances, and toxic substances. Recently EPA approved two innovative revisions of the New Jersey State Implementation Plan that, DEP asserts, will maintain both air quality and a healthy business climate in the state. Non-coal burning air pollutant sources will be allowed to "bubble" (average) their sulfur dioxide emission rates when establishing compliance with emission standards (as opposed to requiring that each facility individually meet the standard). Sources voluntarily converting to clean or pollution-controlled coal burning will be permitted to burn higher sulfur oil prior to conversion to help offset the costs of conversion.

DEP has also set standards for air contaminant emissions from landfills, from the cleanup and treatment systems for hazardous waste sites, and for hazardous waste incineration. Air pollution considerations were likewise developed as criteria for siting commercial hazardous waste disposal facilities. A good deal of controversy surrounds the proposed guidelines DEP drew up to aid those assessing proper pollution control technology for resource recovery facilities (which burn garbage and are currently seen as one of the state's solutions to the mounting garbage disposal crisis). The Department of the Public Advocate and environmental groups question both the stringency of the proposed guidelines and the available technology to effectively control emissions from large-scale resource recovery plants.

Acid Rain

New Jersey has been in the forefront in bringing national attention to the acid rain issue. Within the state the legislature has appropriated $100,000 for research on acid rain damage. Projects currently underway study acid rain effects on our lakes and streams along the Kittatinny Ridge and in the Pinelands. Other DEP-sponsored research includes an assessment of crop damage and a study to determine the means to measure materials damage.

On the national scene Governor Kean has spearheaded a special acid rain policy initiative. Under the premise that acid rain is a national problem and all states must contribute to its cleanup, New Jersey, working with the Coalition of Northeast Governors (CONEG), has endorsed an acid rain control policy. If adopted by the federal government, this would provide for meaningful sulfur dioxide emission controls for all major emitting sources in the nation. The costs to comply would be distributed among all states in an equitable manner according to the amount of pollution emitted by each state.

Other Environmental Quality Programs

Pesticide control includes administering certification examinations and registering users, dealers, businesses, and pesticide products. The Department of Environmental Protection made major revisions in the pesticide regulatory code in 1983, including programs to register pesticide operators and dealers, an aquatic permit program for pesticide applications to water systems, and public notification requirements prior to large scale applications. A model ordinance was also developed to be used as guidance for local governments in developing pesticide ordinances for their communities.

New Jersey's Pesticide/Toxic Substance Laboratory is the first such facility in the nation. The laboratory's expertise is in toxic pollutant analysis. It has the capacity to analyze samples ranging from air and water to sludge, oil, and industrial residues.

The New Jersey Noise Control Act of 1971 made New Jersey the first state in the nation to control noise pollution through legislation. The act authorizes DEP to regulate excessive noises that may be detrimental to public health. A system of regional federal noise abatement offices and the EPA central noise abatement office were closed in 1981 due to federal budget cuts. The New Jersey program, however, continues limited operations, staffed in part by senior citizen volunteers who investigate claims. With the support and assistance of the Noise Control Council, model ordinances for both stationary and mobile sources of noise were prepared and are available for use by municipalities. As a result of a major enforcement action in the early 1980s a large steel mill in New Jersey invested $3 million in noise control, the most comprehensive noise abatement program ever undertaken in the nation.

Radiation protection responsibilities in DEP include regulating the use of radiation sources and materials (including chest and dental x-rays), preparing plans dealing with radiological emergencies such as the Essex County site contaminated by radon gas, and administering a program to license and maintain educational standards for nuclear medicine and x-ray technologists. New Jersey has been active in the development and implementation of emergency plans for accidents that may occur at the nuclear power plants operating in or near New Jersey. In 1983 DEP developed a Nuclear Engineering Program to perform assessments of the dangers in the event of a nuclear power plant accident.

Land Resources

New Jersey purchased its first public lands for conservation purposes in 1905. Some years later, in 1932, the fish and game agency started purchasing lands suitable for fishing and hunting. Not until the 1950s, however, with the purchase of almost 96,000 acres of the Wharton Tract in the Pinelands and the subsequent purchase of 123,422 acres under the first phase of the Green Acres Open Space Land Conservation Program, did the state government acquire land for itself in sizeable amounts.

Open Space
The preservation of open space has become increasingly recognized by the public as an important function of government. Open space is vital to protect essential sources of water; to control erosion and flooding; to preserve woodlands, wildlife, and plants; to cleanse the air; to keep unique natural sites intact; and, of equal importance, to give citizens opportunities for recreation and an appreciation of their natural surroundings.

The New Jersey Open Space Policy Plan estimates a total need of just over one million acres of open space for the state. This is based on a "balanced land use standard" which sets aside 4 percent of the state's total area for federal open space; 10 percent of the state's total area for state open space; 7 percent of developable land (excluding steep slopes, wetlands, and federal and state open space) for county open space; and 3 percent of developed or developable land for municipal open space.

Figure 10.2

Major Conservation and Open Space Areas

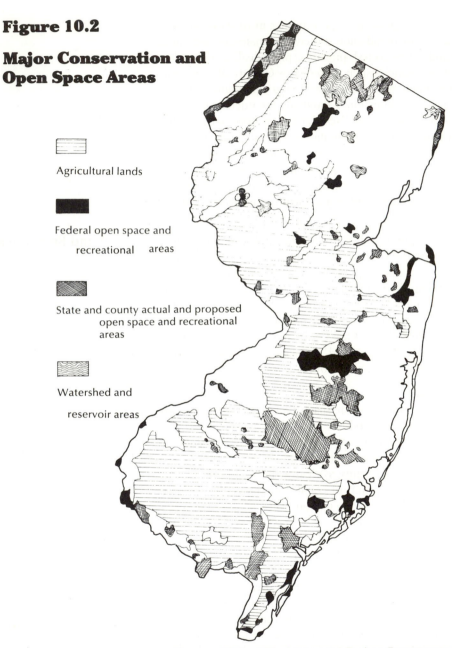

Agricultural lands

Federal open space and recreational areas

State and county actual and proposed open space and recreational areas

Watershed and reservoir areas

Sources: **Office of Environmental Review, Department of Environmental Protection, Division of Rural Resources, Department of Agriculture.**

236

Indeed in New Jersey open space is maintained by each of these levels of government as well as by interstate agencies and private and commercial enterprises. Currently 646,000 acres of open space in New Jersey are publicly owned, while 159,000 acres are privately held.

Federal, interstate, and regional agencies together hold title to 112,000 acres of open space in New Jersey. The National Park Service, an agency of the Department of the Interior, has responsibility for four recreational areas in New Jersey: the Morristown National Historical Park (Jockey Hollow) in Morris County; the Edison Laboratory National Historic Site in West Orange, Essex County; the Delaware Water Gap National Recreation Area comprising thirty-five miles of the Delaware River in New Jersey and Pennsylvania; and the Gateway National Recreation Area at Sandy Hook in Monmouth County. The United States Fish and Wildlife Service, also in the Department of the Interior, maintains five national wildlife refuges: Brigantine in Atlantic County, Great Swamp in Morris County, Blood Point in Burlington County, and Killacohook and Supawawna in Salem County.

Due to the efforts of private conservationists as early as 1897, the New Jersey Palisades, which overlook the Hudson River, remain tree-clad today rather than built up. This thirteen mile stretch north of the George Washington Bridge is one of eighteen parks of the Palisades Interstate Park in New Jersey and New York operated by a bistate commission. Most of the New Jersey portion (2,437 acres) was acquired by John D. Rockefeller, Jr, and donated to the park system in 1935.

The Pinelands, a unique tract containing 760 square miles of pine and oak forest located largely in Burlington and Ocean Counties, is a national and state land-use unit. The area is the first National Reserve and includes state parks, forests, wildlife management areas, and many acres of privately owned land managed under the Pinelands Protection Act of 1979.

Protection of open space and environmentally sensitive lands in the coastal area is also a state responsibility. Because the protection of the Pinelands, coastal lands, and the Hackensack Meadowlands are important examples of New

Jersey's best efforts in land-use management, all three are discussed in chapter 11 which deals with land-use issues.

The State of New Jersey has preserved open space through a system of state parks and forests, historic sites, and recreational areas. The power to procure open space rests with the Department of Environmental Protection. It may acquire land or rights in land by purchase, by gifts, or by eminent domain when the land is to be used for a state park or forest, as a watershed, or as a historic site. DEP may also acquire freshwater lakes and the surrounding lands.

State Parks and Forests

New Jersey's Divison of Parks and Forestry has been providing outdoor recreation and forest management programs since the beginning of the twentieth century. The State Park Service provides for the maintenance, operation and protection of thirty-five state parks, eleven state forests, five recreation areas, thirty-three natural areas, twenty-five historic sites, and three state marinas. The newest and most heavily visited of these facilities is Liberty State Park in Hudson County. (See the most recent annual edition of *Fitzgerald's Legislative Manual: State of New Jersey* for a description of these state facilities.)

While the primary focus of park management is preservation of natural areas and recreation, the State Forestry Service was created to manage the forest environment for mixed uses: to provide recreational opportunities; to produce forest products; and to conserve land, water, timber, and wildlife. Forestry concerns also include preventing insect and disease damage and protecting life and property threatened by forest fires.

New Jersey has many state-owned historic sites that are open to the public. Most are managed jointly by the State Park Service or the Office of New Jersey Heritage. The latter operates a federally certified historic preservation program. The office identifies and lists historic sites for the state and national historic registers, reviews publicly funded projects on recognized historic sites, certifies projects for federal preservation tax incentives, and administers matching survey and planning grants. Through creative use of federal preservation tax incentives, the heritage program also includes inner-city projects which have helped provide hundreds of new housing units.

Under the Office of Natural Lands Management are grouped a number of functions aimed at preserving open space. Specifically, this office identifies and develops strategies to protect unique, rare, endangered, and scenic habitats. The office is responsible for planning and implementing the Wild and Scenic River System, the State Trail System, and the newly-passed Open Lands Management Act. Identification of potential natural areas and development of management plans for the thirty-three natural areas already designated, such as the Island Beach Natural Area, is another responsibility of this office. The office also staffs the Natural Lands Trust, a non-profit corporation established to accept donations of land for preservation.

The Green Acres Program

The Green Acres Program was born out of a 1961 bond issue that demonstrated the voters' belief that a highly urbanized state must set aside a sufficient amount of open space. This conviction was reaffirmed as voters approved subsequent bond issues in 1971, 1974, 1978, and 1983 for a total of $675 million. As part of the $135 million Green Acres Bond Act approved by the voters in 1983, a Green Trust Fund was established. This is an innovative, low-interest loan program for local government designed to maintain acquisition and development capability far beyond the limitations of past bond issues. Since the trust is a revolving loan program, as one community pays off its loan, funds become available for land acquisition by another community.

The impact of Green Acres purchases have been felt by state agencies as well as local municipalities. Expansion of the Pinelands holdings, state parks, forests, and wildlife management areas all have resulted from the Green Acres bond issues. The matching grants for county and municipal open space have greatly expanded local open space and recreational facilities. Many municipal governments coordinate their acquisition of lands for recreation with local school boards to establish facilities on or adjacent to public school grounds. There are over 2,830 municipal parks and recreation areas developed for outdoor games and sports, bicycle and hiking trails, and playgrounds.

While urban dwellers and local municipalities benefit from the state's program of preserving open space, other important beneficiaries are New Jersey's fish, game, and wildlife.

Fish, Game, and Wildlife   One tends to think of New Jersey resorts primarily as seashore facilities, yet there are more than eight hundred inland lakes and fourteen hundred miles of trout streams for recreational purposes. New Jersey is also considered among the best deer-hunting states in the country, with more deer per square mile in its woods than are found in Maine's forests. Maintenance of hunting and fishing opportunities is an important complement to New Jersey's important tourism industry. Maintenance of commercial fishing and shellfishing is also vital to the state's economy.

The Division of Fish, Game, and Wildlife is responsible for the protection and management of New Jersey's fish and wildlife resources. To achieve its goal of maintaining the density and diversity of New Jersey's wildlife resources, the division licenses hunters, provides hunter and trapper education, enforces game laws, and manages native species. The state operates three game farms, three fish hatcheries, and several wildlife research stations. License fees plus some federal aid make this division largely self-supporting.

The Nongame and Endangered Wildlife Program is supported in part by a check-off allowing New Jersey residents to contribute to the fund when they file their state income tax returns. Currently there are thirty-five species on the state's endangered list, but some gains have been made by the division in increasing both the peregrine falcon and bald eagle populations in New Jersey. Wild turkeys have also been reintroduced in New Jersey, raising the population to a level where turkey hunting was recently allowed for the first time in one hundred years.

New Jersey has also joined many other states in developing a state Duck Stamp program to provide funds for the purchase, management, improvement, and protection of wetlands which are vital to the waterfowl. The program includes both requiring a duck stamp for hunters and selling limited edition prints and medallions reproduced from the stamp design.

Policies of fish and wildlife management are formulated by the Department of Environmental Protection and the Fish and Game Council, which is made up of sportsmen, farmers, commercial fishermen, members of the commercial fishing industries, and citizens dedicated to helping preserve New Jersey's fish, game, and wildlife.

The Marine Fisheries Council and the Shell Fisheries Council work with DEP to preserve and manage commercial fishing resources. Traditionally, clams and oysters have been an important part of New Jersey's commercial fishing industry. The state owns all underwater lands including 75,000 acres of natural clam and oyster "bottoms" and many acres of oyster planting grounds along the Atlantic shore and in the Delaware Bay. The state protects the shellfish beds from exploitation and assists commercial fishing by preventing overharvesting and by licensing those who harvest shellfish. This industry has been seriously threatened by pollution because shellfish, acting as filtering agents in the water, retain in their bodies harmful bacteria from polluted waters. The clams, however, purge themselves of harmful organisms if they are relocated to pure waters for a short time. New Jersey cooperates with commercial clammers by helping transport clams from polluted areas, such as Raritan Bay, to unpolluted areas, such as one leased in Great Bay. The oyster harvest has been affected not only by pollution but also by disease. The state works with the oyster industry to protect the oyster grounds and to control the pollution that threatens them.

Solid Waste

Most New Jersey citizens are aware of garbage—they carry it out (several pounds per person each day), they watch it build up during garbage strikes, and they are bombarded with media coverage of the solid waste disposal crisis. Many citizens try to do something about garbage; they voluntarily separate their newspapers, glass bottles, and metal cans for recycling.

The garbage coming from residential, commercial, and institutional sources (schools and hospitals primarily), is made up of paper (40 to 60 percent), glass containers (10 percent), miscellaneous trash (10 percent) metal cans and tubes (8 to 10 percent), yard wastes (7 to 10 percent), food wastes (5 to 7 percent), and plastic containers (2 to 5 percent). Most of this garbage is collected by tax-supported municipal services (often through a contract with a private hauler), although in some towns individuals contract directly with private collectors.

New Jersey produces approximately eleven million tons of solid waste each year, to which is added another two or three million from other waste. If this solid waste were all baled and piled up, New Jersey would create new mountain ranges each year.

With the exception of small amounts that are recycled, composted, or incinerated, the bulk of this garbage currently goes to sanitary landfills. These are dump sites meeting basic state standards for reduction of litter, odor, and pollution. Generally, the waste is covered with a layer of dirt. Once garbage is dumped in a landfill, however, the problem may not end.

Landfills in New Jersey have problems: eventually all may leak and pose a threat to the environment. Poorly designed or poorly operated landfills cause more problems, both when they are active and after they have been closed. If methane gas generated by decomposing garbage is not vented or recovered, it may migrate into nearby homes and buildings. Leakage is a problem when liquids in the waste (landfills may not accept liquid waste) or decomposing garbage mix with rainwater. The resulting liquids (leachate) may seep into underground or surface water supplies and contaminate them. Odors, litter, and pests (such as rats and gulls) result from landfills not adequately covered and maintained. In addition, the traffic created by heavy trucks using the landfill may annoy neighbors and cause excessive wear on local roads. Finally, in all too many cases, hazardous and toxic wastes such as paints, dry cleaning fluid, or batteries are mixed with ordinary household trash and dumped at landfills. Other hazardous and toxic wastes are, from time to time, dumped illegally at some landfills.

Landfills will probably always be needed—in conjunction with recycling and resource recovery systems. Every waste treatment method leaves some residue, and landfills are also needed as backup facilities in case of operating problems at resource recovery facilities or employee strikes. Recognizing this, DEP has taken steps to reduce the adverse effects of landfills on the environment. DEP regulations prohibit contruction of sanitary landfills that will allow wastes to come in contact with surface or groundwater, or in which leachate impairs the quality of surface or groundwater as established by DEP classification standards. Dust, odor, insect, and rodent control are also required as are specific procedures for daily, intermediate, and final cover. New facilities must install gas venting and monitoring systems, and they may be required in existing landfills if methane gases are detected beyond the landfill area. What may be deposited in a landfill is also carefully regulated. The disposal of hazardous or radioactive waste in sanitary landfills is prohibited, and operators soon will not be allowed to accept liquid sewage sludge or septic waste or other liquids, unless they install liners and leachate collection and treatment systems.

Even with these regulations, landfill problems still exist and it is no wonder that municipality after municipality says "not in our back yard" when siting of a new landfill is proposed for their area. The same resistance is offered to proposed resource recovery facilities (plants to burn solid waste and generate steam as a saleable by-product). Yet there are only three options for dealing with solid waste, and each is logically part of the disposal solution. Recycling removes valuable materials and reduces the volume. Burning in a resource recovery facility disposes of much of the volume of solid waste. The remaining ash would be landfilled unless alternative and productive uses (such as using the ash to construct roadbeds) are approved by DEP.

Currently DEP is requiring the counties to move ahead with plans for dealing with their solid wastes. Since many of

Figure 10.3

New Jersey Laws Governing the Disposal of Solid and Hazardous Wastes

Solid Waste Management Act (N.J.S.A. 13:1E *et seq.*) Originally passed in 1970 and amended several times since, this act gives DEP the power to supervise the collection and disposal of solid and hazardous waste. It calls for the coordination of collection and disposal activities through the creation of 22 solid waste districts (one for each county plus the Hackensack Meadowlands District) and encourages the use of recycling and resource recovery. It also includes civil and criminal penalties for violations.

Major Hazardous Waste Facilities Siting Act (N.J.S.A. 13:1E-51 *et seq.*) supplements the Solid Waste Management Act. It defines hazardous waste facilities and established the Hazardous Waste Facilities Siting Commission to review DEP proposed siting criteria, prepare a Hazardous Waste Siting Plan, and propose and adopt site designations.

Solid Waste Utility Control Act (N.J.S.A. 48:13a-1 *et seq.*) gives the Board of Public Utilities (formerly the Public Utilities Commission) the power to license and regulate solid waste collection and disposal facilities, set rates, and establish franchise areas. Registration with DEP is a prerequisite for licensing.

The Recycling Act (N.J.S.A. 13:1E-92 *et seq.*) supplements the Solid Waste Management Act. It implements a statewide recycling plan and imposes a 12¢ per cubic yard tax on landfilled waste for distribution to local governments as grants and to recycling businesses as low interest loans. After 1986, the tax becomes 6¢ per cubic yard.

Sanitary Landfill Facility Closure and Contingency Fund (N.J.S.A. 13:1E-100 *et seq.*) imposes a 15¢ per cubic yard (or .2¢ per gallon) tax on landfilled waste to establish a fund which will pay damages resulting from improper operation or closure of landfills. Facility owners and operators must develop plans covering closure and post-closure care. The act also directs landfill operators to establish escrow accounts at 30¢ per cubic yard (or .4¢ per gallon) for costs incurred in closure and post-closure.

Natural Resources Bond Act of 1980 (N.J.S.A. 5:12-117.1) provides for the sale of $50 million in general obligation bonds to be used as grants and loans to fund the development of resource recovery systems. Another $95 million is earmarked for sewage treatment and water supply facilities, dam restoration projects and harbor clean-up projects.

Spill Compensation and Control Act (N.J.S.A. 58:10-23.1 *et seq.*) requires that all spills or other discharges of hazardous substances be reported to the DEP. The act provides for a fund for prompt containment and removal of a discharge and for swift and adequate compensation to persons damaged by a discharge.

Hazardous Discharge Bond Act (P.L. 1981, C. 275) authorizes the issuance of $100 million in state bonds for the identification, clean-up, and removal of hazardous discharge.

Pretreatment Standards for Sewerage, etc. (N.J.S.A. 58:11-49 to 58) authorizes the adoption and enforcement of rules and regulations requiring the treatment of certain wastes prior to their discharge into sewerage systems.

Water Pollution Control Act (N.J.S.A. 58:10A-1 *et seq.*) authorizes the DEP to adopt and enforce rules and regulation to prevent, control or abate water pollution.

Pesticide Control Act (N.J.S.A. 26:2C-1 *et seq.*) authorizes the DEP to adopt and enforce regulations governing the sale, use, and application of all pesticides.

Air Pollution Control Act (N.J.S.A. 26:2C-1 *et seq.*) provides for the control of air contaminants, installation or alteration of control apparatus, enforcement of procedures, and issuance of penalties.

Causing or Risking Widespread Injury or Damage (N.J.S.A. 2C:17-2) makes it a second degree crime to purposely or knowingly unlawfully cause or release any harmful or destructive substance into the environment. Violations punishable by 5 to 10 years in prison and/or $100,000 fine per count. Corporate fines range to $300,000 per count.

N.J.S.A. means New Jersey Statutes Annotated. The numbers to the left of the colon indicate the chapter; those to the right are subchapter and section.

Source: **Reprinted with permission from** *Throwing It Away in New Jersey: A Comprehensive Look at Waste Disposal*, **written by Barbara Eisler in 1983 for the American Lung Association of New Jersey with support from the New Jersey Department of Environmental Protection. (This and other Lung Association publications provide valuable and well-written information on New Jersey environmental problems.)**

the major landfills are closing and new landfills are not being sited, the majority of the counties are planning resource recovery plants. The first major facility expected to be completed will be that of Essex County. While the Essex plant, as presently planned, will have sophisticated pollution control equipment to remove hydrochloric acid and particulate emissions, environmentalists raise many questions about the dangers of solid wastes escaping into the air and causing pollution problems. They argue that high technology and continuous monitoring of the emissions from a resource recovery plant are necessary to prevent those pollution problems.

The Department of the Public Advocate, in a nontechnical "white paper," has raised questions about the potential health and environmental hazards of emissions and of residue from incineration. The white paper argues that the state should permit the construction and operation of resource recovery facilities but only with tough environmental regulations. The report further urges the state to require counties to have strong recycling programs to separate and eliminate much of the waste stream that otherwise would be burned.

Regulation of the Solid Waste Industry

The first federal legislation dealing with solid waste problems was the Solid Waste Disposal Act of 1965. Limited money was provided for the states to develop solid waste management plans. The Resource Recovery Act of 1970 encouraged the recycling and reclamation of materials. Then, as the problems of hazardous waste became increasingly evident, the U.S. Congress passed the Resource Conservation and Recovery Act (RCRA) of 1976. The section on non-hazardous waste prohibits open dumping on the land and requires the closing or upgrading of existing dumps that fail to meet land disposal standards. The law also requires the various states to promulgate their own guidelines for acceptable solid waste management.

New Jersey's involvement in regulating solid waste began in 1958 with an amendment to the State Sanitary Code declaring open dumps a nuisance and empowering local boards of health to take action against them. In 1970 amendments added to the code required solid waste disposal facilities to register with the state and also provided operating standards for landfills including a provision requiring the owners to submit engineering designs for review.

In 1970 the newly created Department of Environmental Protection assumed the solid waste regulatory powers formerly wielded by the Department of Health. In that same year, the legislature passed two significant pieces of legislation. The first was the Solid Waste Management Act which gave DEP broad new powers to supervise the collection and disposal of solid waste. Regional solutions to solid waste disposal were mandated, a Solid Waste Advisory Council was established, and penalties for violations of up to one thousand dollars per day were authorized.

The other legislation resulted from a long investigation by the State Commission of Investigation into problems and corruption among waste haulers and landfill operations. The Solid Waste Utility Control Act of 1970 declared that solid waste collection and disposal operations were public utilities and as such would be licensed and regulated by the Board of Public Utilities (BPU), part of the Department of Energy. (See chapter 9) The BPU certifies operators of solid waste facilities after they have been investigated by the State Police; issues franchises, sets areas where an operator has exclusive rights to conduct business; and reviews proposed solid waste plans prepared by the counties.

In 1974 transfer stations, incinerators, and resource recovery facilities were brought under DEP regulation. The following year twenty-two solid waste management districts, one for each county and for the Hackensack Meadowlands District, were created, and DEP was required to develop a statewide plan encouraging the maximum use of resource recovery procedures. The passage of the New Jersey Recycling Act in 1981 made a recycling program in each solid waste district mandatory. An Office of Recycling was established as a joint project of the Department of Environmental Protection and the Department of Energy. The office is located in the Department of Energy. The Kean administration is now proposing legislation to make recycling mandatory after several years of promoting local recycling projects through a grant program funded by a twelve cents per cubic yard surcharge on all solid waste disposed of in New Jersey landfills.

A waste reduction mechanism that works well in a number of other states is the requirement of a deposit on beverage containers. By placing a cash value on all beer and soft drink containers, litter is reduced significantly, the volume of solid waste going to landfills is decreased, and energy and raw materials are saved. Despite strong lobbying for such a mandatory beverage container deposit law (the "bottle bill") by many groups in New Jersey, such legislation has not yet been passed. Marshalled against the legislation are those who fear it will harm New Jersey's large glass and container industry, those who fear it will compete with present recycling programs, and some retailers who would be involved in handling returned containers and refunding deposits.

Policy review, guidance, and public input for these various programs are provided on the state level by the Solid Waste Advisory Council. Members represent the general public, the solid waste industry, and the departments of Community Affairs, Health, Agriculture, and Energy, the latter represented by the president of the Board of Public Utilities. Each solid waste management district also has a Solid Waste Advisory Council (SWAC).

Hazardous Wastes

For many years hazardous wastes were not treated as a disposal problem separate from solid waste. In fact, all too often hazardous wastes were landfilled right along with other wastes. Only recently has disposal of hazardous wastes been recognized as a problem. Some have entered our surface and underground drinking water supplies. Others have polluted the air as they evaporate, are improperly burned, or explode, as they did at the Chemical Control Corporation in Elizabeth in 1980. The density and nature of New Jersey industry, with its many chemical and petroleum products plants, make hazardous waste disposal an especially pressing issue in this state. Indeed, experts estimate that the geographically small state of New Jersey produces approximately 8 percent of the nation's hazardous wastes. As a result New Jersey has more abandoned hazardous waste disposal sites scheduled for cleanup than any other state. Cleaning up yesterday's hazardous wastes is only part of the challenge. Reducing the quantity of hazardous wastes is the ultimate challenge. Regulating the production and disposal of hazardous wastes currently being generated is also necessary. Both the federal and state governments have addressed these issues with legislation and programs.

Federal Hazardous Waste Programs
The New Jersey congressional delegation has been especially active in initiating and supporting federal legislation dealing with hazardous wastes. In the 1970s and early 1980s a number of important laws were passed that began to address the issues of hazardous waste cleanup and disposal. In the mid-1980s the New Jersey congressional delegation and citizens' groups continue to press for additional cleanup funding and for strict adherence to the original intent of these environmental laws.

The federal laws dealing with hazardous wastes range from the Resource Conservation and Recovery Act of 1976 to the Comprehensive Environmental Response, Compensation, and Liability (Superfund) Act of 1981. They include provisions of the Clean Air Act, the Clean Water Act, the Safe Drinking Water Act, and the Marine Protection, Research, and Sanctuaries (Ocean Dumping) Act. Other laws directly affect the production, transportation, and disposal of hazardous materials and wastes.

State Hazardous Waste Initiatives
During the second half of the 1970s New Jersey became actively involved in controlling hazardous wastes. In 1976, after DEP closed the Kin-Buc landfill in Edison due to pollutants leaching into the Raritan River, the legislature passed the Spill Compensation and Control Act. This law prohibited the discharge of hazardous substances and also provided funding for cleanup of some hazardous waste dumps. In 1978 New Jersey initiated a manifest system to track hazardous waste from generator to disposal site, taking action even before federal regulations for such a program were developed. The Solid Waste Management Act of 1970 was amended in 1980 to make illegal the transport of any hazardous waste to an unauthorized facility, or for the disposal, storage, or treatment of those wastes not in compli-

ance with DEP regulations. In 1981 the Hazardous Waste Facilities Siting Act was passed.

The Major Hazardous Waste Facilities Siting Act provides a mechanism for the siting and construction of major commercial, off-site treatment and disposal facilities which are either new or which plan to expand by more than 50 percent and which have a storage capacity of more than 250,000 gallons. The New Jersey Hazardous Waste Facilities Siting Commission is composed of nine members (three county or municipal elected or appointed officials, three employed by the industry involved, and three representing environmental or public interest organizations) appointed by the governor for staggered three-year terms. The commission is attached to DEP but independent of DEP control. The task of the commission is to prepare a Hazardous Waste Facilities Plan specifying the number and type of needed new facilities and to propose and adopt site designations. The site choices will be based upon criteria adopted by DEP with the advice of the Hazardous Waste Advisory Council. The criteria set forth by DEP in 1983 include objectives to provide a stable structure for the facility, safe transportation of the hazardous wastes to the site, and protection of human population, surface water, groundwater, environmentally sensitive areas, and air quality. In order to minimize the number and size of sites selected, the commission is currently studying ways to reduce the amount of hazardous wastes generated and to recycle at least some of the wastes.

The Division of Waste Management

In 1982 DEP reorganized the Solid Waste Administration and the Bureau of Hazardous Waste into the new Division of Waste Management (DWM) with responsibility for solid waste programs, those dealing with hazardous waste treatment and disposal, and the evaluation and cleanup of spills and abandoned dump sites.

The Division of Waste Management, through its Hazardous Site Mitigation Administration (HSMA), is currently addressing the problems posed by years of illegal and uncontrolled disposal of hazardous wastes. Due to aggressive identification and assessment of hazardous waste sites, New

Jersey leads the way in competition for federal Superfund cleanup grants. The HSMA works with EPA for cleanup of those sites on the National Priorities List (for Superfund grants) and also contracts for cleanup of other New Jersey sites using the State's Spill Compensation Fund and the Hazardous Discharge Fund. The Management Plan for the Cleanup of Hazardous Waste Sites in New Jersey 1983–1986, prepared by HSMA, is a systematic approach to enforcement and cleanup and also identifies future funding needs and sources. Other divisions within DEP deal with regulation and enforcement of hazardous wastes as they relate to water and air quality.

Enforcement responsibilities are also shared with the Department of Law and Public Safety. (See chapter 14.) The Interagency Strike Force, established by Governor Brendon Byrne (governor from 1974–1982), focused on seeking out and prosecuting illegal dumpers of hazardous wastes (the so-called "midnight dumpers" who find convenient places for disposing of their illegal cargoes). The Hazardous Waste Strike Force in the Department of Law and Public Safety continues this fight against illegal dumpers. In addition, the Department of Law and Public Safety and DEP have joined in the Northeast Hazardous Waste Coordination Committee, a multi-state effort to address the problem of illegal transportation, storage, and disposal of hazardous wastes. This coordinated approach includes both training programs for field investigators and prosecutors, and an information system allowing states and the federal government not only to exchange technical investigative data but also to more effectively enforce the manifest system for hazardous wastes.

Radioactive Wastes

America has an increasing supply of radioactive wastes. They include both high-level wastes (primarily spent fuel rods from nuclear generating plants), and low-level wastes (typically industrial, medical, and research wastes such as protective clothing, paper, and glass equipment contaminated with a radioactive substance). Both are regulated by the federal government. However, low-level wastes are by

definition all radioactive wastes not included in the definition of high-level wastes. This relegates wastes from nuclear
reactors—both the dry waste (clothing, rags, and tools) and
wet wastes (resins and sludges from cleaning the cooling
water)—to low-level waste facilities. However, the wet
wastes from nuclear reactors have much longer half-lives
than the other low-level wastes and therefore must be segregated from the environment for many more years—for
some of the elements segregation for three hundred years
is recommended.

Disposal of these low-level wastes have in the past been
handled either by on-site storage until they decay to the
point where they can be handled as ordinary waste (medical
wastes are often in this category), or they have been shipped
to six radioactive landfills around the country. Because of
serious erosion problems and migration of radioactivity beyond the confines of the storage trenches, three of these
sites were closed during the 1970s. The remaining three facilities (Barnwell, South Carolina; Hanford, Washington;
and Beatty, Nevada) are expected in 1986 to close their
doors to wastes from states other than joined in compact
with the facilities' host state.

Under the terms of the federal Low-level Radioactive
Waste Policy Act of 1980 congress mandated that states
either form regional compacts or make in-state arrangements for their own wastes by 1986. New Jersey, to date,
has been unsuccessful in forming a workable and lasting
compact with other states.

High-level radioactive wastes, while a federal responsibility, affect the state in several ways. Most of the wastes are
currently stored on-site in temporary storage pools at the
nuclear reactor facilities. While awaiting development of
a permanent national storage facility for high-level wastes,
some of the spent fuel rods are being shipped from facilities
that have no more temporary storage space to facilities
that have space.

Shipments of high-level radioactive wastes, under current federal court rulings and federal regulations, may not
be banned by state or local governments. Notification is
given to the governor of the state through which shipments
will pass seven days ahead of the shipment, but that infor-

mation is not made public. Citizen groups are calling for changes which would allow strong state regulation of such shipments in concert with the federal regulations. In particular, they advocate pre-notification of state and local authorities before each shipment; regulation and enforcement of the packaging, vehicle inspection, driver training, route selection, and in-transit storage of the wastes; development of safer shipping casks for the wastes; and application of these regulations to military as well as civilian wastes.

This law, which became effective in 1984, establishes a comprehensive system for the disclosure and dissemination of information about hazardous substances in the workplace and in the environment. The act is a legislative response to growing concern about the potential adverse effects these substances may have upon the health, safety, and welfare of the public.

The Worker and Community Right to Know Act

The law is being administered jointly by the departments of Health, Environmental Protection, Labor, and Treasury. The state departments of Health and Environmental Protection are responsible for determining which substances are hazardous. To date some 2,100 substances have been so designated. By a given date, under the current plan, each employer must assure that every container holding any of the designated hazardous substances on their premises bears a label showing the chemical name or the trade-secret registry number assigned to the substance.

Forty-two thousand businesses and manufacturers in the state will be surveyed in order to determine which of these hazardous substances and how much of each is being used or stored. State-prepared health and safety data sheets must then be placed on file at the business and in the state and county departments of health. This information will be accessible to everyone: employees, citizens, and health and emergency response personnel. The law also requires labeling of all containers, valves, and pipelines that contain hazardous substances.

Enforcement provisions and citizen oversight could make Right to Know a significant tool for monitoring and controlling the release of hazardous substances into the environment.

Implementation of the law for industries covered by the federal Occupation Health and Safety Act (OSHA) regulations is currently being held up while the state appeals a federal court ruling that OSHA regulations supercede this state law.

11.

The Public Advocate,
The Public Defender,
and Land Use

I n 1974 the New Jersey Legislature created the Department of the Public Advocate (DPA). For the first time in the history of the country a cabinet-level agency, supported by general taxes, existed to provide legal representation for the public. The agency is empowered to represent the public interest in quasi-judicial proceedings before state regulatory agencies; to initiate litigation on behalf of mental patients, the developmentally disabled, and prisoners; and to institute legal proceedings on behalf of the public in any broad social concern.

Creation of the Department of the Public Advocate stemmed from concerns that, while the decisions of government agencies have a great impact on the public, nevertheless the public essentially has been excluded from the administrative, adjudicative, and rule-making processes. Other concerns addressed by the legislation creating the DPA included fear that agencies created to regulate private industry on the behalf of the public sometimes became captives of the industries they were designed to regulate; that some agencies established to provide services or assistance to the public have not always protected the public interest; and that the citizens' inability to control these governmental decisions which seriously affect their lives leads to erosion of confidence in government. That the diverse programs of the DPA have been models for many other states indicates these concerns are not unique to New Jersey.

THE PUBLIC
ADVOCATE AND
THE PUBLIC
DEFENDER

The Office of
the Public Defender

The nucleus of the Department of the Public Advocate is the Office of the Public Defender. This agency was established in 1967 to provide legal representation for indigent defendants charged with indictable offenses as well as for juveniles with indigent parents or guardians in cases where there was the possibility the juvenile would be committed to an institution. The Office of the Public Defender was established in response to a series of judicial decisions mandating the state to provide a paid lawyer for every indigent criminal defendant.

Now incorporated into the Department of the Public Advocate, the combined agencies are headed by one person, appointed by the governor with the consent of the senate, and holding both the title of the Public Advocate and the Public Defender. By statute the public defender's term of office is five years while that of the public advocate is at the pleasure of the governor. (It is possible that these posts could be held by two separate persons.)

Eighty-five percent of the resources of the DPA are devoted to the activities of the Office of the Public Defender. By far the largest activity is representation of indigent criminal defendants in trials and appeals. Since the restoration of capital punishment in 1982, a special budget has allowed for training and activities focused on death penalty cases. Eighty such cases in the first twenty months alone required the services of a public defender. The office also provides legal representation for accused parole violators and represents the rights of inmates in county jails. (See Chapter 12, Corrections.)

The Juvenile Administration Unit provides legal representation for institutionalized juveniles and investigates alleged cases of abuse or violation of rights. They also advocate for educational programs in juvenile facilities and challenge inappropriate placements of juveniles.

The work of the Public Defender in advocating the rights of inmates is complemented by the Office of the Ombudsman within the Department of Corrections. This largely independent agency represents the rights of those confined within state correctional facilities.

The public advocate is a cabinet-level officer acting as the voice of the people—those not directly involved in policy making but whose lives are affected by those decisions. Often in the face of adverse public opinion, the public advocate champions the rights of the individual, upholding the rights of those with the least power—the poor, the mentally ill, the developmentally disabled, those in prison, and minorities. In other activities the public advocate argues on behalf of the public as a whole—in utility rate-setting cases, for example.

Activities of the Public Advocate

Advocacy for the Mentally Ill and the Developmentally Disabled
Through field offices and class action suits the rights of the mentally ill are protected. Employment discrimination, the rights of patients acquitted of criminal charges on the basis of insanity, and community placement for the mentally ill are some areas of DPA activity. The department has also involved itself in a landmark case arguing the right of hospitalized psychiatric patients to refuse certain mind-altering drugs.

A program to advocate for the rights of the developmentally disabled is jointly funded by the federal and New Jersey governments. The developmentally disabled population includes the mentally retarded; victims of cerebral palsy, epilepsy, dyslexia, and autism; as well as those with lifelong physical disabilities. The program concerns itself with issues such as appropriateness of placements, educational programs, transportation, housing, barrier free buildings, employment discrimination, and receipt by these individuals of state and federal assistance. (See chapter 13, Services for the Mentally Ill, and Services for the Mentally Retarded.)

Advocacy for the General Public
To ensure that the interests of the public are adequately represented in rate setting decisions, the DPA is a party to rate setting for public utilities. (See chapter 9, Public Utilities.) The public advocate's involvement is financed by an assessment on the utility seeking the rate hike. A major issue ad-

dressed by the DPA is protecting electric utility customers from having to pay for costs stemming from nuclear power plant shutdowns and mismanagement, especially the Three Mile Island nuclear generating plant accident. DPA staff also studies ways to stimulate effective auto insurance reform, ways to promote affordable health care for the disadvantaged, and ways to minimize subscriber costs for Blue Cross and Blue Shield medical insurance coverage.

DPA also serves as the state's ombudsman in resolving problems citizens face in dealing with government agencies. Thousands of requests for assistance received over the telephone "hot line," by mail, and in person are investigated. Through persistent prodding and negotiation many of the complaints are successfully resolved. When patterns of complaints emerge, changes in procedures or legislation are initiated. Such actions have resulted, for example, in changes to insure compliance with the Open Public Meeting Act and to assure adequate numbers of food stamp issuance centers.

The Office of Dispute Settlement uses mediation and arbitration to avoid court action in resolving a number of disputes predominantly in the areas of housing, local government, state agencies, and environmental matters. By offering an alternative to litigation through the overburdened state court system, the DPA often provides less costly and more timely resolution of conflicts. Under a contract with the Department of Community Affairs this office also provides mediation and conciliation services for the New Home Warranty Program. (See chapter 12, Housing and Development.) In addition, training in the skills of negotiation and mediation is provided to interested citizens and officials.

Public Interest Advocacy

The nation's first and only government sponsored "public interest law firm" is the New Jersey Division of Public Interest Advocacy. This division captures the lion's share of headlines for the DPA as it engages in legal actions, administrative interventions, and negotiations on behalf of broad public interests. "Public interest" is defined by the statute creating the Department of the Public Advocate as an interest or right arising from the constitution, decisions of court, common law, or other laws of the United States or of New Jersey, belonging to the citizens of New Jersey or to a broad class of such citizens. The public advocate has sole discretion to represent or refrain from representing the public interest in any proceeding. The courts have upheld the public advocate's discretion in numerous court challenges.

Public interest advocacy was made part of the DPA in recognition of the fact that, with the exception of special citizen groups who have substantial financial resources, the public was not being represented in administrative proceedings which have a great impact on the public. The division determines if an adjudicatory or rule-making hearing of any state agency will affect a broad public interest. If so ruled, the division can institute litigation on behalf of the public against federal, state, county, and local government. Arbitrary and illegal governmental action can thus be challenged by citizens who previously have been unable to obtain representation.

Headlines in the newspaper frequently point to the activity of the Division of Public Interest Advocacy in the areas of housing, energy, the environment, employment, health, and education. Results of the division's efforts include guarantees of public access to New Jersey beaches, assurance that low-income people will not be barred from living in coastal area developments, protection of elderly and handicapped residents facing eviction from apartments being converted to cooperatives or condominiums, and provisions for medical treatment for the poor. But the division's involvement in the Mount Laurel zoning suit has probably had the most impact on all the citizens of New Jersey.

The Mount Laurel Decisions
Planning activities have not been a priority for New Jersey government. Land-use planning has been largely left to the municipalities, and, in the absence of state guidelines setting standards for local zoning ordinances, the municipalities have focused on local interests in their land-use decisions. Local dependence on the property tax as the major

source of revenue caused many municipalities to adopt what is termed "fiscal zoning," a policy of using zoning powers to maximize tax revenues rather than to satisfy long-range planning needs. To attract ratables (sources of property tax revenue) and minimize tax burdens, these suburban municipalities zone much of their land for single-family houses on large lots, and little or no land for higher density moderate- and low-income housing; they seek "clean" industry; and often they postpone the acquisition of land for recreational use. This policy, because it lures the middle class and light industry to the suburbs, results in a pattern of development called sprawl—a scattering of residences and industry over large amounts of land. At the same time, the older cities are saddled with lower-income residents, fewer jobs, and a shrunken tax base.

The reluctance of communities to zone for higher density housing, and the absence of legislative response, led the New Jersey Supreme Court to assume a leadership role in assigning to certain comunities obligations to provide housing for moderate- and low-income people.

The New Jersey Supreme Court found, in a 1975 suit against the Township of Mount Laurel that although the zoning ordinance did permit a variety of upper-income residential uses, it had intentionally discriminated against low-income housing. Along with finding the Mount Laurel Township zoning ordinance deficient, the court found that the zoning techniques utilized by municipalities statewide contribute to a shortage of low- and moderate-income housing. In addition, the court held that because Mount Laurel belongs to a class of municipalities defined as "developing," it had an obligation to provide the opportunity for the development of its fair share of low- and moderate-income housing for the present and prospective regional need.

Low- and moderate-income housing has been defined in 1984 dollars for the different regions in New Jersey. For example, in the region encompassing Essex, Union, Morris, and Sussex counties, low-income families of four are defined as those earning up to $16,000 and moderate-income families are those earning up to $25,000. By contrast, in Camden, Burlington, and Gloucester, counties in the south, low income is defined as earning up to $14,000 and moderate income up to $22,000.

In the years following the 1975 Mount Laurel decision, government entities debated just what was meant by the court ruling—and no low- and moderate-income housing was built in the township of Mount Laurel. In January 1983 the New Jersey Supreme Court handed down the Mount Laurel II decision which clarified and strengthened the 1975 decision. While the details of the court-mandated obligation to provide low- and moderate-income housing run to many pages, the philosophical basis of the court ruling, as written by Chief Justice Robert Wilentz, is worth repeating here:

> The constitutional basis for the *Mount Laurel* doctrine remains the same. The constitutional power to zone, delegated to the municipalities subject to legislation, is but one portion of the police power and, as such, must be exercised for the general welfare. When the exercise of that power by a municipality affects something as fundamental as housing, the general welfare includes more than the welfare of that municipality and its citizens: it also includes the general welfare—in this case the housing needs— of those residing outside the municipality but within the region that contributes to the housing demand within the municipality. Municipal land use regulations that conflict with the general welfare thus defined abuse the police power and are unconstitutional. In particular, these regulations that do not provide the requisite opportunity for a fair share of the region's need for low and moderate income housing conflict with the general welfare and violate the state constitutional requirements of substantive due process and equal protection.
>
> It would be useful to remind ourselves that the doctrine does not arise from some theoretical analysis of our Constitution, but rather from underlying concepts of fundamental fairness in the exercise of governmental power. The basis for the constitutional obligation is simple: the State controls the use of land, *all* of the land. In exercising that control it cannot favor rich over poor. It cannot legislatively set aside dilapidated housing in ur-

ban ghettos for the poor and decent housing elsewhere for everyone else. The government that controls this land represents everyone. While the State may not have the ability to eliminate poverty, it cannot use that condition as the basis for imposing further disadvantages. And the same applies to the municipality, to which this control over land has been constitutionally delegated.

The clarity of the constitutional obligation is seen most simply by imagining what this state could be like were this claim never to be recognized and enforced: poor people forever zoned out of substantial areas of the state, not because housing could not be built for them but because they are not wanted; poor people forced to live in urban slums forever not because suburbia, developing rural areas, fully developed residential sections, seashore resorts, and other attractive locations could not accommodate them, but simply because they are not wanted. It is a vision not only at variance with the requirement that the zoning power be used for the general welfare but with all concepts of fundamental fairness and decency that underpin many constitutional obligations.

(*South Burlington County* NAACP v. Mt. *Laurel Township* 92 NJ 158)

The ruling goes on to define which municipalities have a constitutional obligation to provide a realistic housing opportunity for a fair share of the region's low- and moderate-income people both at the present time and in the future. It then defines two responsibilities that municipalities have in meeting their Mount Laurel obligation. First, they must remove all municipally created barriers to the construction of their fair share of low- and moderate-income housing. For the areas designated to accommodate this housing market, the zoning and subdivision restrictions can be only those necessary to protect health and safety. The court points to the federal Department of Housing and Urban Development (HUD) Minimum Property Standards as a logical starting point in establishing these minimum restrictions.

Second, the municipality is obligated to encourage or require developers to use housing subsidies. When federal or

state housing subsidies are available, the municipality must
actively pursue them. When they are not available, a municipality must consider incentive zoning and mandatory
set-asides. Incentive zoning gives rewards, such as increased
densities, to developers providing a percentage of lower-
income housing. (The developer can put more housing
units on a piece of land than normally allowed.) Mandatory
set-asides require a developer to provide a certain percentage of the development—often 20 percent—as low- and
moderate-income housing. Municipalities must also consider zoning substantial areas for mobile homes and other
types of low-cost housing.

The Mount Laurel II decision set up a mechanism to
speed the process of creating low- and moderate-income
housing. Within the court opinion is provision for "developer's remedies"; if a developer proves that a municipality is
in a growth area and has not complied with the provisions
of the Mount Laurel ruling, the developer is entitled to a
court order issuing a building permit for the development.
The developer must act in good faith and first seek to obtain
relief without litigation. If the developer prevails, the permit shall be issued unless the municipality is able to prove
that the proposed development is clearly contrary to sound
land-use planning. To be eligible to use the developer's
remedies, the developer's proposal must contain a substantial amount of low- and moderate-income housing (20 percent is seen as a reasonable minimum).

While the philosophy and rules for establishing low- and
moderate-income housing are set by the Supreme Court,
the Department of the Public Advocate has been instrumental in seeing that the court rulings are translated
into action.

The Division of Public Interest Advocacy joined both
Mount Laurel suits as well as other suits against municipalities to bring them into conformity with the Mount Laurel
decision guidelines. At the request of the Morris Fair Housing Council and the NAACP, the division was the plaintiff
(one who brings action) in the lawsuit against the municipalities in Morris County. This lawsuit was initiated both
because it was believed that there was a broad pattern of ex-
clusionary zoning practices in the county, and because

such a suit, it was expected, would provoke zoning reforms on a statewide basis as municipalities sought to avoid their own involvement in costly litigation.

The Mount Laurel decisions and subsequent suits have brought the power of state government squarely into conflict with perceived home rule prerogatives which local citizens had assumed left them very much in charge of the destinies of their municipalities. In addition, municipalities involved in lawsuits based on the Mount Laurel decision are faced with considerable legal fees to defend the suits, plus heavy legal and consulting fees to devise a plan for housing acceptable to the court. Confronted with the reality that the obligation to assume a fair share of low- and moderate-income housing is now the law, taxpayers in those communities involved are faced with supporting the additional services such as schools and police and fire protection that the new housing units may require of the municipality.

In response to widespread concern about the impact on municipalities of these court decisions, the legislature is considering a number of proposals. These include creating a series of regional housing councils or a single state affordable housing council, methods to mediate disputes between municipalities and builders without resorting to the courts, ways to arrive at a more accurate determination of the number of low- and moderate-income housing units needed for each area, subsidies for low- and moderate-income housing possibly funded through an increase in the realty transfer tax, and ways by which municipalities can meet part of their obligation by contributing financially to rehabilitation of housing in urban areas.

LAND-USE PLANNING

Planning and zoning are the means by which governments control or affect the growth and development of a community or region along desirable lines. Planning is concerned with such matters as physical layout, provision of essential services and facilities, protection of natural resources, the accommodation of anticipated population and economic change, and maintenance of the ambience desired by the community residents.

Zoning, a major tool for carrying out planning goals, has

two aspects. The first involves dividing an area into districts or zones—residential, business, industrial—and then regulating the use of land and buildings within these zones. The second deals with regulation of building heights, lot sizes, yard dimensions, road widths, and other relevant physical elements.

State and Federal Planning

New Jersey's first laws governing zoning came in the 1920s after many municipalities had started writing their own land-use ordinances. Planning boards were established only after enabling state legislation in 1930. The years following World War II were ones of rapid development; commitment to land-use principles was often obviously lacking. With the depletion of land as a natural resource, the mushrooming of metropolitan areas, and the leapfrogging of housing developments into rural areas, the pressure to plan the use of land increased.

Planning by various levels of government assumed increasing importance in later decades. The federal government required local government units to assume planning responsibilities as a prerequisite to receiving financial assistance. In metropolitan areas it supported planning on a regional basis. The 1960s and 1970s saw many federal programs reflecting this emphasis, but by the 1980s federal attention had turned elsewhere.

New Jersey's Municipal Land-Use Law, enacted in 1975, was a complete revision and codification of existing laws, recognizing the need for more judicious and uniform handling of the problems of development. Developers were guaranteed timely action on their applications. The powers of planning boards and zoning boards of adjustment were more clearly defined. Master plans written by each municipality had to be reviewed and updated every five years and had to contain a statement of objectives and consideration of land use, housing, traffic, utility service, community facilities, recreation, land conservation, and energy conservation.

During the years of federal encouragement of land-use planning, a Division of State and Regional Planning functioned within the Department of Community Affairs. It was charged with preparing and maintaining both a compre-

Figure 11.1

Development Choices for New Jersey

(Recommendations of the Regional Plan Association,
New Jersey Committee)

Increase the compactness of metropolitan and nonmetropolitan areas—New Jersey has a larger share of its population residing within metropolitan areas but outside central cities than any other state in the nation. Farmland continues to be lost to development and New Jersey's older cities continue to lose population.

Increase mass transit availability—despite rising gasoline prices, a stepped-up population dispersal in the 1970s has contributed even further to the erosion of public transit usage.

Produce affordable housing to accommodate more varied market demands and social needs—while New Jersey's total population has remained nearly static over the last decade, the number of households has exploded: smaller families, single parent families, more young adults and single individuals, and more elderly.

Accelerate rehabilitation, reuse, redevelopment and infill in existing metropolitan and nonmetropolitan areas, with a special emphasis on conserving existing structures and facilities—New Jersey's compact cities and older suburbs, close to public transit, offer substantial opportunities for redevelopment and infill.

Specific recommendations for achieving the above goals:

■ Rehabilitation standards—New Jersey should consider revising its standards for rehabilitation by not requiring older buildings converted for adaptive reuse to conform with all new building construction standards.

■ Performance-based standards—New Jersey should encourage a shift to the use of performance-based standards, wherever possible, in construction codes instead of requiring use of specific materials.

■ Improving capital availability—New Jersey should more aggressively address the problem of lack of capital for multi-family rehabilitation, especially in buildings with more than four units.

266

■ Zoning—municipalities should consider permitting, where appropriate, the conversion of single family homes to include small rental units. These conversions are already taking place illegally without benefit of local code enforcement.

■ Inclusionary housing—New Jersey, in cooperation with its local governments, should develop inclusionary housing programs with the incentives necessary to make them happen.

■ Transit financing—while transit consumers should pay a fair share of the system's operating expenses, automobile-based revenue sources should be used to provide the public share of cost.

Source: Adapted, with permission, from "Development Choices for New Jersey," prepared in 1981 by the New Jersey Committee of Regional Plan Association, Kathleen W. Rae, Director

Note: The Regional Plan Association (RPA) is a privately funded, nongovernmental agency formed in 1929 to work for the efficient and attractive development of the region's thirty-one counties, including fourteen in northern and central New Jersey and others in New York and Connecticut. RPA serves as counsel for the whole region, advocating for the entire economy, not for a single industry or a particular section.

hensive state development plan and a capital improvements program; assisting and coordinating regional planning activities; and disbursing federal funds for planning programs. To facilitate the handling of these charges, the division created a State Development Guide Plan which delineated four specific kinds of area, each to be used for a different purpose: growth, agriculture, open space, and limited growth.

Land-Use Planning and the Mount Laurel Decisions

In the sixties and seventies many municipalities traditionally, for financial advantage, zoned to include tax-paying business and industry and to exclude dense populations that require additional human services such as schools. The first requirement to include all income groups in the zoning provisions came with the Mount Laurel decisions when the New Jersey Supreme Court stepped into the zoning picture. Acting on a suit brought by fair housing groups, the supreme court decided that a developing community must provide for affordable housing for low- and moderate- income groups in its zoning. The court used the State Development Guide Plan as a basis for determining what areas were developing and thus liable for a low- and moderate-income housing responsibility.

The Mount Laurel II decision not only set forth specific requirements for municipal land-use plans, it also advocated land-use planning on a statewide basis.

The lessons of history are clear, even if rarely learned. One of those lessons is that unplanned growth has a price: natural resources are destroyed, open spaces are despoiled, agricultural land is rendered forever unproductive, and people settle without regard to the enormous cost of the public facilities needed to support them. Cities decay; established infrastructures deteriorate for lack of funds; and taxpayers shudder under a financial burden of public expenditures resulting in part from uncontrolled migration to anywhere anyone wants to settle, roads leading to places they should never be—a pattern of total neglect of sensible conservation of resources, funds, prior public investment, and just plain common sense. These costs in New Jersey, the most highly urbanized state in the nation, are staggering, and our knowledge of our limited ability to support them has become acute. More than money is involved, for natural and man-made physical resources are irreversibly damaged. Statewide comprehensive planning is no longer simply desirable, it is a necessity recognized by both the federal and state governments.

(*South Burlington County* NAACP *v. Mt. Laurel Township* 92 NJ 158)

Given the history of strong home rule sentiment in New Jersey, state land-use planning has not been a politically popular issue. However, the costs of failure to plan cohesively the siting of shopping centers, housing developments, highways, and sewer systems, are increasing. Pressures to find regional solutions to the challenges posed by housing problems, flooding disasters, transportation crises, and solid waste disposal may make land-use planning a more popular concept in the future. Other states with less strong home rule biases have developed successful regional and statewide land-use plans and offer New Jersey useful models. (Note: For an in-depth discussion of a number of these issues, see *New Jersey Reporter*, September 1984, devoted to the topic "Home Rule in New Jersey.")

New Jersey has, however, taken the lead in regional planning in three environmentally and economically important areas: the Pinelands, the coastal zone, and the Hackensack Meadowlands. While the Pinelands and the coastal area are regulated by agencies associated with the Department of Enrivonmental Protection, and the Hackensack Meadowlands by an agency associated with the Department of Community Affairs, they will be discussed here as examples of successful and far-reaching land-use planning units. In fact, the National Conference of State Legislatures in 1983 called the Pinelands Comprehensive Management Plan a model land-use plan for the nation.

The Pinelands

The Pinelands, sometimes called the Pine Barrens, is a unique tract containing 760 square miles of pine and oak forest located largely in Burlington and Ocean Counties. The area covers a vast underground body of water equivalent to a lake of 2,000 square miles in surface and 37 feet in depth. Though enormous in size, this aquifer is unusually vulnerable to pollution since it is close to the surface, and the sandy soil above it is not a good filtering agent to remove surface pollutants.

The area contains vast commercial cranberry and blueberry bogs, historical ironworking sites, wild and scenic rivers, and a number of small towns. The western edge of the Pinelands is accessible to the Philadelphia area and has a region of lakes surrounded by homes. The eastern edge feels the population pressure from the employment boom in Atlantic City. To the north is Fort Dix, a vast military reserve.

The Pinelands emerged as a national and state land-use unit after a decade of conflict between opposing forces— those who sought to preserve the natural area and those who sought development, those who wanted state and national intervention and those who adhered to local control principles. Issues came to a head when local businessmen and landowners sought to win approval for a regional international jetport in the Pinelands. Morris County environmentalists, faced with a similar threat, bought up the land of the Great Swamp and donated it to the federal government as a nature preserve. Following this example, Pinelands enthusiasts won the support of Brendan T. Byrne (governor 1974–1982) for their efforts to preserve the area.

A Pinelands area equal to about 20 percent of New Jersey's total land area was identified as needing protection or preservation. Over a period of years federal, state, and private funds were used to purchase a third of the land. State land purchases continue in the mid-1980s. Land left in private hands is regulated to prevent environmentally unsound development and/or threats to the purity of the surface and underground water resources.

The Pinelands was designated as the nation's first National Reserve by the United States secretary of the interior in 1978. Recognizing the unique partnership between state and federal land-use agencies, the New Jersey Legislature

adopted the Pinelands Protection Act, signed into law by
Governor Byrne in 1979. In this land management act care
was given to develop ways to safeguard the resources of the
Pinelands while maintaining the life-style and habitat of the
indigenous population.

The act provides for a Pinelands Commission of fifteen
members. Seven of these are appointed by the counties of
the area (Atlantic, Burlington, Camden, Cape May, Cumberland, Gloucester, and Ocean); seven are named by New
Jersey's governor; and one by the United States secretary of
the interior. The commission is empowered to hire an executive director and staff. One of their first tasks was to develop a comprehensive management plan to

■ maintain a contiguous tract of land in its natural state,
■ safeguard the essential character of the Pinelands
environment,
■ protect the quality of the surface and ground water,
■ promote compatible agricultural and recreational
uses,
■ and encourage appropriate residential, commercial
and industrial patterns of development.

The Comprehensive Management Plan implemented in
1981 and reviewed every three years requires all municipalities entirely or partially in the Pinelands to bring their master plans and zoning regulations into conformity with the
comprehensive plan for the Pinelands. The plan designates
appropriate uses for various areas within the Pinelands, establishing a preservation area where little growth is permitted in order to protect the most vulnerable environmental
areas and a protection area in which more development
is permitted.

In view of the restrictions on development that the comprehensive plan places on many landowners, a development credits system was devised. The comprehensive plan
provides for a system of transferable Pinelands Development Credits (PDC's). These provide a mechanism for landowners in environmentally sensitive areas to share in the
economic benefits of increasing land values by trading or
selling their PDCs to developers through a bank established
for that purpose. These accumulated development credits
will permit development of residential growth near existing

development, in traditional village settings, and near employment centers. They will discourage growth near fragile ecological areas, wetlands, and important agricultural acreage. The system of allocation recognizes the elevated value of farmland and provides fewer development credits per acre to owners of non-productive wetlands.

This system of transferable development rights has important implications for other land-use issues as well—specifically, for Mount Laurel housing issues and for preserving farmland in agricultural areas.

Coastal Zone Land Management

The coastal area of New Jersey represents 18 percent of the state's land and includes ocean and bay beaches, wetlands, pine forests, the intracoastal waterway, and prime agricultural land. It encompasses old, established residential communities, urban resort areas, newly developing suburbs, and ocean-oriented resort and recreation towns. Also in this area is Atlantic City which has become one of the nation's prime entertainment capitals as people flock to the gambling casinos.

The Wetlands Act of 1970 describes this coastal area where the land meets the sea as an area which

> protects the land from the force of the sea, moderates our weather, provides a home for water fowl and for two-thirds of all our fish and shellfish, and assists in absorbing sewage discharge by the rivers of the land.

There are 245,000 acres of wetlands mapped in eleven coastal counties, of which 242,000 are under state regulatory control. Prior to regulation, more than 1,900 acres of wetlands were indiscriminately destroyed each year. Since regulation began in 1973, the loss has been cut drastically.

The Wetlands Act of 1970 assigns to the Department of Environmental Protection (see chapter 10) responsibility for reviewing impact statements and building plans and for issuing construction permits for development proposed in mapped wetland areas.

Federal aid for planning of land use in coastal areas was granted under the Coastal Zone Management Act of 1972.

Financial assistance, according to this act, was given to states in three one-year grants to plan, establish regulations, and administer their coastal regions.

With this encouragement New Jersey passed the Coastal Area Facilities Review Act of 1973 (CAFRA), designating the Department of Environmental Protection as the regional planning agency for the coastal district. Under CAFRA, DEP and local governments share land use responsibilities. The department's regulatory power includes the location and construction of housing developments of twenty-five or more units, most major industrial and commercial projects, and sewer and energy facilities. These developments and facilities are weighed against the requirements of the comprehensive management strategy prepared by the department. The goals are to preserve such natural and constructed features as wetlands, barrier beaches, dunes, forest areas, and historical sites. Definitions of areas where different forms of development should be encouraged or discouraged are included within the comprehensive management strategy.

Under this system local governments retain regulatory powers over land use such as subdivisions, zoning ordinances, and building standards. However, those developments subject to CAFRA review must win not only local government approval, but also approval by the Department of Environmental Protection.

The Mount Laurel II decision has had an impact on CAFRA projects; in 1983 the New Jersey Supreme Court upheld the Department of Environmental Protection's authority to enforce its policy on affordable housing as a condition of a CAFRA permit. Another decision ensures that New Jersey's ocean beaches will remain open to the public rather than being closed off by private development.

The Hackensack Meadowlands

The Meadowlands—the marshes and salt-water swamps along the Hackensack River surrounding Secaucus—have tantalized developers for centuries. Despite the land's potential value, all plans were mired in a trio of obstacles: the costs of reclamation, title questions, and fragmented governmental control (fourteen municipalities in two counties with fourteen zoning boards and sixteen planning boards).

To surmount these difficulties, the Hackensack Meadowlands Development Commission (HMDC) was created in a highly controversial law enacted at the end of 1968. The commission's legislative mandate was to provide for the orderly development of the Meadowlands district, protect and preserve 19,730 acres of valuable wetlands in Bergen and Hudson counties, and provide disposal facilities for the accelerating solid waste tonnage entering the Meadowlands from 118 northern New Jersey communities (who supported the Meadowlands legislation in exchange for the right to continue sending their solid waste to the district in perpetuity).

The HMDC consists of six residents of the district, appointed by the governor with the consent of the senate, and the commissioner of the Department of Community Affairs, ex officio. In delineating the commission's powers the law attempts to balance the agency's overall interests with those of the affected municipalities, but the agency nonetheless has the land-use powers necessary to insure that a district master plan can be implemented.

The master plan for the Meadowlands district was presented in two stages. The first stage, adopted in 1970, set forth the objectives and standards of the commission and established interim zoning, building, subdivision, and environmental standards. The HMDC later presented a comprehensive land-use plan which proposed a balanced community with residential, commercial, and recreational uses and which emphasized environmental restoration.

The powers to enforce the provisions of the master plan and the comprehensive land-use plan rest with the HMDC. The agency reviews all building applications, issues permits for development that conforms with the master plan, and sets building and subdivision standards. Municipalities' plans that fall under the purview of the master plan must be approved by the HMDC. The commission also has the power to condemn and acquire lands. It may issue bonds for capital improvements and land acquisition, although most of the agency's funding comes from the revenues from the Meadowlands Sports Complex and from state appropriations.

National attention was drawn to the Meadowlands with

the completion of the New Jersey Sports and Exposition Authority (the Meadowlands Sports Complex). With three football teams, indoor and outdoor soccer, basketball, and hockey teams playing regular schedules and an occasional tennis spectacular adding to the bill, the sports complex has put New Jersey on the map in the sports world. In addition, the racetrack with its schedule of thoroughbred and harness racing has been a popular and highly profitable part of the complex. A baseball facility has been approved and a bid for the summer Olympics is in the talking stage. The sports complex has, according to some social scientists, had a positive influence on many New Jersey residents' sense of pride and identification with their state.

The profitability of the sports complex allows the authority to pay back the interest and principal on the bonds that financed building the facilities; in addition, 40 percent of the net profits supports the Hackensack Meadowlands Development Commission and its activities. Additional sports complex profits built and operate the environmental education center located in DeKorte State Park within the Meadowlands, and there is still a surplus of profits left to turn over to the state general revenue fund.

Equally successful has been the industrial, commercial, and housing development of the Meadowlands. Approximately 50,000 new jobs have been created in the area, and its proximity to Manhattan makes it increasingly attractive. With this success, though, have come increasing problems in handling the traffic. The thirty-two square mile Meadowlands sits astride the major throughways connecting Manhattan with the New Jersey suburbs. Yet the development pattern in the Meadowlands does not encourage use of public transportation—the jobs are too dispersed. Obvious planning challenges still exist for the development commission.

Garbage has been the largest challenge to the Meadowlands since the formation of the development area. Before the marshes were drained and filled, the Meadowlands were used mainly as an open dump, with the additional aroma of hog farms adding to the ambience. Part of the original mandate for the HMDC was to continue to deal with the solid waste created in the area. This has been done creatively.

The acreage devoted to landfill operations has shrunk drastically. In the early 1980s, with the help of federal funds, a $6.9 million solid waste baler was installed. Not only did the baler greatly reduce the mass of the solid waste, it created compact bales which were used to fill low areas and create future recreational acreage. Resource recovery plants are now being considered as the long range solution for the garbage problem, and the HMDC is helping finance a solid waste recovery plant in Newark in return for a planned termination of Essex County dumping in the Meadowlands by 1987. Similar arrangements are being made with other solid waste districts.

12.
Community Affairs, Corrections, and Health

High on the list of problems facing many New Jersey communities are those stemming directly from the state's rapid urbanization—or more specifically rapid suburbanization. This process has placed heavy demands on cities and towns to provide housing, facilities, and services for a changing population. Growth in the suburbs also contributes to shrinking populations and related problems in the older cities.

The Department of Community Affairs (DCA) was created in 1967 to provide a state-led attack on these problems by regrouping into one department state agencies concerned with local government. However, in 1976 an attempt to economize threatened the department with extinction. Brendan T. Byrne (Governor 1974–1982) offered proposals to dismantle the DCA, parceling out its various agencies among other departments, but the legislature refused to act on this executive request.

The department, led by a commissioner appointed by the governor with the consent of the senate, has been shaped in part by the federal housing and urban-aid programs that DCA administers. Federal regulations stipulated that local community development agencies organized under the supervision of the DCA include the "maximum feasible participation" of the people whom the programs were designed to assist. One result has been the political education and empowerment of leaders in the groups being served. Out of this have come department programs aimed at support of, and advocacy for, self-help efforts of the urban

COMMUNITY AFFAIRS

277

poor, Hispanics, senior citizens, and women. The current functions of the DCA reflect this and the continuing priorities in housing and community resources; the department's main program areas are local government services, housing and development, and community resources.

Local Government Services

Channeling federal and state urban-aid funds to municipalities and providing supervision and technical assistance to local and county governments are the major functions of the Division of Local Government Services. The bulk of federal and state urban assistance funds that flow through the division are not targeted to specific budget items; a major exception is the Safe and Clean Neighborhoods Program providing funds designated for police and fire departments. Along with direct involvement in some federal and state assistance programs, the division also serves as a clearinghouse for information on other federal- and state-aid programs, on general municipal law, and on matters of concern to local governments.

The DCA has responsibility, mainly in the financial area, for supervising local governments—counties, municipalities, school districts, and local financing authorities. (See chapter 6, Long-term Capital Financing.) Since the state's credit is linked to the credit of its local governments, this financial supervision has statewide importance. The high ratings given municipal and school bonds on Wall Street reflect the high regard the financial community has for the DCA's system of local financial regulation.

The Division of Local Government Services also provides a variety of technical assistance in management areas. Budget preparation, accounting systems, borrowing, and auditing procedures are all regulated by the division to assure a sound local financial base.

Although all counties and municipalities must have their budgets approved by the division, occasionally a unit of government ends up in a financial crisis. In the most serious situations the division takes over all or part of fiscal management. When technical assistance, training, and direct division administration of the finances have restored fiscal stability, control is returned to the local government unit.

Besides these financially oriented services, the division also assists individuals and families during emergencies such as floods, which periodically inundate parts of the state.

Federal housing initiatives in the 1960s and 1970s had a significant impact on New Jersey: public housing projects, urban renewal, housing for the elderly and handicapped, and categorical community development grants were all part of the program. Then in the early 1980s federal priorities were reordered, and new, less costly solutions to housing problems were explored. Renovation and rehabilitation of existing housing was one new focus of federal programs, and more responsibility was placed on the shoulders of the private sector working in concert with local governments to build affordable housing for lower-income Americans. The New Jersey Mount Laurel II decision (see chapter 11, Land-Use Planning and the Mount Laurel Decisions) details many ways that changes in zoning, building codes, and other government requirements can help private industry build affordable housing for moderate-income families. However, there is general agreement that housing for low-income citizens will continue to need heavy subsidies, and that the federal government remains the most viable source of those funds.

The momentum for addressing housing projects has not come entirely from federal initiatives and the Mount Laurel decisions. The government of New Jersey became active in the housing field following the Newark riot in 1967 which left twenty-six dead and $10 million in property damage. The Governor's Select Commission on Civil Disorder conducted an investigation and concluded that the lack of decent housing, jobs, and education were root causes of the civil disorder. The legislature responded by enacting a package of significant community restoration laws which gave the Department of Community Affairs additional powers and responsibilities. But progress has been slow. A shortage of money, high land and construction costs, large-lot zoning, and high property taxes, all combine to present formidable obstacles to providing sufficient housing units for New Jersey. To maximize available monies the department has

Housing and Development

devised a combination of aid programs to take advantage of available federal, state, and private resources. The legacy of federal programs is shown in figure 12.1.

Community Resources

Federal funds for poverty programs go to community action agencies that are composed in part of those people whom the programs were designed to assist. Administrative support and technical assistance for these programs come from the Division of Community Resources. Working with the local agencies, it administers programs for target populations:

- Community Action Programs (CAP) for New Jersey's most disadvantaged citizens
- Community Services Block Grant Program for services to low-income individuals
- Head Start Programs for disadvantaged youngsters
- Low-income energy conservation program for weatherizing homes for qualifying individuals
- Tournament of Champions for the physically disabled, and Special Olympics for the mentally retarded
- Legal services for the needy

Office of Hispanic Affairs
In recognition of the needs of the growing Hispanic community in New Jersey, the legislature created an Office of Hispanic Affairs to provide financial and technical assistance to existing Hispanic agencies. Funding comes from both state funds and federal social services block grant funds matched on a three dollars (federal) to one dollar (state) basis. Many of the Hispanic agencies are community action organizations offering multiple services: for example, jobs counseling, translation/interpretation, family planning, and day care.

Division on Aging
While the Office of Hispanic Affairs is a recent addition to the Department of Community Affairs, an agency focusing on senior citizens has been in existence since the late 1950s. Although many programs directly affecting senior citizens are housed in the Department of Human Services,

Figure 12.1

The Legacy of Federal Housing Programs

Public Housing Projects. These were built and operated by local housing authorities for low- and middle-income groups, including senior citizens. Recently, most new construction has been targeted for senior citizens. Now federal funds are becoming available for the modernization and rehabilitation of the older projects.

Urban Renewal. Federal funds for removal of blighted areas to make possible investment in the urban centers were channeled through local redevelopment authorities. Cleared land has been used for a variety of purposes—industrial, commercial, low-cost housing, and luxury high-rise buildings. Developments are planned that will strengthen the economic base of urban areas, making it more possible for cities to provide services to their low-income populations. Urban renewal funds are now available to municipalities through Community Development Block Grants.

Federal Housing and Community Development Act of 1974. This program for Community Development Block Grants replaces categorical aid programs such as urban renewal and Model Cities. Now communities submit applications for funds, setting forth both their needs and their proposals for meeting those needs. Funds are distributed according to a formula based on population, extent of poverty, and housing allocation.

Moderate Rehabilitation Program. New Jersey was selected to participate in the federal Department of Housing and Urban Development (HUD) Rental Rehabilitation Demonstration Program. Combining private and public financing, this program will illustrate how to rehabilitate private rental units in six New Jersey cities.

Handicapped Housing Assistance Project. Originally aimed at providing housing for those mentally and physically handicapped citizens in low- or moderate-income categories, this project now focuses on establishing and enforcing standards for barrier-free construction in all subsidized housing and commercial buildings.

Rental Assistance Program. Low- and moderate-income people are assisted in finding housing units of their choice for which they pay up to 30 percent of their income. The remainder is subsidized by grants from the federal government, administered by the DCA. Special help is now being given the handicapped, the disabled, and the mentally ill who have been recently released from institutions.

Federal Housing Administration (FHA) and Veterans Administration (VA). Each has a mortgage loan program that, since the end of World War II, has provided opportunities for the middle class to become homeowners. A by-product of these programs was encouragement of the exodus from the cities to single-family dwellings in the suburbs.

Figure 12.2

New Jersey Housing Initiatives

New Jersey Housing and Mortgage Finance Agency. Formed in 1984 by the merger of the Mortgage Finance Agency and the Housing Finance Agency, this new agency allows a flexible response to the new forms of federal assistance for housing as they become available. The mortgage money is targeted for qualified first-time home-buyers in urban centers and is designed to increase owner-occupied residences in order to help stabilize and revitalize eligible neighborhoods. Single-family, multi-family, and condominium buildings can all be financed through this agency.

Housing Demonstration Program. This revolving loan fund, supported by annual state appropriations, assists nonprofit housing sponsors who need money to initiate the construction or rehabilitation of moderate-income housing. A special project of the fund financed life safety improvements for temporary shelters for the homeless.

Rooming and Boarding House Regulation. Following a series of disastrous fires, the legislature enacted laws requiring the licensing of all rooming and boarding home operators and the inspection of all such facilities by the DCA. As a result, more than 100 such homes have been closed, and standards for the others have been increased. A companion Life Safety Improvement Act made it possible for the DCA to offer loans for the installation of life safety improvements in such buildings. These loans are repaid from appropriations by the legislature and from the Casino Revenue Fund if the tenants are of low and moderate income, seniors, or disabled citizens. Code enforcement and housing inspection also apply both to all multi-family dwellings of three or more units and to hotels.

Uniform Construction Code. DCA administers directly or trains and certifies the competency of local officials to administer both a uniform construction code for the entire state and a system of one-stop service for construction permit applications. National standards for building, plumbing, and electrical work are incorporated into the New Jersey code.

Uniform Fire Safety Code. Adopted in 1983, the code provides for the establishment and enforcement of minimum standards for all buildings except one-and two-family dwellings. Fire inspections are required before the registration and licensing of public buildings including hotels, convention centers, and apartment buildings of six or more stories. The registration procedure permits the commissioner to close any building failing inspection until violations of code are corrected. Responding to concerns raised by the fatal amusement park fire in 1984, the New Jersey Fire Safety Commission has recommended new fire safety requirements for all amusement park buildings and plans to establish a 24-hour, toll-free hotline for people to report suspected fire code violations at amusement parks.

New Home Warranty Builders Registration Act. Builders are required to register with the DCA and provide warranties of up to ten years to protect buyers against shoddy work.

Assistance for the Homeless. Individuals and families, who, for reasons beyond their control, are homeless or threatened with the loss of housing through inability to pay their rent, mortgage, or other housing costs will be helped on a temporary basis by a fund administered by the Division of Housing. The funds may also be used to encourage the construction of affordable housing by subsidizing interest costs.

Special Assistance to Atlantic City Residents. Legislation originally passed in 1978, extended for three years in 1981, and for six years in 1984, grants extra protection to tenants threatened with removal from their homes in Atlantic City through the conversion or demolition of their buildings.

Casino Reinvestment Development Authority (See also Figure 9.1). This 1984 political compromise restructures the casino reinvestment requirements and for the first three years of the program mandates that all investments must be for housing and community redevelopment projects in Atlantic City.

it is the Division on Aging in the Department of Community Affairs that acts as advocate for, and watchdog over, programs for New Jersey's older citizens. The success of the legislative initiatives of the Divison on Aging is evidenced by the many programs targeted at this population, especially those funded by the tax on casino revenues. The political clout of those championing the needs of older citizens is recognized by the legislature.

Funds from the division are allocated on a formula basis to county offices on aging which administer local programs. These consist of nutrition programs (including home-delivered meals), transportation, homemaker and home health aide services, volunteer support, counseling, recreation, and local advocacy programs. In addition, the division provides training for those working with older citizens, a hot-line for information to senior citizens, and a program to hire older workers. New initiatives include a pilot program to prevent residents of senior citizen housing from being institutionalized unnecessarily.

Ombudsman for the Institutionalized Elderly

Separate from the Division on Aging is the Office of the Ombudsman for the Institutionalized Elderly which operates on a legislative mandate to protect the health and safety of elderly New Jerseyans who are in nursing homes, hospitals, and boarding or rooming houses. The office not only investigates and seeks to resolve individual complaints, but also drafts recommendations for corrective action or legislation in areas where there are repeated problems. When abuses of institutionalized elderly are frequent and repeated, the office has the power to take court action. As a result of office actions, corrective measures have been taken in both the boarding and rooming house and the nursing home industries.

Division on Women

Working with the women's organizations in New Jersey, this division advocates legislation and programs to help women. The division especially emphasizes the improvement of women's economic status. Research, education, and legislation in the areas of displaced homemakers, prevention of domestic violence, and enforcement of child support payments have been other focuses of much division energy. Task forces on child care and on sexual harassment on the job have been established. The division funds certain programs for displaced homemakers and shelters for battered women, as well as a crisis intervention and information service. Working with the division is the Advisory Commission on the Status of Women, a governor-appointed eleven-member commission formed to advise the executive branch on women's issues.

Inspite of possible duplication of programs, a growing number of advocates for children are urging passage of legislation to create a Division on Children within the Department of Community Affairs in order to better coordinate efforts in the state.

One of the oldest state responsibilities, the maintainence of correctional facilities, was given departmental status in 1976 when the Department of Institutions and Agencies was divided to form two new departments—the Department of Human Services and the Department of Corrections. The legislative act creating the Department of Corrections defined its purpose:

CORRECTIONS

> . . . to protect the public and provide for the custody, care, discipline, training and treatment of persons committed to state correctional institutions or on parole; to supervise and assist in the treatment and training of persons in local correctional and detention facilities, so that such persons may be prepared for release and reintegration into the community; and to cooperate with other law enforcement agencies of the state to encourage a more unified system of criminal justice.

The legislature further defined the need to
■ provide maximum security confinement for those offenders whose demonstrated propensity to acts of violence requires their separation from the community;
■ develop alternatives to conventional incarceration for

those offenders who can be dealt with more effectively in less restrictive community-based facilities and programs;

■ and separate juvenile offenders from adult offenders and develop programs and services for juvenile offenders that recognize their special needs.

The legislature further finds and declares that

■ the environment for incarcerated persons should encourage the possibilities of rehabilitation and reintegration into community life;

■ and the incarcerated offender should be protected from victimization within the institution.

A commissioner of corrections, appointed by the governor with the consent of the senate, heads the Department of Corrections. The department's role in carrying out the legislative mandate for dealing with convicted offenders is divided into two sections—institutions and parole.

State Correctional Institutions

Offenders sentenced for state crimes are either given suspended sentences and placed on probation (see chapter 4, Probation), assigned to an alternative program, or remanded to a correctional facility. (Persons found guilty of federal crimes and committed to an institution are sent to federal correctional facilities or to local institutions under contract with the federal government.)

County Correctional Institutions

An offender sentenced to an institution for a term of one year or less serves the term in the county jail unless there is a county penitentiary or workhouse. Sentenced offenders may be committed to county penitentiaries for a maximum of eighteen months. Also housed in the county jails are persons awaiting trial—both those who cannot raise bail and are not released on their own recognizance, and those charged with offenses so serious that the judges will not set bail. Because of current overcrowding in state prisons, county facilities are also being used to house state prisoners until space is available in state facilities. Other state prisoners are kept in county facilities on a long-term basis under the CAP plan. (See this chapter, Prison Overcrowding.)

A convicted offender sentenced to a term of more than

one year is sent to a state prison, the correctional institution for women, or one of the youth correctional facilities, depending on age and sex.

State Prison Complex—for Adult Males

The state prisons for adult males are Trenton in Mercer County, Rahway in Middlesex County, Leesburg and the nearby Southern States I and II in Cumberland County, and Mid-State at Fort Dix in Burlington County. Camden in Camden County and Newark in Essex County are under construction.

A maximum security prison readjustment unit at Trenton Psychiatric Hospital is operated by the Department of Corrections and used to house incorrigible inmates and special cases. A capital sentence unit with a capacity of twenty-four single cells was designated at Trenton State Prison in 1983. The Adult Diagnostic and Treatment Center (the only correctional facility in the nation solely devoted to treating sex offenders) is located in Middlesex County.

The Corrrectional Institution for Women

Located at Clinton in Hunterdon County, this is the only state correctional institution for adult females. This cottage-type facility has academic classes at all levels and a work-release program under which the women are employed in nearby communities. The facility also provides services for adult male offenders over the age of fifty who are housed in a separate cottage.

Youth Correctional Institution Complex

The youth correctional institutions are Yardville and Bordentown in Burlington County and Annandale in Hunterdon County. The Youth Reception and Correction Center at Yardville receives and classifies juvenile and adult male offenders in separate reception units. Bordentown is a medium security facility for older youths.

Other facilities for young people needing supervision are provided by the Division of Juvenile Services in the Department of Corrections. These facilities include Jamesburg Training School for Boys (supervised cottage living for juvenile delinquents), the Training School for Boys at Skillman (specializing in youngsters who have serious behavioral problems and who have not responded to treatment within their own communities), and twenty-two other residential programs for youthful offenders, both committed and probationary (ranging from the Forked River Game Farm where boys raise pheasants for New Jersey hunters, to the Pinelands facility where the boys' first assignment was to renovate the abandoned hunters' lodge that became their residence). Each of these residential sites provides a work program, education, and group interaction or therapy. Young people assigned to these facilities require correctional handling but are not convicted of violent crimes and are considered minimum security risks. The residential programs are short-term, usually under six months. Contact with families and community is maintained with weekend furloughs home granted for good behavior.

Community-Centered Corrections Programs

The acknowledged failure of imprisonment alone to curb crime and reduce recidivism has led to a nationwide search for alternative and supplementary methods of rehabilitation. One approach being tried in New Jersey is the modification of the regimented and isolated institutional environment. "Cottages" and other small units on prison grounds and at satellite locations are designed to create more intimate and less depersonalized surroundings within large institutions. To reduce further the abrupt transition from a closed society to an open one, halfway houses and community treatment centers are becoming available to a limited number of prisoners prior to release. In 1984 about eighty adult males and females were housed in contract halfway houses; two community treatment centers, one for males and one for females, were available in Newark for a total of sixty-four beds.

Prison Programs

United States Chief Justice Warren Burger in 1984 called American prisons "an appalling failure for civilized people" and urged that prisons provide more opportunities for work, study, and recreation in preparation for the productive life outside the prison. One barrier to this reform is the lack of money for staff and program space. An even more difficult barrier is that which prevents prison-made products from competing on the open market. By law in New Jersey prison-made goods may be sold only to state and local governments to reduce the impact on the free market. In addition, these "state use industries" are required to be self-supporting but have a limited market. As a result, the program tends to provide jobs only for the more skilled and work-oriented longer-term prisoners. A minimum number of jobs are provided for production of such goods as license plates, baked goods, and clothing. Other jobs on prison property, and at other state institutions where prisoners work, are of an unskilled or semi-skilled nature—laundry and food services, maintenance, farming and dairying, grounds keeping, conservation activities—and are often inappropriate as job training for inmates who must return to urban surroundings.

As a partial remedy for this situation a 1969 law authorized work release programs for inmates of state correctional institutions. Selected inmates are permitted to leave the institution during normal working hours to work for regular employers in the community, returning at night to the institution or to a designated minimum custodial facility. From their pay, the inmates contribute toward their own maintenance at the institution and toward the support of any dependents. This law also permits selected inmates to leave at stipulated times to assist their families during periods of need.

Education and counseling are provided in varying degrees for inmates of the state correctional institutions. Juveniles must take some formal schooling; other prisoners may take basic adult education, high school equivalency courses, and college courses. Social education (education to alter the prisoner's basic social skills and attitudes), recreational programs, vocational training, special education, work opportunities, and counseling round out the treatment program.

Psychological consultants conduct admission interviews. Individual therapy is rarely provided, but there are group counseling sessions in all the reformatories and institutions for juveniles—similar programs are provided at the state prisons. Inmates receive medical and dental treatment at all institutions.

Office of the Ombudsman

The Office of the Ombudsman, within the Department of Corrections, provides a medium through which inmates can seek redress for problems and complaints outside of established operational units. The office operates independently from prison administration; this detatchment enables the development of trust, confidentiality of information, and objectivity between the ombudsman and the inmate. Ombudsmen deal with violations of due process, observe that basic living standards are met, and respond to allegations of staff brutality. The Department of the Public Advocate (see chapter 11, Activities of the Public Advocate) also provides services in this area to inmates.

Parole

The second section of the Department of Corrections deals with parole. The Parole Board, composed of seven members appointed by the governor, is independent of the Bureau of Parole within the Department of Corrections. The function of the Parole Board is to decide whether an offender is ready for parole—a conditional release from an institution. If parolees successfully reenter society during a stated period, without becoming involved in trouble with the law, they are discharged; if not, they must return to the institution. The 1979 revisions of the criminal code restricted eligibility for parole until completion of minimum sentence. On the other hand, the Parole Act of 1979 set forth a new philosophy for parole—it presumes an offender is eligible for parole after serving a specified time unless documentation by the Parole Board dictates otherwise. An inmate can be denied release only if the board is convinced that there is a substantial likelihood the convict will commit another crime or pose a threat to the community, or if the conditions set for the convict's release, such as participation in drug or alcohol rehabilitation programs, cannot be provided outside of prison.

Legislation went into effect in 1984 ensuring the rights of

victims of first and second degree crimes to testify at parole hearings. The new system applies to offenders convicted of first degree crimes (murder, aggravated sexual assault, or armed robbery, for example) and second degree crimes (aggravated assault, sexual assault, extortion, or bribery, for example). County prosecutors are now required to notify in writing every victim of a first or second degree crime, telling them of their right to appear before the parole board when the convict becomes eligible to be considered for release. Included with the notification is a registration form which victims wishing to participate may send to the parole board. This participation is voluntary and would not involve confronting the convict, face to face. Confidentiality may be demanded by victims fearful of reprisals. Victims will be invited to explain whether the crime caused any continuing physical, psychological or emotional harm, loss of earnings, or ability to work. These statements may affect the conditions set for parole, such as payment of restitution.

County prosecutors have the right to appeal New Jersey Parole Board decisions releasing inmates, according to a 1984 New Jersey Supreme Court ruling. The prosecutor, as the primary representative of the state in law enforcement matters within a county, represents the interests of the public when participating in parole hearings. While the parole board is not required to spell out their reasons for granting parole, the court ruling encouraged them to do so in cases in which prosecutors participate in the parole eligibility hearings.

Bureau of Parole

When released from confinement by the independent parole board, a paroled convict comes under the supervision of the Bureau of Parole in the Department of Corrections. An amendment to the Parole Act of 1979 expanded the responsibilities of the Bureau of Parole to include supervision of county parolees and supervision of the very young offenders as well. Also the bureau is responsible for collecting payments from offenders, for example, fines, payments to the Violent Crimes Victim Compensation Board, and restitution.

Parolees, under the Parole Act of 1979, have additional

due process protections when accused of violations of parole. Now attorneys, public defenders, and probable cause hearings become part of the process. No longer can the Parole Bureau take action against parolees regardless of their admission of guilt. The Parole Act also removed the power of arrest from the Parole Bureau, an additional effort to protect the due process rights of the parolee.

The work load of the Parole Bureau increased dramatically when the Parole Act of 1979 also brought county parolees under the bureau's supervision. In 1976 the average case load for each parole officer was forty-eight; in 1980 it was fifty-two; however, in 1984 it averaged eighty parolees per officer. The 1985 budget contains money to hire additional staff and reduce case loads to about sixty parolees per officer.

Prison Overcrowding

Originally imprisonment was viewed as punishment for violating the law. Over the years, the focus shifted: imprisonment came to be viewed as a means of rehabilitation. Society expected correctional institutions to "fix" violators of the law in such a way that when they return to society they would become law-abiding citizens. Yet the hoped-for rehabilitation has not taken place. The recidivism rate, a relapse to criminal ways, remains high. Currently about 40 percent of adult males in secure correctional facilities are recidivists.

Public disillusion with rehabilitation and distress at increasing victimization of innocent people by habitual criminals has led in recent years to a changing emphasis. We appear to be returning to the older view of imprisonment as punishment. A growing number of people appear now merely to want violent criminals off the streets and restrained in prisons.

As a result, more offenders are being sent to prison and are staying there longer than in past years. But appropriations by the legislature to build and maintain correctional facilities have not kept pace with use. The inevitable result of a changed mandate for corrections without sufficient funding to administer that mandate has been the over-crowding of the state's correctional institutions.

Recent Criminal Justice Legislation

In 1979 the legislature responded to public concern about crime by passing a revised Code of Criminal Justice which provided for a number of changes in criminal sentencing procedures. (See figure 4.4) The seriousness of the crime was established as the primary determinant of the sentence. Guidelines were established for the courts, indicating appropriate sentence ranges for various classifications of crime. For the first time in recent history there were mandatory minimum sentences, and prisoners were ineligible for parole until that minimum time had been served. An amendment to the code in 1981 permitted mandatory minimum sentences for any crime and required a mandatory minimum sentence of not less than three years whenever a firearm was used in committing a crime. The only exception was in cases of fourth degree crime where the minimum mandatory sentence was made eighteen months. The 1981 amendment went on to require for second offenders extended term sentences approximately double the conventional sentence. By 1984 50 percent of all incoming inmates had mandatory minimum sentences.

In 1982 capital punishment was reinstated in New Jersey, and in 1983 legislation mandated lethal injection as the method of capital punishment. (Under the previous death penalty law, execution was by electrocution in the electric chair at Trenton State Prison. The last such execution took place in 1963.)

Along with new legislation mandating longer minimum prison sentences, the New Jersey courts have put into place a Speedy Trial Program which has resulted in a substantial increase in the number of persons tried and sentenced each year. Under this program sentencing increased from approximately 14,000 in 1980 to 18,000 in 1981. The result was a 75 percent jump in New Jersey's prison population between 1980 and 1983 (from 6,199 on September 30, 1980 to 10,872 on June 30, 1983). Projections for the 1988 adult male prison population top 15,000. (See chapter 4

Probation, for court programs that affect the Department of Corrections.)

Correctional Facilities Construction

Issues of philosophy aside, the challenge for the Department of Corrections in the 1980s is to find space to house this influx of sentenced criminals. Bricks and mortar become the focus of discussion as solutions are explored. Rehabilitation of old buildings, conversion of recreation space to dormitory use, installation of trailers and prefabricated units, and use of county facilities have all become part of the solution. With funds from an institutions bond issue approved in 1980 and from the Correctional Facilities Construction Bond Act of 1982, a major building program for prisons has been initiated.

County Assistance Program (CAP)

Both Governors Byrne and Kean issued executive orders authorizing the Department of Corrections to utilize all state and county facilities for housing state prisoners. At the peak of overcrowding, December 1982, close to 1600 offenders waited in county jails for space to become available in state institutions. Currently funds from the 1982 bond issue have been allocated to fourteen counties participating in the County Assistance Program. Under provisions of this program interested counties may apply for funds to assist in expansion of existing correctional facilities or for construction of new jails. Each county receiving CAP funds agrees to house a designated number of state inmates in their new or expanded facilities as a partial repayment for funds received. Through the CAP program the state will gain almost 700 beds for state inmates in county facilities. The goal is to house a select group of nonviolent state offenders in their own counties, in close proximity to family and support services to aid their reintegration into the community.

New State Prisons

Mid-State Correctional Facility. In the early 1980s Governor Kean negotiated with the United States Department of Defense and obtained a lease on the stockade facility at Fort Dix. This became the 500-bed Mid-State Correctional Facility.

Southern State I and II. A new medium security prison composed of two units (448 beds opened in 1983 and 560 beds opened in 1984) was built in less than a year by utilizing prefabricated building units. The new prison is located close to the existing prison at Leesburg in Cumberland County.

Conventional Construction. New facilities are being added at Trenton State Prison and the Rahway State Prison Minimum Security Compound. Two new medium security facilities are being constructed in Newark (1,000 beds) and Camden (450 beds).

The Correctional Facilities Construction Bond Act of 1982 will result in a total of nearly 5,300 new state prison beds by 1988. Of that number, 1,243 beds were added in 1983 alone.

Alternatives to Incarceration

By mid-1985 the Intensive Supervision Program (ISP) is expected to provide an alternative to incarceration for 350 to 500 persons—about the number of inmates housed in a new prison unit. ISP selects certain persons convicted of nonviolent crimes having no mandatory minimum sentences to participate in an intensive probationary period of from one to five years. After approximately two months in prison, these people are released to the supervision of a probation officer and various community sponsors. Participants must either work or attend school full-time, remain drug free, and meet the conditions set by the sentencing judge. They must either see or talk to their ISP probation officer a minimum of twenty times a month. In 1984 the program cost between $4000 and $5000 per person compared with the $15,700 average cost to keep an inmate in a state prison for a year. ISP is administered by the Probation Services in the Administrative Office of the Court (see chapter 4), in cooperation with the Department of Corrections.

Another alternative program releases alcohol- or drug-dependent young adults with indeterminate sentences for nonviolent crimes to residential treatment programs. The program being developed as a joint venture of the Parole

Board and the Departments of Corrections and Health would provide ninety days of mental health treatment, vocational training, and alcohol and drug rehabilitation in community settings. This program, while serving a relatively small number of inmates, is expected to be much less expensive than incarceration and is focused on modifying the behavior patterns that lead to criminal activities, thus reducing recidivism.

For current descriptions and statistics on the correctional facilities in New Jersey, see the annual *Fitzgerald's Legislative Manual: State of New Jersey*, current year edition.

HEALTH

After decades of agitation by the Medical Society of New Jersey and others concerned with the link between poor sanitation and poor health, the legislature created the New Jersey Board of Health in 1877. At first it had little power, but over the years it became the head of the Department of Health and acquired the power to issue a body of sanitary regulations known as the State Sanitary Code.

The Department of Health

The structure of the current Department of Health was developed in 1937; the state board of health was abolished, a commissioner became head of the department, and a new public health council inherited the power to issue the State Sanitary Code.

The commissioner, appointed by the governor with the consent of the senate, must be a licensed physician who has acquired either at least five years of full-time administrative experience in a public health agency or has experience in the field of community health facilities planning, and at least ten years of full-time experience in community medical service. As the head and chief administrative officer of the Department of Health, the commissioner is free to organize the department into divisions, subject to the approval of the Public Health Council. The commissioner sets policy with the advice of a number of governing and advisory boards attached to the Department of Health. Appointments to these policy-making boards are generally made by either the governor or the commissioner; only the members of the hospital rate setting commission are paid for their work on the board.

Programs of the Department of Health

The New Jersey Department of Health administers a multitude of programs to achieve these goals:

- The prevention of the spread of diseases within New Jersey
- The prevention or reduction of the major causes of illness and death in the state, particularly as they relate to the most vulnerable populations
- The assurance of quality health care at a reasonable cost for New Jersey residents

To accomplish these goals, the Department of Health receives operating funds from three basic sources: federal grants (mostly passed on to fund local services), state monies, and the private and public grant-making communities. In the early 1980s approximately 60 percent of the department's revenues came from federal funds, 35 percent from state appropriations, and 5 percent from other funding sources. Federal block grant eligibility has been instrumental in both funding and guiding the nature of programs offered by the department.

In carrying out its duties to promote public health and prevent disease, the department itself does not generally offer services, because of its limited personnel. Rather, it offers advisory, supervisory, technical, and sometimes financial aid. Many of the department's programs involve education, both of the general public and of health care personnel. Workshops and courses are given in a variety of areas affecting public health; grants are awarded to enable health care workers to extend their training; and demonstration projects are set up in hospitals. (See figure 12.3)

Establishing and Enforcing the Sanitary Code

The Public Health Council is primarily responsible for promulgating the rules and regulations contained in the State Sanitary Code. These cover all subjects affecting public health including the prevention of disease. Specific provisions of the code regulate local boards of health and their

Figure 12.3

A Sampler of New Jersey Health Programs

FEDERAL BLOCK GRANT—MATERNAL AND CHILD HEALTH SERVICES

Woman, Infants, and Children (WIC) Special Supplemental Food Program: Aims at improving the nutritional status and health of mothers and children during critical phases of growth and development.

Preventive Health Care for Pregnant Mothers and Young Children

Sudden Infant Death Syndrome (SIDS): Establishes a network of counseling and group support services for families experiencing the loss of an infant from any cause including SIDS.

Handicapped or Crippled Children (and those suffering from conditions leading to handicaps or crippling): Makes diagnostic and corrective medical services available on a limited basis.

Lead-Based Paint Poisoning Prevention Program

Adolescent Pregnancy Program

FEDERAL BLOCK GRANT—PREVENTIVE HEALTH AND HEALTH SERVICES

Hypertension Prevention and Control Program

Emergency Medical Services Program: Provides training in areas of care and in use of communications systems.

Rodent Control Program: Targets cities with significant rat infestations.

Health Education Risk Reduction Program: Targets risk factors—smoking, misuse of alcohol and drugs, poor nutrition, stress, lack of exercise, accidents, and hypertension.

Comprehensive Public Health Services: Includes a program of asbestos removal and a program for response to emergencies both man-made and natural.

Rape Services and Prevention Program: Provides better emergency care and after-care for rape victims and develops statewide public informational and educational materials on rape prevention and care of the victim.

NEW JERSEY PROGRAMS—PREVENTION AND DETECTION.

Childhood Immunization: Purchases vaccine doses and distributes them to local sites where children are innoculated against polio, diphtheria, measles, rubella, and mumps.

Sexually Transmitted Diseases (STD): Provides screening services in clinics.

Metabolic Disorders in Newborn Infants: Routinely screens newborn infants for metabolic disorders that can lead to mental retardation.

Accidental Poisoning: Provides a 24 hour, centralized poison information and education system, linked by computer to national poison control centers.

NEW JERSEY PROGRAMS—TREATMENT

Migrant Workers and Refugees: Contracts with local agencies to provide primary health care to these individuals.

Renal Disease: Provides financial aid to eligible victims receiving dialysis treatment at approved centers.

Hemophilia: Provides blood products, treatment, and financial and technical assistance at three comprehensive hemophilia treatment centers.

Tuberculosis: Contracts with local agencies to assure detection and proper treatment of this disease, which persists in inner-city poverty areas.

personnel as well as reportable diseases, birds and animals, laboratories, burial and disinterment of the dead, campgrounds, and refuse disposal. The code has the force and effect of law and is to be enforced by all local boards of health and all law enforcement officials in the state. However, local boards of health may pass additional ordinances and regulations that they feel are necessary for their own municipalities, as long as they do not conflict with state laws or code provisions. In addition to prescribing the minimum program and minimum performance standards that local health boards must meet, the council establishes the qualifications for licensing such public health personnel as health officers, sanitary inspectors, plumbing inspectors, and food and drug inspectors.

Local Boards of Health. The Local Health Services Act of 1976 established a statewide network of local health departments with set minimum standards. Each municipality is required to provide health services in five essential areas:

- Administration, including vital records and statistics
- Environmental health, including bathing areas, camps, food service, housing, mobile home parks and camp grounds, insect and rodent control
- Communicable diseases, including acute communicable diseases, rabies, tuberculosis, venereal disease control
- Maternal and child health, including control of lead poisoning
- Chronic disease, including services for those afflicted with cancer, diabetes, heart and circulatory diseases

Administration of Local Programs. These services must be administered by a full-time, licensed public health officer, but municipalities may work cooperatively to expand their financial base and contract for services from other health agencies.

State Aid. The Office of Local Health and Regional Operations is the principal liaison between the New Jersey Department of Health and the local health department. The office aims to strengthen all public health programs by providing priority health funds to municipal, county, and regional health departments, and by offering technical assistance towards improving these services on a regional basis. Many federal and state funded health programs, which are implemented on the local, county, or regional level, are administered by this agency.

Other State Health Services

By remaining flexible, the Department of Health is able to meet a myriad of health needs and respond to changes in those needs.

Alcohol, Narcotic, and Drug Abuse Control. Prevention and treatment are the two thrusts of this program. Educational efforts are designed to make drug use unglamorous to young people; other prevention efforts are directed towards early detection and intervention. The state's fourteen state-operated drug treatment clinics were converted to private, nonprofit corporations to maintain the current treatment system at a lower cost. The treatment programs include an outpatient methadone maintenance program for heroin addicts. Similar efforts in prevention and treatment are undertaken for the state's half million alcoholics.

Consumer Health Services. This group of programs aims at preventing food-related illnesses, the misbranding or adulteration of drugs and cosmetics, and the spread of animal diseases—especially rabies—transmittable to humans. Field inspectors periodically visit food and drug establishments and public facilities to ensure compliance with the State Sanitary Code.

Prevention of Epidemics. State efforts are targeted on the prevention, control, and eventual eradication of communicable diseases. Epidemiologists are available to determine the factors responsible for disease outbreaks and to develop appropriate control measures. They also provide testing and care for exposed individuals.

Environmental and Occupational Health. Data is being gathered on New Jersey's environment and the risks associated with specific occupations. Field personnel are inspecting schools, state institutions, and other government buildings to determine potential exposure to asbestos fibers; a program to remedy dangerous asbestos situations is being developed. Units are available to investigate occupational and health emergencies.

State Laboratory Services. The Public Health and Environmental Laboratories perform comprehensive analytical and diagnostic tests in bacteriology, chemistry, serology, virology, and inborn errors of metabolism. These same laboratories test for pesticides in foodstuffs, isolate and identify infectious agents, ensure the freshness of milk and other dairy products transported across state lines, analyze potentially contaminated foods, and provide an immediate and accurate diagnosis of rabies. Environmental testing is also conducted; water, air, and soil samples are analyzed for evidences of toxic and other hazardous substances. The laboratories are also responsible for determining the asbestos level in various state facilities.

Health Care Facilities

The programs so far delineated have focused on the New Jersey Department of Health's first two goals: the prevention of the spread of diseases within New Jersey, and the prevention or reduction of the major causes of illness and death in the state. Understanding the third goal, assurance of quality health care at a reasonable cost, necessitates a discussion of health care facilities.

In recent years health care costs have risen almost twice as fast as the consumer price index, and health care costs as a percentage of the gross national product (GNP) have risen from about 5 percent in 1960 to more than 10 percent in 1982. Several factors have contributed to this dramatic upward cost pressure. The number of people sixty-five and older continues to increase faster than the population as a whole, and it is this segment of the population that requires a greater proportion of health care expenditures. In addition, the recent development and use of high technology treatments tend to extend life expectancy and force medical costs upward. High technology medicine also tends to drive health care labor costs up, since skilled workers are more often needed to operate sophisticated new equipment. Added to these factors are the presence of Medicare and Medicaid programs, which, for the first time, give some new segments of the population access to a wide range of health services.

In light of these factors and to improve implementation of federal legislation, New Jersey passed the Health Care Facilities Planning Act in 1971. This act established the

Department of Health as the sole agency to license and reg- ulate health care facilities in the state. A thirteen-member Health Care Administration Board (HCAB) appointed by the governor reviews and approves the rules and regulations proposed by the commissioner of health.

In 1972 the legislature created the New Jersey Health Care Facilities Financing Authority to meet the capital needs of New Jersey hospitals and other health care insti- tutions at the lowest possible cost through the sale of tax- exempt government bonds. The commissioner of the De- partment of Health is ex-officio chairman of the authority, and the Department of Health is responsible for setting standards for design, construction, and operations of health care facilities, for licensing them, and for inspecting each at least once a year.

Certificates of Need

The core of the 1971 Health Care Facilities Planning Act reads:

> No health care facility shall be constructed or expanded and no new health care services shall be instituted . . . except upon application for and receipt of a certificate of need.

This law, therefore, regulates the construction or expansion of health care facilities or services by determining whether or not a cost effective need exists. An application for a certif- icate of need is first reviewed by regional health system agencies. The application then goes to the State Health Coordinating Council, which makes the final recommen- dation to the commissioner. If the commissioner denies the application for a certificate of need, appeals go to the Health Care Administration Board. This same board is re- sponsible for setting both the standards for certificates of need and hospital rates.

Hospital Rate Setting and Diagnostic Related Groups (DRGS)

The 1971 Health Care Facilities Planning Act, which cre- ated the certificate of need process, also authorized the establishment and maintenance of a uniform cost-accounting system for health care institutions. In addition, it conferred upon the Department of Health authority to set the reimbursement rates for health care facilities. The Hospital Rate Setting Commission sets the schedule of rates for each hospital, adjusting those rates according to factors unique to the institution (such as size, location, and nature of the population served).

In the areas of hospital rate setting and certificates of need New Jersey leads the nation in developing programs that later become national standards. The Diagnostic Related Groups (DRG) cost-containment system was pioneered by the New Jersey Department of Health in the early 1980s; in 1983 the federal Medicare program adopted its own version of the system.

Under the DRG system hospital rates are based on the average cost of treating 467 diagnoses, covering nearly every reason for hospitalization. Rates are derived from treatment costs in a base period and then increased for inflation each year. Because hospitals lose money if they spend more than the DRG rate to treat a patient, they have incentive to use only the necessary tests and to keep patients in the hospital only as long as needed.

13.
Human Services

The majority of New Jersey social service programs, agencies, and institutions are under the direction of the Department of Human Services. The department's jurisdiction includes the state's developmental centers and community-based residences for the mentally retarded; psychiatric hospitals, mental health centers, and community-based residences for the mentally ill; foster homes, group homes, and treatment facilities for children and adolescents; certain day care centers; and for veterans nursing homes and a cemetery.

The department administers federal funds appropriated for these services, as well as Medicaid and public welfare assistance. Programs for the blind and visually impaired, a foster grandparent program, and veterans' services also come under the auspices of the department. By far the largest employer in the state government, the Department of Human Services is second only to education in state dollars received. The largest program in human services is Medicaid.

Faced with a loss of federal funds in the early 1980s, the State of New Jersey maintained human services program levels in most instances by using state funds. The remaining federal funds are most heavily committed to supporting public welfare and to Medicaid, but federal monies also support a sizeable percentage of the budgets for Youth and Family Services and for the Commission for the Blind. Services for the mentally ill and the mentally retarded are largely supported with state funds, as are veterans' services. (See figure 13.1.)

Figure 13.1

Department of Human Services
Revenue Sources (FY 1985) ($000's)

Division	Federal	State	Other*	Total
Public Welfare	$ 440,850	$ 275,970	$ 87,544	$ 804,364
Medical Assistance	508,279	572,895	113,000**	1,194,174
Youth and Family Services	76,241	83,417	18,825	178,483
Commission for the Blind	5.329	6,483	0	11,812
Mental Health and Hospitals	15,843***	178,213	801	194,857
Mental Retardation	93,948	185,792	18,171	297,911
Veterans' Services	0	16,898	0	16,898
Management and Budget	12,901	10,533	165	23,599
Capital Budget				
Capital Projects	0	0	0	0
Debt Service	0	0	27,729	27,729
Sub-total	$1,153,391	$1,330,201	$266,235	$2,749,827
Department Pass-thru (of Federal Funds)				
Food Stamps	$ 285,887	$ 0	$ 0	$ 285,887
Supplemental Security Income (SSI)	189,300	0	0	189,300
Sub-total	$ 475,187	$ 0	$ 0	$ 475,187
TOTAL	$1,628,578	$1,330,201	$266,235	$3,225,014

  * Includes State Facilities Education Act, county reimbursements, restricted grants (federal public, private), legally responsible relatives, other government benefits.
  ** Casino revenues.
  *** Includes Education funds.

The functions of welfare and social services were administered by the Department of Institutions and Agencies, which
included most charitable and correctional institutions, until
1976. In that year the department was split, forming two
new departments—Human Services and Corrections.

The Department of Human Services is headed by a commissioner appointed by the governor with the approval of
the senate after consultation with the New Jersey Board of
Human Services. The commissioner is the principal executive officer and administrative head of the department.

The commissioner has jurisdiction over all department-
oriented institutions and agencies, with the power to establish policies so that each unit can function as an integral
part of the general system. The commissioner can designate
specific functions for each institution as well as the category
of people each will serve.

The New Jersey Board of Human Services consults with
and advises the commissioner on the administration of the
department and its institutions and agencies. Particular
concerns of the board are long-range planning and policy-
making for the entire system of state institutions. The board
has twelve members, nine appointed by the governor to
four-year terms. The other three are ex-officio members, including the governor and the commissioners of human services and health. Current practice has been to hold board
meetings at different state institutions during the year.

The commissioner and the state board have the power to
inspect all similar public and private institutions, and they,
or their agents, must semiannually inspect all public and
private residential facilities for the mentally retarded. If an
investigation reveals violation of laws or improper or inadequate treatment of patients, the board or the commissioner
may apply for a court order to remedy conditions considered improper.

By the time the Department of Human Services was created, the pattern of a citizen board for each institution was
firmly entrenched. Citizen boards had come about partly in
an attempt to emulate the boards of trustees of similar private institutions and partly in a hope to insulate the institutions from political pressures. Despite repeated attempts to
abolish them, these citizen boards continue today.

The Department of Human Services

In the early 1980s, under the leadership of Commissioner George J. Albanese, the department underwent major reorganization in order to integrate management services, streamline program administration, and utilize modern management techniques. Restructuring in the Division of Youth and Family Services, for example, reduced management levels and put more case workers in the field. Development of an Office of Information Systems aided computerization of a number of departmental functions and allowed for more special projects to be undertaken. The computerized child support enforcement project along with the Family Assistance Management Information System, both largely funded by a federal grant, will be a cost-effective way to reduce fraud and increase compliance with court-ordered child support. Responding to other federal incentives, additional programs aimed at reducing fraud and abuse of the social services were instituted; included in this response is technical aid to county agencies that directly administer much of the welfare assistance.

Welfare Services

Welfare is the term used for government and private programs that provide food, money, and other necessities for needy people. In early times responsibility for caring for the poor usually fell upon family members and neighbors. Only when poverty became too great or widespread for individual families to handle did the government offer some relief. During the Middle Ages the church and other religious groups assumed much of the responsibility for helping the poor. Merchant and craft guilds met the needs of their own members. As far back as 1601, when the English Parliament passed the Elizabethan Poor Law, government acknowledged its accountability. That law made the local governmental units, called parishes, responsible for their own poor, providing for the taxation of parishioners to support the needy in each parish.

Early welfare laws in the United States resembled those of Great Britain. By the early 1900s many states required their cities and counties to provide support for the aged, the blind, and for fatherless children. Some state governments assumed the costs of this aid.

In New Jersey those programs that have traditionally been considered welfare are under the direction of the Division of Public Welfare. Established in 1950, the division in 1962 acquired a fifteen-member citizen board to set policies and review division activities. In 1976 the division was transferred to the newly formed Department of Human Services.

The most widely known welfare programs are those classified as categorical assistance, i.e., assistance to those in certain categories of need. These programs are federal in origin; they were designed in 1934–1935 as part of the overall Social Security program to help certain needy groups whose localities could not or would not assist them. Federal funding remains an important part of these programs.

Aid to Families with Dependent Children (AFDC)

Under the AFDC program payments are made for needy children under the age of eighteen to their parents or relatives with whom they are living. To qualify for this aid, a family must include one or more dependent children who have been deprived of support or care because of the death, continued absence from the home, or incapacity of a parent. In certain circumstances, it also provides help to families where both parents are in the home but do not have enough income to support their children adequately. In 1984 approximately 130,000 New Jersey families were receiving AFDC grants, and one child in every five in New Jersey was living on a welfare grant.

Each state runs its own AFDC program, directly administered by a welfare board in each county, under the supervision of the state Division of Public Welfare, and in accordance with federal and state laws and regulations. Each county board is composed of five citizens and two freeholders appointed by the board of freeholders (the county governing board). An appointed director administers the program.

The aid is drawn from federal, state, and local funds. Approximately one-half of the cost is borne by the federal government; the state pays 37½ percent and the counties pay 12½ percent. The counties, however, are not reimbursed for their administrative costs.

Aid to the Working Poor

The Omnibus Budget Reconciliation Act of 1981 changed federal regulations for Aid to Families with Dependent Children to target assistance to the very neediest. This was done by setting a total income limit of 150 percent of the state's need standard, and by changing the manner in which earned income was considered when figuring eligibility for aid. As a result, many of the working poor are no longer eligible to receive AFDC. This change removed about 10,000 New Jersey families from AFDC eligibility and the accompanying Medicaid benefits as well.

Along with changing eligibility standards for AFDC, the Budget Reconciliation Act encouraged states to develop work alternatives so families would be able to move from welfare depenency to job-based self-sufficiency. New Jersey took advantage of several of these new program options including the WIN (Work Incentive) Demonstration Program to increase employment and training opportunities for AFDC clients, and the grant diversion option which allows for reprogramming of welfare grant dollars into training resources.

Food Stamps

This federal program is administered by the Department of Human Services, but all costs are paid by the federal government. The program is designed to supplement the nutritional needs of AFDC recipients and other low-income households, such as the underemployed and the aged poor.

Supplemental Security Income
(SSI)

Direct federal income maintenance payments are made to the aged, blind, and disabled at a stipulated minimum level. These payments are separate from the regular Social Security Payments. New Jersey supplements the federal payments to meet state standards for minimum income maintenance.

General Assistance

This large nonfederal program provides funds for the needy who are not eligible for federal programs. While general assistance is a responsibility of the municipalities, those towns that request state aid and meet state standards are partially reimbursed by the state government. In order to qualify for these state payments, a municipality must have a local assistance board composed of three or five unsalaried members appointed by the municipality's governing body. Each board, in turn, appoints a qualified welfare director, who must administer general assistance by periodic investigation of all welfare cases, aiding needy persons to achieve self-support or aid from other agencies, keeping records, and committing individuals to state or county institutions when such care is necessary. Under this aid program the allocation of maintenance and hospitalization expenditures is 75 percent state and 25 percent municipal.

For several years New Jersey has had a General Assistance Employability Program which places employable recipients at public work sites in their municipalities so that recipients provide labor equal in value to the amount of their grants. This program also assists with developing job-seeking skills to reduce welfare dependency.

Refugee Assistance
These programs are entirely federally funded for the first three years of refugee residence and are administered by county welfare agencies. Legal immigrants from Indochina, Eastern Europe, and other areas where the refugees have experienced persecution, and entrants from Cuba and Haiti, have been eligible for these programs in recent years.

Home Energy Assistance
This program distributes funds to help low-income families pay their home heating bills.

Nature of Welfare Grants
The amount of assistance given to those on welfare in a monthly cash grant is based on a schedule prepared by the Division of Public Welfare. The grant, which varies only with family size, is based on average costs of personal and household needs, including a shelter cost representing the average among welfare families. The flat grant is to cover rent, clothing, food, and utility expenses. The cost of medi-

cal care is paid directly to the provider of the medical service through the Medicaid program. Limited funds may be obtained for such miscellaneous circumstances as emergencies, day care, homemaker service, and job training allowances. Most households receiving public assistance are eligible for federal food stamps which enables them to obtain food free of charge or at reduced prices, depending on their incomes. Social services, such as family planning and educational counseling, are available to AFDC recipients in some counties. Legally responsible relatives of recipients are obliged to reimburse the county welfare boards to the extent of their financial ability.

Medical Assistance and Health Services

In 1970 a separate division was established to handle Medicaid benefits to eligible public assistance clients. New programs added to the division, the Pharmaceutical Assistance to the Aged and Disabled (PAAD) and Lifeline (which helps senior and disabled citizens meet the increasing cost of utilities), are funded with casino revenue tax and state fund monies.

Medicaid

Joint federal-state Medicaid programs provide for the medical and health needs of over 525,000 low-income New Jersey citizens. Medicaid covers physician services; services from dentists, chiropractors, psychologists, podiatrists, and optometrists; a preventive care program for children (the Early and Periodic Screening, Diagnosis, and Treatment program); prescribed drugs; inpatient and outpatient hospital care; home health and personal care; certain health maintenance organizations; clinic services, including family planning, and rehabilitation centers as well as comprehensive health care clinics; mental health services; eyeglasses, hearing aids, artificial limbs and braces; medical supplies and equipment; X-ray and laboratory services; ambulance and invalid coach; and transportation for medical services.

A state may participate if its plan meets the minimum federal requirements for eligibility and for services to be furnished. New Jersey's plan, inaugurated in 1970, provides the required coverage and services for families with dependent children and families of the working poor who are eligible for or receive public assistance through a county welfare board; the aged, blind, and disabled eligible for or receiving federal Supplemental Security Income (SSI); children in foster care, private adoption agencies, or on a subsidized adoption program; indigent persons in long-term care facilities; poor people in state psychiatric hospitals; those eligible for federal refugee assistance programs; and low-income pregnant women.

Federal commitment to coverage of Medicaid costs was being limited by the mid-1980s, thereby leaving the states with an increasing share of the cost. In addition, changes in federal funding for Medicare increased state expenses for Medicaid.

Medicare

While Medicaid is a state-federal program for the poor, Medicare is a federal insurance program for the aged and disabled. Medicare (Part A) covers hospital visits and up to one hundred days of skilled nursing home care for most people who have paid into the Social Security Trust Fund. Medicare (Part B) coverage of physician and ancillary services is offered as an optional plan, for a monthly fee. Virtually all parts of Medicare require cost sharing by the patient. New Jersey, through the Division of Medical Assistance and Health Services, pays for the medical insurance (Medicare Part B) and all cost-sharing responsibilities of the eligible client up to division reimbursement limits. Thus, federal cutbacks in Medicare (by requiring additional cost sharing) directly affect New Jersey's Medicaid costs.

Efforts to Contain Health Care Costs

The activities of the Division of Medical Assistance and Health Services (DMAHS) account for the expenditure of more than $1 billion annually, of which over $600 million is in state funds. Moreover, the cost of services in this category has been increasing in recent years at an annual rate of about 14 percent, against an average annual increase of only 10 percent in the state's resources. Accordingly, the potential in this area for escalating financial strains on the state is enormous.

(Excerpted from the "Summary, Division of Medical Assistance and Health Services, Governor's Management Improvement Program" October 5, 1983)

This statement of the problem faced by New Jersey is important in light of the dramatic rise in the amount budgeted for medical assistance and health services (from $352 million in 1980 to $613 million in 1985) and the percentage of the total state budget of $7.5 billion in 1985 (medical assistance and health care accounted for 8 percent of that total budget). However, some progress is being made in slowing the increase of these costs in New Jersey.

Community Care for the Elderly. DMAHS has made significant progress in overcoming an institutional bias in the federal Medicaid regulations that was manifested by an unequal Medicaid income standard between community residents and nursing home patients. This bias encouraged nursing home placement as the only alternative covered by Medicaid for many elderly patients needing care. Through a federal waiver, the income standard was equalized, and under the Community Care program for the elderly and disabled those eligible have the alternative of receiving an array of community support programs enabling them to remain in community residence.

Home Care for the Disabled. Through another waiver program certain hospitalized or institutionalized disabled adults and children eligible for Medicaid only while in an institutional setting could retain their eligibility when discharged and cared for by family members at home.

These waivers are contingent upon the costs of home and community treatment being less than institutional care.

Other Experimental Programs. In 1984 several pilot programs operated to test ways to reduce medical and health care costs. In conjunction with the Community Care program, some recipients of Aid to Families with Dependent Children are being trained to provide specialized home care for the elderly. Another pilot program allows Medicaid eligible clients to receive prepaid health care from a health maintenance organization (HMO). This helps to stabilize costs for Medicaid. Yet another experimental program allows Medicaid recipients to enroll with a single physician who will act as their case manager. The goal of this program is not only to improve care but also to reduce costly non-emergency use of hospital emergency rooms. This is also a prepaid program under which enrolled physicians receive a per capita payment for each Medicaid recipient instead of a fee for service for each contact with a patient.

In the early days of New Jersey the mentally ill were confined in county almshouses and jails. In a number of the jails they were further confined in chains. By the early 1840s, sentiment for a state asylum grew in the expectation that it would provide greater safety for the citizens, more humane care for the insane, and, through medical treatment, more likelihood for their recovery and rehabilitation. Although the legislature approved the idea in principle, it added the proviso that it be done "as soon as the finances of the State will warrant a sufficient appropriation."

No funds had been provided by the time Dorothea Dix, the social crusader, arrived in New Jersey. In a January 1845 memorial to the legislature she stated:

> [that New Jersey had] ample means, was unembarrassed by state debts, and prosperous in all her public relations, and more private channels of business. [She concluded] Gentlemen, it is believed that the time has arrived for action upon the . . . resolutions. The finances of the State will warrant a sufficient appropriation for the establishment of a State Hospital for the Insane and Idiots of New Jersey.

Two months later the legislature appropriated the funds for the Trenton State Hospital.

The state's needs soon outgrew the new hospital. While waiting for the establishment of a second state institution, a number of counties opened asylums of their own or made special additions to their almshouses to provide for the care

Services for the Mentally Ill

of the insane. In 1876 the second state asylum, the State Hospital at Greystone Park, was opened.

For a century the "humane" treatment of the mentally ill was most often confinement in a state mental institution— the psychiatric hospitals. But by the 1950s, with the advent of drug therapies which permitted swifter discharge of many patients, the average daily population in these facilities dropped dramatically. At the same time admissions rose as more people sought or were referred for help and entered the psychiatric hospitals for short-term treatment.

Along with the miracle drug therapies came new support for serving patients by returning them to community living through halfway houses or residential centers rather than keeping them at a state hospital.

Community-Based Mental Health Services

Now more than 90 percent of people receiving mental health care services in New Jersey are treated through the state network of public and private community agencies. In contrast less than 10 percent were admitted to state hospitals (10,000 people in 1983), and the stay was generally short (average daily population in the state hospitals was 3,600 in 1983).

In 1957 the New Jersey Legislature passed the Community Mental Health Services Act providing state aid for these community agencies. In 1963 federal funding was added through the federal Community Mental Health Centers Act. This legislation mandated basic services in order to support community-based centers and to avoid commitment of patients to institutions. In 1975 the legislation was expanded to include funding for services for children, the elderly, drug abusers, and alcoholics.

As outlined in the state legislation, each county is required to have a county mental health board of appointed citizens which annually assesses local needs and submits priority recommendations to the state for approval and funding. Along with citizen involvement on the mental health boards, citizens are deeply involved as volunteers in providing a significant part of the community support as well as the public awareness and information campaigns.

Included in the range of mental health care services are clinical services, social services, rehabilitation, education, and individual and systems advocacy for people with critical and chronic conditions that prevent them from functioning independently. Local service areas are mandated to provide a minimum basic range of mental health programs and to cooperate in regional and statewide programs to provide special services. The basic local service components include emergency screening (through which people are admitted to mental health services), short-term acute inpatient care, day care, outpatient care, consultation and education, residential services, and individual and systems advocacy for clients. Services are to be provided locally if at all possible. In keeping with modern treatment concepts and with civil rights guidelines, efforts are made to provide treatment in the least restrictive settings and to limit inpatient confinement to the shortest time compatible with accepted treatment standards and needs.

The system is financed with public funds including federal grants, state appropriations, state aid to local programs, county and municipal government appropriations. Public funds are supplemented in many cases by private sources and by insurance reimbursements and payments by individuals based on their ability to pay. Unfortunately, maintenance of the old and costly residential psychiatric hospitals continues to take a disproportionate share of the mental health budget at the expense of the more cost-effective community-based mental health programs.

Specialized Services
Diversified and specialized mental health services have been developed to meet the needs of particular population groups and individuals, and to reflect federal and state legal mandates and program guidelines.

For children a new community-based system of six regional children's crisis intervention services now provides up to twenty-eight days of inpatient psychiatric care. This network replaces the primary reliance of ten years ago on adolescent and children's units in four state psychiatric hospitals. With expanding community support services most children are now treated in the regional centers and returned to their homes and community agencies for further treatment and care. When necessary, longer term inpatient services are provided for children under age fourteen at the Arthur Brisbane Child Treatment Center in Allaire and for adolescents ages fourteen to seventeen in the adolescent treatment unit which is operated in a separate group of buildings on the grounds of Trenton Psychiatric Hospital. A network of more than thirty crisis intervention, residential, and day care programs for children is also part of the special children's service system.

To provide more appropriate living arrangements for persons previously confined on a long-term basis to state hospitals, an expanding network of residential settings (more than eight hundred in 1984) is maintained throughout the state. These facilities range from more than fifty group homes to over two hundred apartments, with supervisory staff and support services provided for clients according to their needs.

The network to serve the elderly mentally ill includes the Glen Gardner Center for Geriatrics and the special geriatric units in the other state hospitals—Trenton, Greystone, Marlboro, and Ancora. Additional placements in nursing homes are being created through agreements with proprietors and with the Department of Health, permitting the transfer of clients remaining inappropriately in state hospitals.

Special individualized programs are being developed for people with multiple handicaps and dependencies, including the mentally ill who are alcohol or drug abusers, retarded, deaf, blind, or otherwise physically impaired or disabled.

In the 1980s the system finds itself faced with a growing population of disabled and dependent persons between twenty and thirty-four years old. This group, known as the young chronics, has special needs for housing alternatives as well as special treatment needs which are often related to drug and alcohol abuse.

A separate facility, the Forensic Psychiatric Hospital, was developed on the grounds of the Trenton Psychiatric Hospital as a special institution for clients judged not guilty of crimes by reason of insanity, incompetent to stand trial, or so dangerous as to require confinement and treatment in a secure setting.

The major responsibility for the care of New Jersey's retarded citizens rests with the Division of Mental Retardation (DMR). In 1983 about six thousand mentally retarded people were served in the state institutions and about five thousand were served in the community.

Expansion of the population served by DMR was recommended by the Developmental Disabilities Council which, in a 1982 report, recommended that DMR extend services to persons with cerebral palsy, spina bifida, epilepsy, autism, and other handicapping conditions. However, while DMR does provide some services for autistic people, their current focus remains on the population more narrowly defined as mentally retarded.

Intermediate Care Facilities

The state's traditional service approach for the mentally retarded was to provide "training schools" for those whose families could not care for them at home. In the 1970s about eight thousand residents were housed in eight residential facilities featuring large wards and basic custodial care. However, a Medicaid program initiated in 1971, and made more attractive to states like New Jersey in 1977, established and helped finance a new approach—Intermediate Care Facilities for Mentally Retarded (ICF/MR). Under this program, the federal government gives financial aid for staff, maintenance, and administration of facilities meeting federal standards for less restrictive settings that emphasize the development of clients' potential.

Responding to federal financial incentives and embracing the goal of more stimulating and less restrictive settings for their clients, DMR used a combination of funding sources to convert a large share of their beds for the mentally retarded to ICF/MR facilities. Large open wards were converted to series of air-conditioned rooms for two to four residents with more home-like furnishings and additional recreational space. The direct care staff to resident ratio improved from highs of 1:13 to a more workable 1:8.5. More

Services for the Mentally Retarded

abundant professional and support services were also made available. In recognition of this change within the facilities, legislation enacted in 1983 changed the names of most state training schools to developmental centers. The long-range plan is to complete conversion of all facilities to ICF/MR standards by 1989.

Community Residential Placement

At the same time state training schools were being converted to developmental centers, another major goal of DMR was development of community residential placements for persons inappropriately placed in state institutions. By 1989 half of the DMR population will be served in community residential placement, and only those who are severely handicapped will remain in the developmental centers. No longer will the state institutions be the primary source of residential service for the mentally retarded.

Aided by state bond issue monies, federal Housing and Urban Development funds, and community care waiver programs involving Medicaid ICF/MR funds (see this chapter, Medical Assistance and Health Services for similar federal waivers for community care), DMR was able to place about two thousand clients in community settings in 1983 with an additional nine hundred situated in "purchase of care" facilities, private institutions for the retarded which take state clients on a contract basis. The community residential facilities include skill development homes, group homes and supervised apartments, adult foster care, unsupervised apartments, purchase-of-care services, and home assistance.

Other DMR Programs

DMR runs a variety of supportive services including day programs run in conjunction with the departments of education and labor, support services for families caring for a mentally retarded relative; and aid in securing specialized equipment used by some retarded people.

Guardianship is provided by DMR for a large number of clients. DMR accepts the legal responsibility to protect the clients' rights, see that their needs are met, and protect them from abuse, neglect, or exploitation. Self-advocacy training is a new program helping the mentally retarded better assert themselves and protect their own rights.

The Division of Youth and Family Services (DYFS) seeks to protect, strengthen, promote, and preserve family life. When children are endangered within that family setting, however, DYFS steps in to offer protective services. They also provide care for orphans, wards of the state, and those children who are freed for adoption. Children requiring physical or mental health services and who meet eligibility standards are also supervised by DYFS. The division operates an emergency reception and child diagnostic center, several residential treatment centers, and a number of group homes and day care centers. Additional care is purchased for New Jersey children on a contract basis from private institutions and community-based providers, usually within New Jersey. DYFS also has responsibility for inspecting and licensing a wide range of facilities that care for children, ranging from child care centers to residential facilities.

Efforts to prevent child abuse and disruption of family life focus community services on families in crisis. Identification of high risk families and provision of services before crises occur are important objectives of DYFS. Families in crisis may receive a number of services including

■ in-home services such as teaching homemakers and parent aides;

■ partial care including day care, after school care, and camp;

■ emergency responses to, and intervention in, crisis situations;

■ case management services to assure the plan for a family is coordinated and completed;

■ and general social services.

For those children who must be removed from the home because family problems are not resolved or because the children are in need of protection, residential care is provided. As funding becomes available, more community residential options, including group homes for adolescents and additional foster homes, are planned. Increasing reimburse-

Services to Youth and Families

ment to foster homes is viewed as one way to recruit more foster families.

Permanent placement for children whose families are unable to care for them even after supportive services have been provided is essential for the children's well-being. Barriers to permanent placements are being addressed. Special permanency planning workers seek to find relatives with whom the children can live or, in some cases, DYFS seeks court guardianship and termination of parental rights so the child can be freed for adoption. The cases of all children placed out of their homes are reviewed periodically by the Child Placement Review Boards (composed of citizen volunteers) who make recommendations to the court on the appropriateness of the plan for the children's care.

In 1984 a subsidized adoption bill was passed eliminating financial disincentives to the adoption of hard-to-place children, especially those with ongoing medical or mental health needs. When fully funded, this law is designed to enable new adoptive parents to receive compensation equal to that of foster parents. This law is especially important in removing financial barriers impeding foster parents from more often adopting their foster children who are freed for adoption.

Services to Veterans

The Division of Veterans Programs and Special Services administers two veterans nursing facilities, one located in Menlo Park and the other in Vineland. A third veterans nursing facility is under construction in Paramus. The division will also administer the New Jersey Veterans Memorial Cemetery to be located in Arneytown, Burlington County. This facility, funded with federal and state monies, will have more than 110,000 burial plots.

The Bureau of Veterans Services operates sixteen local offices throughout the state. These offices assist New Jersey veterans in obtaining state and federal benefits including pension, insurance, civil service veterans preference, state property tax exemptions, educational and disability grants, and financial aid.

The division also provides assistance to the New Jersey Agent Orange Commission, a legislative study commission.

This group has been working to establish possible links between various illnesses reported by veterans and the use of herbicides in Vietnam. It also coordinates various social services to Vietnam veterans.

14.

Law, Public Safety, and Defense

The preservation of order is perceived in our society as one of the most important aspects of government. Many law enforcement functions in New Jersey are gathered together in the Department of Law and Public Safety: the Law Division, the Division of Criminal Justice, the New Jersey State Police, the New Jersey Racing Commission, and the divisions for Gaming Enforcement, Alcoholic Beverage Control, Motor Vehicles, Civil Rights, and Consumer Affairs.

Not included in the Department of Law and Public Safety, but important to the preservation of order and therefore discussed in this chapter, are the State Commission of Investigation, the Office of the United States Attorney, and the New Jersey Department of Defense.

At the top of the pyramid of law enforcement officers is the attorney general, the chief law enforcement official of the state and head of the Department of Law and Public Safety. Each New Jersey constitution since 1776 has provided for an attorney general. Since 1814 the post has been filled by the governor with the consent of the senate, although only since the 1947 constitution has the attorney general's term been made concurrent with that of the governor. Prior to this the attorney general's term was five years, two more than the term of the governor. Therefore, governors frequently had to work with hostile attorneys general. In 1947 Alfred E. Driscoll (governor 1947–1950), unsuccessful in

THE DEPARTMENT OF LAW AND PUBLIC SAFETY

persuading the incumbent attorney general to resign, induced the legislature to let the governor have a personal counsel. This post still exists. The attorney general, along with the secretary of state, still serves a constitutionally mandated four-year term and may be removed by the governor only "for cause"—unlike the rest of the cabinet officers who serve at the governor's pleasure.

The powers and duties of the attorney general have been altered periodically by the legislature. Under the 1948 reorganization of the executive branch, the attorney general was put in charge of the newly created Department of Law and Public Safety, composed of previously independent agencies. Each was made a division within the department. The attorney general's supervisory powers over these divisions, and many of those subsequently added, are nevertheless limited: largely because of the former independent status of many of the agencies, most division heads are appointed by the governor with the consent of the senate.

The Law Division

The Division of Law acts as the lawyer for the state government. Assistant and deputy attorneys general, under the supervision of the state attorney general, staff this division. Some departments such as Banking are assigned a deputy attorney general on a full-time basis to provide legal assistance and to examine contracts and other legal documents.

Criminal Justice

The Criminal Justice Act of 1970 lodged the ultimate responsibility for law enforcement with the state, more particularly with the attorney general operating through the Division of Criminal Justice. The law gave the attorney general original jurisdiction to investigate and prosecute criminal offenses of statewide significance, those involving multi-county criminal activity, and those requiring sophisticated and complex strategies normally beyond the scope of local and county agencies.

The director of the division is appointed by the attorney general and serves at the attorney general's pleasure. Special sections within the division focus on a particular industry or enforcement of a specific law: the Anti-Trust Section investigates price fixing and collusion within an industry; the Casino Control Section prosecutes cases involving casino gambling in Atlantic City; the Economic Crime Section prosecutes cases of public contract fraud, unemployment insurance fraud, embezzlement, and frauds against the private sector; the Health Services Section investigates and prosecutes Medicaid fraud and criminal activities victimizing nursing home residents; and the Environmental Prosecutions Section focuses on the investigation and prosecution of anti-competitive, racketeering, and other illegal practices in the solid waste industry. This section is also responsible for the investigation of illegal handling of hazardous wastes and for screening waste industry license applicants to deter the infiltration of undesirable people into the waste disposal industry.

The Division of Criminal Justice also handles all criminal appeal cases in the state to insure that the state's interest in criminal matters is represented consistently and with the highest quality. The division likewise monitors all cases involving the capital punishment law. Law enforcement on the local level is also supervised by the division.

Supervision of County Prosecutors

The chief law enforcement official in a county is the county prosecutor (the equivalent of the district attorney in other states). The county prosecutor is appointed by the governor with the consent of the senate and, usually, upon the recommendation of the county chairman of the governor's political party. The prosecutor's term is five years and until a successor is appointed. The county bears the cost of salary and office for the county prosecutor.

The county prosecutor is responsible to the governor, the attorney general, and the assignment judge of the superior court vicinage. In effect, the prosecutor is supervised by the Criminal Justice Division so that effective and uniform enforcement of criminal law will be promoted throughout the state. To this end the division conducts periodic evaluations of each prosecutor's office, analyzes the annual reports, assists in investigations, acts as a clearinghouse, and otherwise coordinates criminal law enforcement in the state. County prosecutors, local police departments, and all other law enforcement agencies in the state are expected to cooperate with the division.

The Criminal Justice Division also trains the county prosecutors; during the early 1980s this training focused on helping county prosecutors handle more complex crimes. These include certain toxic and hazardous waste cases, incidents of "white-collar" crime and Medicaid fraud, and matters involving illicit trafficking in controlled dangerous substances by health care professionals. By training county personnel to handle these cases occurring in their locale, the division is freed to focus on the organized crime and multi-county aspects of these criminal activities.

The attorney general may also supersede or substitute for county prosecutors at the request of the governor or upon the written request of a grand jury, board of freeholders, or the vicinage assignment judge. This power includes the authority to intervene in the investigation or prosecution of individual criminal cases, including appeals of criminal convictions, either upon the attorney general's own initiative or upon the request of the county prosecutor. This power is especially vital since the bulk of the investigation and prosecution of crime in New Jersey is conducted by county prosecutors.

County prosecutors wield much discretionary power. They decide whether or not to conduct investigations and how thoroughly they are to be conducted; they decide whether or not to bring an alleged offender before a grand jury; they control what evidence a grand jury hears; they decide whether or not to recommend a lighter sentence to the judge in return for a plea of guilty (called plea bargaining); they decide whether or not to ask a judge for permission to drop a case even though a grand jury has returned an indictment. The quality of law enforcement in a county is directly affected by its prosecutor. (See chapter 4, The State Courts, and figure 4.3.)

Local police forces and their detective staffs (where they exist) perform much of the original detective work and arrest of suspects. County prosecutors and their staffs of detectives and investigators, however, have overall responsibility.

As the chief law enforcement officers of the counties,

the prosecutors work closely with, and may direct, the mayor and police department of any municipality in law enforcement matters. Prosecutors may conduct raids and make arrests without notifying municipal police. And they may call upon the attorney general and the State Police for assistance.

To allow county prosecutors to concentrate on more serious crimes, lesser offenses such as traffic violations and disorderly persons offenses are handled by municipal police and tried by municipal courts. Except where a defendant has waived the right to indictment by a grand jury, the prosecutor must first present each case pursued by the prosecutor's office to a grand jury.

The county prosecutor's position as the primary law enforcement officer in the county is reinforced by an ability to draw on federal funds. Local and countywide projects funded by the State Law Enforcement Planning Agency (SLEPA) must originate through the office of the county prosecutor.

State Law Enforcement Planning Agency (SLEPA)

The goal of this agency is to develop a comprehensive plan for improving the criminal and juvenile justice system in New Jersey. The agency also has responsibilities for coordinating the development of programs and projects for which federal matching funds are available. The federal funds currently come from the Juvenile Justice and Delinquency Prevention Act of 1974 and the Justice Assistance Act of 1983 which replaced the federal Law Enforcement Assistance Administration (LEAA). One of the most important projects funded by SLEPA to date was a study done by the Administrative Office of the Courts to devise a plan and a funding design for a fully unified court system in New Jersey. (See chapter 4).

SLEPA is composed of unsalaried members, including the Superintendent of State Police, mayors of several large cities, the Chief Justice of the New Jersey Supreme Court, the Director of the Administrative Office of the Courts, and other powerful officials in state and local government. The attorney general chairs the agency, which is technically in, but effectively not of, the Department of Law and Public Safety.

Office of the State Medical Examiner

All violent or suspicious deaths and those that constitute a threat to public health are investigated by the Office of the State Medical Examiner within the Division of Criminal Justice. A state medical examiner, who is a licensed physician and a qualified forensic pathologist, is appointed by the governor with the consent of the senate to head the office for a five-year term. This officer, in turn, supervises the county medical examiners (the post of coroner was abolished). Statewide rules and regulations for the scientific investigation of deaths are established by the office, and modern laboratory facilities are available for use by the county medical examiners. By court order the state medical examiner may supersede the medical examiner of any county.

The State Police

The original mandate of the State Police was to furnish police protection to the state's rural areas. However, since their establishment in 1921 as an independent agency, and their assignment in 1948 to the Department of Law and Public Safety, the role of the State Police in law enforcement has expanded dramatically.

The Division of State Police is under the leadership of a superintendent appointed by the governor with the consent of the senate. In 1980 the Superintendent of the State Police was also designated the State Director of Emergency Management, thus taking over the civil defense functions for the state. Approximately 2200 male and female troopers, organized on a paramilitary basis, and 900 civilians staff the State Police force. There are five commands—northern, central, and southern New Jersey, plus the New Jersey Turnpike, and the Garden State Parkway commands.

Patrol

The most visible function of the State Police is enforcing traffic laws and providing emergency services on toll roads, state highways, and local roads in rural areas. Beyond that troopers also protect life and property and enforce laws on the coastal and in-land waters and enforce all criminal and marine laws and regulations. The State Police, working with other law enforcement agencies, have been active in enforcement of laws concerning illegal drugs brought into the Northeast via the New Jersey coast and small airports.

Investigations

Regulatory and other agencies in the Department of Law and Public Safety use the State Police to conduct investigations. They may also conduct investigations on their own initiative or when ordered to do so by the governor or the attorney general. As a result, they investigate on an on-going basis many aspects of horseracing, casino gambling, other forms of gaming, and the production and sale of alcoholic beverages. They also investigate organized crime, official corruption, arson, fugitives from justice, and auto theft. In conjunction with local and federal authorities, State Police conduct narcotics and gambling raids as well.

In 1984, responding to national concern about the thousands of children reported missing each year, Attorney General Kimmelman established a Missing Persons Unit within the Criminal Investigation Section of the State Police. When local police cannot locate a missing juvenile, information is fed immediately through the State Police into the National Crime Information Center for storage in the national crime computer.

Security Responsibilities

State troopers function as aides and personal security agents for the governor and the attorney general and their families. Other troopers are responsible, along with the capitol police and security guards, for the security of state offices and personnel within the capitol complex, as well as for escorting state monies.

Services to other Law Enforcement Agencies

The State Police aid local law enforcement agencies in a number of ways. The Major Crime Unit assists all law enforcement agencies in the investigation of homicides, kidnappings for ransom, arson, and any incident resulting in the death of, or by, a sworn member of the Division of State Police. Intelligence is collected and disseminated to the various law enforcement agencies concerning the involvement of organized crime in all areas of investigation.

The four regional State Police forensic crime laboratories serve the state's law enforcement agencies by analyzing specimens related to criminal investigations. The State Police also provide expert witnesses for court appearances and conduct a wide range of training activities in the forensic sciences.

The Uniform Crime Reporting Unit of the State Police gathers, classifies, and analyzes crime statistics from each police agency in the state. Reports are made by municipalities for each of the seven serious "index" crimes ranging from homicide to auto theft.

The State Police also have major responsibilities in professionalizing the county and municipal police through the Police Training Commission. This group, which includes the Superintendent of State Police and the commissioners of Education and Higher Education, develops curriculums and assures that the basic training at the fourteen police training academies meets state standards. By law, all municipal and county law enforcement officers must pass a basic training course before being permanently appointed.

Emergency Management

The State Police are responsible for coordinating emergency response activities in compliance with the Federal Emergency Management Act. They maintain a State Emergency Operating Center as well as a warning system in the event of attack. Activities include overseeing emergency response nuclear incident drills at the state's nuclear generating stations as well as handling overall coordination of water emergencies—working with the National Guard and other agencies to distribute potable water to residents. State Police helicopters are also available for medical evacuations.

The New Jersey Racing Commission

By the early 1890s racing interests so dominated and corrupted the New Jersey Legislature that the citizens rebelled and in 1893 voted in an entirely new set of legislators. Racing was crippled first by law and then by a 1897 constitutional amendment that prohibited gambling. Racing was not restored until 1939 with the adoption of another constitutional amendment permitting pari-mutuel betting at racetracks. In pari-mutuel betting on horses, those who bet on the winning horse share the total stakes, less a small percentage to the management. The bets are registered on a machine called a pari-mutuel. In 1966 voters authorized additional racing during evening hours. Racing on Sundays is still banned in New Jersey.

Administration of the law regulating racing is the responsibility of the New Jersey Racing Commission in the Department of Law and Public Safety. The commission is a seven-member, unsalaried, bipartisan body, appointed by the governor with the consent of the senate for overlapping six-year terms. The commission has the power to grant permits to operate horse race meets where pari-mutuel wagering is allowed. The commission's permit for a new racing site is provisional, however, subject to the approval by voters of both the county and the municipality in which the track is located.

New Jersey has five racetracks—one for harness racing, two for thoroughbred racing, and two, the Meadowlands and the Garden State, for both types of racing.

State law establishes the maximum number of days for each type of track. The commission allocates the racing days among the tracks, usually in order to reduce competition among them and with tracks in neighboring states.

Regulation of Gambling and Gaming Activities

The power to regulate and to police gambling and gaming in New Jersey resides in a number of departments and agencies. Many of those agencies, however, are attached administratively to the Department of Law and Public Safety.

Casino Gambling in Atlantic City

As noted in chapter 1 the New Jersey Constitution prohibits the legislature from authorizing gambling in the state except as approved by the voters. In the early 1970s casino gambling became the focus of a group of individuals (legislators, businessmen, real estate brokers, entertainment people, private citizens) interested in rebuilding and revitalizing the tourist center of Atlantic City. The subject engendered passionate response from both its supporters and detractors, bringing legal, religious, and business leaders into the fray. In 1974 a constitutional amendment authorizing gambling casinos was proposed but failed adoption. Again in 1976 an amendment was offered to the voters empowering the "legislature to establish and regulate gambling casinos in Atlantic City," with a tax on revenues to be paid into a special fund applied solely to aiding senior and disabled citizens through property tax rebates and other benefits. This time the amendment was approved, and the first gambling casinos in the state were sanctioned.

Regulation of casino gambling is shared between the Casino Control Commission, an agency technically in, but effectively not of, the Department of Treasury, which promulgates rules and regulations, and the Division of Gaming Enforcement in the Department of Law and Public Safety, which enforces those rules and regulations. While the commission issues licenses to casinos as well as licenses and work permits to employees, the Division of Gaming Enforcement conducts investigations before licensure. The division also investigates and prosecutes all violations of the Casino Control Act and the rules and regulations promulgated by the commission.

In order to accomplish this, the division established itself as a functioning regulatory agency with a highly specialized staff with offices in Trenton, Atlantic City, and Absecon. The division director is appointed by the governor with the consent of the senate. The governor with the consent of the senate also appoints the five members of the Casino Control Commission. These commissioners are full-time, salaried appointees serving for staggered five-year terms.

As a further safeguard in the system established to keep corruption out of the casino gambling industry, the Executive Commission on Ethical Standards, an agency technically in, but effectively not of, the Department of Law and Public Safety (see chapter 2), is vested with responsibility for enforcing sections of the Casino Control Act. This commission watches for any conflict of interest by members and employees, and their families, of the Casino Control Commission and the Division of Gaming Enforcement.

Other Gambling and Gaming Activities

Voters in New Jersey have approved other gambling and gaming activities including the state lottery, bingo and raffles, and games of chance at amusement parks, resorts, and agricultural fairs. In each case part of the revenue from licensing and taxing these activities is reinvested in the machinery to police the industry—both against consumer fraud and against infiltration by known criminals.

When voters approved a state lottery in 1969, a Division of the State Lottery was established in the Department of the Treasury. (See chapter 6.) The division director, appointed by the governor with the consent of the senate, is advised by a five-member, unsalaried commission.

The Legalized Games of Chance Control Commission within the Division of Consumer Affairs in the Department of Law and Public Safety regulates the bingo games and raffles operated by certain types of organizations such as religious, civic, patriotic, educational, and senior citizens' groups. These games can be conducted only in those communities that have voted by referendum to allow them, and the entire net proceeds must be devoted to "educational, charitable, patriotic, religious, or public-spirited use." By 1977 voters in almost all of New Jersey's municipalities had authorized either bingo or raffles or both, in some places even on Sunday. The laws implementing the constitutional amendments permitting these games also contain restrictions on such details as legal participants (those over eighteen years of age), methods of advertising, and the amount of prize money. Licenses are issued by the municipalities to organizations that have been approved by the Legalized Games of Chance Control Commission.

The Office of Amusement Games Control administers, supervises, and enforces the laws concerning the playing of games of skill or chance for an inexpensive merchandise prize at recognized amusement parks, at resorts, and at agricultural fairs and exhibitions approved by the Department of Agriculture. Licenses for operating the games, which are obtained from the municipalities, can be issued only in those municipalities where the voters have approved by referendum the law permitting these games. The Office of Amusement Games Control is housed in the Division of

Alcoholic Beverage Control; the division director also serves as the commissioner of the Office of Amusement Games Control.

Alcoholic Beverage Control

New Jersey has strict laws regulating the manufacture, distribution, and sale of alcoholic beverages; these are enforced by the Division of Alcoholic Beverage Control. The director of the division is appointed by the governor with the consent of the senate to serve during the governor's term. The director appoints investigators and inspectors; these officers may make arrests without having warrants for violations committed in their presence.

As an administrative agency the division also establishes regulations, conducts investigations (usually on the basis of tips or complaints), and enforces compliance with state laws and its own regulations at hearings or in court. Violations that can subject a licensee to suspension or revocation of license privileges include selling liquor to a person under twenty-one years of age or permitting illegal activities on the premises.

Licenses or permits are required for every commercial activity involving alcoholic beverages. Some types are issued by the division and others by the municipalities. The division issues licenses to manufacturers and wholesalers, and permits for sales representatives, specific social affairs by organizations, and noncommercial home wine-making. Municipalities issue almost all retail sales licenses and set the fees, within statutory limits. Each keeps the fees for the licenses it issues.

The high number of liquor licenses issued in the 1930s after the repeal of prohibition was a source of trouble to a number of New Jersey cities. Accordingly, laws were passed to limit the issuance of new retail licenses. Based on a community's population at the latest federal census, the limit is one tavern license for every three thousand residents and one package store license for every seventy-five hundred residents. License renewals and transfers are not affected, and the limit does not apply to club licenses that municipalities may issue to bona fide organizations for sale of drinks to members and guests.

Local citizens may vote by referendum to prohibit the sale of liquor; they can also vote by referendum on the hours of sale including whether or not liquor by the drink may be sold on Sunday.

In recent years regulations of the Division of Alcoholic Beverage Control were reviewed to see if they served the public interest. As a result some degree of deregulation has been achieved.

In this most vehicle-congested state in the nation the Division of Motor Vehicles (DMV), lodged within the Department of Law and Public Safety, touches almost everyone. The director of the division is appointed by the governor with the consent of the senate. The motor vehicle and drivers' license fees collected by DMV constitute a major source of tax revenue for New Jersey.

Along with the State Police, DMV has major responsibilities for enforcing motor vehicle and traffic laws and regulations. Through the Office of Highway Safety, DMV develops innovative state and local highway safety programs, in accordance with the objectives of the National Highway Safety Program, and channels the federal funds needed for their implementation. Also included in DMV's diversified services are licensing drivers, handling license revocation, inspecting vehicles for safety and emissions, and vehicle registration.

The Division of Motor Vehicles

Licensing Drivers

DMV is responsible both for issuing licenses (see figure 14.1) and for revoking them when repeated violations of traffic laws occur. The goal of the point system for license revocation (see figure 14.2) is closely related to the violations that cause the most accidents. Driving while intoxicated (DWI) or drunk driving is one of the surest ways for a driver to lose his or her driving privilege. (See figure 14.3).

Drunk Driving Laws

In 1983 and 1984 New Jersey led the nation by passing the country's toughest drunk driving laws. Citizen activists in groups such as Mothers Against Drunk Drivers (MADD),

Figure 14.1

New Jersey Drivers' Licenses

REQUIREMENTS:

- Every resident operator of a motor vehicle must have a New Jersey driver's license.
- Persons moving into the state must obtain licenses within sixty days.
- All licenses are issued for four-year periods.
- Photographs are required on all new licenses.
- Drivers may obtain licenses in person at the fifty privately operated, franchised motor vehicle agencies in the state.
- Once every ten years, drivers are required to take a vision test to see if corrective glasses are needed or if currently used glasses are adequate. Such eye test notifications are sent with normal license renewal notices.

APPLYING FOR A LICENSE:

Permanent

- To apply for a permanent license, an individual must be at least seventeen years old.
- After passing both written and road tests administered by motor vehicle personnel, all new drivers receive probationary licenses for the first two years.

Student

- If enrolled in a driver education course in school or at a commercial driving school, sixteen-year-olds are eligible for student driver's permits.
- Such permits may be used only when accompanied by a qualified instructor—the instructor, not the student, has custody of the permit.
- At age sixteen and one-half, and if behind-the-wheel training has been successfully completed, a student driver may have custody of the permit and may drive between sunrise and sunset when accompanied by a driver with a minimum of three years' experience.

Other

- The basic driver's license permits a holder to drive a car or a moped only.
- To drive a motorcycle, bus, or tractor trailer requires a special test; the specific endorsement is then noted on the driver's license.
- At age fifteen, after passing a road test, an individual may obtain a moped license.

338

Figure 14.2

New Jersey Driver's License Point System

Points toward Suspension of the License. DMV keeps track of a driver's record by adding points whenever a driver is convicted of a moving violation. The more serious the violation, the more points given.

Warning—issued when six or more points are accumulated.

Suspension—imposed when twelve or more points are accumulated.

Removal of Points—up to three points will be subtracted from the total for each year the driver goes without a violation or suspension (but the point total is never reduced below zero). Up to three points will also be removed after completion of an approved driver improvement program.

Offenses Carrying the Most Points (55 offenses carry points)

- Leaving the scene of an accident involving personal injury   8 points
- Racing on the highway   5 points
- Improper passing of a school bus   5 points
- Failure to pass to the right of a vehicle proceeding in the opposite direction   5 points
- Reckless driving   5 points
- Tailgating   5 points
- Exceeding the maximum speed limit by 30 mph or more   5 points

Insurance Surcharge. Motorists who incur six or more points are also subject to an insurance surcharge of $100 for the first six points and $25 for each additional point, payable for three years (for a total of $300 or more). The point surcharge will remain operational as long as a motorist has six or more points on his record for the immediate past three-period. Failure to pay will result in indefinite suspension of all driving privileges.

Figure 14.3

Penalties for Driving While Under the Influence of Alcohol or Drugs

Court-Imposed Fines and Penalties	First Offense	Second Offense	Third Offense
Loss of license	6 mo.–1 yr.	2 yr.	10 yr.
Fine	$250–$400	$500–$1000	$1000
Intoxicated Driver Resource Center	12 hr.	48 hr.	————
Community service	————	30 days	————
Jail	possible 30 days	possible 90 days	180 days

Chemical Test Refusal	First Offense	Second & Subsequent Offenses
Loss of license	6 mo.	2 yrs.
Fine	$250–$500	$250–$500

CONVICTION SURCHARGE

In addition to the court-imposed fines and penalties, anyone arrested and convicted of DWI or a chemical test refusal is subject to an insurance surcharge. Failure to pay the surcharge will result in indefinite suspension of all driving privileges.

DEATH-BY-AUTO PENALTY

In 1984 legislation to supplement those laws aimed at drunk drivers, the penalty for conviction on a death-by-auto charge was raised from a fourth-degree crime (carrying a prison term of up to 18 months) to a third-degree crime carrying a prison term from three to five years. The law also provides for a fine of $7,500, the same as under the old law.

340

Students Against Drunk Driving (SADD), and the New Jersey Coalition for 21 (age for legal drinking) have been cited as instrumental in bringing about the changes.

By law there is a single standard for drunk driving offenses: the level of blood alcohol at which a driver is presumed to be under the influence of alcohol has been set at 0.10 percent. Drunk driving laws apply to a person driving under the influence of any intoxicating substance including narcotic, hallucinogenic, or habit-forming drugs. In action taken by the New Jersey Supreme Court, party hosts are now responsible for damage caused by their drinking guests. Penalties are also imposed on the owner of a vehicle who allows someone to operate the car while intoxicated.

The results of the earliest steps to rid the roads of drunk drivers—highway safety projects including police patrols and roadblocks, and raising the legal drinking age from 19 to 21 effective the first day of 1983—were dramatic. New Jersey traffic deaths for 1983 fell below the 1000 mark for the first time in twenty years.

Motor Vehicle Inspection

All motor vehicles registered in New Jersey must be inspected annually both for exhaust emissions, as part of the state's efforts to meet federal air quality regulations, and for potential safety hazards. Proof of driver's license, insurance, and registration are also checked at this time. Inspections are made by state-owned or leased vehicle inspection stations, or by privately owned reinspection centers. New cars are exempt from such inspection for one year from the date of purchase. In 1985 all commercial vehicles were also required to be inspected for safety and emissions. The rejection rate for initial inspections is about 50 percent (the vehicle must be repaired and reinspected in order to comply with the law), indicating the importance of the program in removing potentially hazardous and polluting vehicles from New Jersey roads.

Vehicle Registration

All motor vehicles, and also boats and outboard motors, operated by residents of New Jersey must be registered with DMV. When a vehicle changes ownership, re-registration is required, and a new certificate of ownership (often called a title) is issued. Registrations are renewed annually, in the same month each year for any particular vehicle.

Registration of vehicles, boats, and motors is not just another way for the state to generate additional revenue; it is an important part of the state's effort to protect drivers from vehicle theft. Around-the-clock information services maintained on registration numbers of stolen vehicles makes it possible to recover some of these vehicles through routine checks of every vehicle stopped for a traffic violation. Also by administering laws controlling the purchase, sale, and transfer of motor vehicles and by issuing salvage certificates for severely damaged cars, DMV has an impact on auto theft. During the early 1980s about 50,000 vehicles were reported stolen annually in New Jersey. While some of these reports were fraudulent—most were real, with vehicles dismanted in illegal "chop shops" and sold as parts to dealers and repair shops. Not only are dismantled cars hard to trace, but also they can command a higher price as parts than they do intact.

In an effort to eliminate the illegal chop shops, legislation passed in 1984 requires major components of cars be marked with identification; it also requires that careful inventory records be kept in auto part facilities.

No-fault Insurance

Motor vehicle insurance is compulsory in New Jersey. In 1973, in an effort to ensure compensation to the victims of motor vehicle accidents, New Jersey embarked on a no-fault insurance program. Under the no-fault concept, accident victims are reimbursed by their own insurance companies for damages regardless of which driver is at fault; injured parties may sue the insurer of the other party for comparative negligence costs only if medical expenses are above a certain "threshold." To ensure that every motor vehicle in New Jersey—cars, trucks, motorcycles, and mopeds—carries minimum personal insurance, evidence of insurance is checked when vehicles are registered. Under this system only about 7 percent of motorists involved in New Jersey accidents do not have up-to-date insurance coverage.

The state's Unsatisfied Claim and Judgment Fund compensates victims of accidents caused by an uninsured driver unable to pay (though insurance is mandatory to obtain registration, some drivers let their insurance lapse), victims of hit-and-run drivers, and those victims who cannot otherwise obtain compensation. Income for this fund is derived from judgments recovered from uninsured drivers and from a tax on automobile liability insurance premiums written in New Jersey. Ineligible for benefits from this fund are owners operating or riding in their own uninsured vehicles, persons driving a car without the owner's permission, and persons driving while on the revoked license list.

Civil Rights

Public protection includes not only government safeguards for the physical safety of an individual, but also safeguards for civil rights and psychological well-being. New Jersey first passed a law against racial discrimination in 1884, a law seldom invoked because the victim had to bring the case to court and bear the costs and publicity.

During World War II both the federal and state governments took steps against discrimination in employment. In 1945, just before the war's end, New Jersey passed a law banning discrimination in employment and creating the Division Against Discrimination to enforce the law. For the first time citizens could turn to an administrative agency for assistance in this area.

The 1947 constitution included a new clause:

No person shall be denied the enjoyment of any civil or military right, nor be discriminated against in the exercise of any civil or military right, nor be segregated in the militia or in the public schools, because of religious principles, race, color, ancestry, or national origin. (Article I, Section 5)

In 1949 the state's statutory prohibition against discrimination in the militia or schools was extended to public accommodations, in 1951 to liability for military service; in 1954 and 1957 to housing aided by public funds; in 1962 to age for employment; in 1966 (in a public contract law) to discrimination in employment by any contractor or sub-contractor supplying goods or services to any governmental agency within the state; and in 1967 to all housing except rentals of rooms in one-family dwellings and of second units in owner-occupied two-family dwellings.

In addition to religion, race, color, and ancestry, several other factors were prohibited as grounds for discrimination: in 1970 discrimination on the basis of marital status and sex for housing, public accommodation, or employment was banned; in 1972 discrimination in employment against the physically handicapped was likewise forbidden; and in 1971 legislation mandated that blind people with guide dogs be accepted in public accommodations.

Upon the outlawing of discrimination because of sex or marital status in 1970, many women promptly brought complaints charging discriminatory pay scales, refusal of employers to hire them in certain jobs, and segregated job advertisements. Later in the decade sex discrimination in the form of sexual harassment became the basis for civil rights suits.

The Division Against Discrimination, within the Department of Education, was renamed the Division on Civil Rights and moved to the Department of Law and Public Safety in 1960. With this change came added emphasis on enforcement. A seven-member citizen Commission on Civil Rights, appointed by the governor with the consent of the senate, consults with and advises the attorney general on the work of this division. The division director is appointed by the attorney general, subject to the approval of the governor and the commission.

The current scope of the Division on Civil Rights includes the protection of equal opportunity in employment, housing, public accommodations, and the extension of credit or making of loans. The goal is to prevent and eliminate practices of discrimination against persons because of race, creed, color, national origin, ancestry, age, sex, marital status, mental or physical handicap, nationality, or selective service (draft) status.

The division cooperates with its counterpart in federal agencies. When a discriminatory practice is not covered by New Jersey law, the New Jersey agency refers the case to the

Figure 14.4

Civil Rights Poster

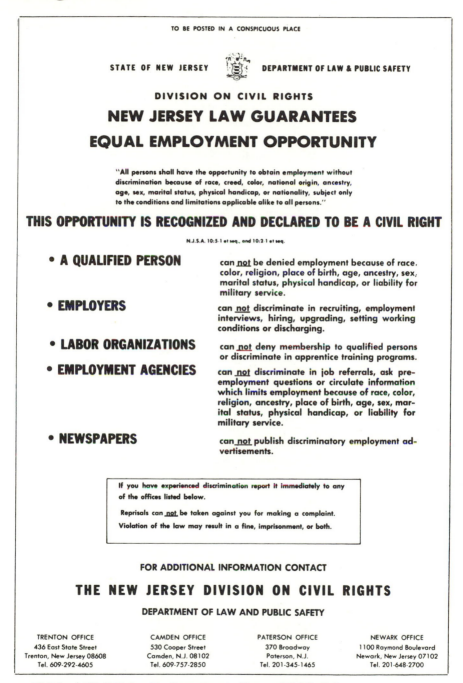

TO BE POSTED IN A CONSPICUOUS PLACE

STATE OF NEW JERSEY   DEPARTMENT OF LAW & PUBLIC SAFETY

DIVISION ON CIVIL RIGHTS
NEW JERSEY LAW GUARANTEES
EQUAL EMPLOYMENT OPPORTUNITY

"All persons shall have the opportunity to obtain employment without
discrimination because of race, creed, color, national origin, ancestry,
age, sex, marital status, physical handicap, or nationality, subject only
to the conditions and limitations applicable alike to all persons."

THIS OPPORTUNITY IS RECOGNIZED AND DECLARED TO BE A CIVIL RIGHT

N.J.S.A. 10:5-1 et seq., and 10:2-1 et seq.

- **A QUALIFIED PERSON** — can <u>not</u> be denied employment because of race. color, religion, place of birth, age, ancestry, sex, marital status, physical handicap, or liability for military service.

- **EMPLOYERS** — can <u>not</u> discriminate in recruiting, employment interviews, hiring, upgrading, setting working conditions or discharging.

- **LABOR ORGANIZATIONS** — can <u>not</u> deny membership to qualified persons or discriminate in apprentice training programs.

- **EMPLOYMENT AGENCIES** — can <u>not</u> discriminate in job referrals, ask pre-employment questions or circulate information which limits employment because of race, color, religion, ancestry, place of birth, age, sex, marital status, physical handicap, or liability for military service.

- **NEWSPAPERS** — can <u>not</u> publish discriminatory employment advertisements.

If you have experienced discrimination report it immediately to any
of the offices listed below.

Reprisals can <u>not</u> be taken against you for making a complaint.

Violation of the law may result in a fine, imprisonment, or both.

FOR ADDITIONAL INFORMATION CONTACT
THE NEW JERSEY DIVISION ON CIVIL RIGHTS
DEPARTMENT OF LAW AND PUBLIC SAFETY

TRENTON OFFICE	CAMDEN OFFICE	PATERSON OFFICE	NEWARK OFFICE
436 East State Street	530 Cooper Street	370 Broadway	1100 Raymond Boulevard
Trenton, New Jersey 08608	Camden, N.J. 08102	Paterson, N.J.	Newark, New Jersey 07102
Tel. 609-292-4605	Tel. 609-757-2850	Tel. 201-345-1465	Tel. 201-648-2700

Source: **Division of Civil Rights, The Department of Law and Public Safety.**

federal agencies charged with enforcing the federal Civil
Rights Act; when complaints fall under the jurisdiction of
the New Jersey law, the federal agencies refer the case to the
New Jersey division for remedial action.

When a complaint of a violation of civil rights is filed
with the New Jersey Division on Civil Rights, an investiga-
tor researches the case to determine whether or not there is
"probable cause." If probable cause is found, resolution is
attempted, first, through a conciliation conference. If that
fails, a public hearing is held before an administrative law
judge. In this hearing the complainant is represented by a
deputy attorney general or, if the complainant wishes, by
his or her own attorney. The final decision is made by the
director of the Division on Civil Rights. Should this decision call for compliance and be ignored, the director may
ask the court to enforce it. In addition, under a New Jersey
Supreme Court decision handed down in 1969, the director
may require discriminators to reimburse victims for financial losses suffered. Later rulings allowed awards also for
pain, humiliation, and mental suffering.

Consumer Affairs

Many laws and numerous state and local regulatory agencies speak for and protect New Jersey consumers. In 1971
growing pressure for more and better consumer protection
led to a reorganization of the state's machinery for handling
problems and an increase in the state's regulatory powers.
The Division of Consumer Affairs was created within the
Department of Law and Public Safety, incorporating the
former Office of Consumer Protection. The division was
given power to proceed against any "unconscionable
commercial practice" and to levy higher fines for noncom-
pliance. The division director is appointed by the governor with the consent of the senate. A Citizen's Consumer
Affairs Advisory Committee, composed of the state director
of Consumer Affairs and nine private citizens appointed
by the governor for unsalaried three-year terms, advises
the division.

The division operates on several fronts. It counsels the
governor and other state officials and bodies on matters related to consumer protection, reviews pending legislation,

and recommends areas for new legislation; it participates in existing consumer education programs; it develops and supervises the local assistance programs; and it supervises the Bureau of Securities, the Office of Weights and Measures, and licensing boards for many groups of professionals. But perhaps the most important activity of the division is acting as the enforcement agency for New Jersey's strong consumer fraud act.

Consumer Fraud Act

New Jersey has one of the strongest consumer fraud acts in the country, prohibiting fraudulent and misleading sales and advertising practices. The Division of Consumer Affairs acts as the enforcement agency. Upon receipt of a complaint, the division holds a hearing. If it finds a violation, it can impose a penalty of two thousand dollars for a first offense and five thousand dollars for a subsequent offense, or it can accept instead the assurance of voluntary compliance with the law. If these measures fail, the attorney general can seek court-imposed sanctions (even to the extent of prohibiting a seller from owning or managing a business in the state), or the case may be turned over to a county prosecutor for criminal prosecution. A complainant may also sue in court for damages; under a 1971 law the complainant may sue for treble damages in cases alleging an unlawful business practice.

Consumer Information and Local Programs

The Division of Consumer Affairs conducts an active public education campaign through the media and via the division's "Tele-Consumer" telephone service which has taped information on numerous consumer issues. Brochures and a booklet on consumer justice are also distributed. Consumers are alerted through press releases about seasonal frauds and product safety concerns. Similar information is provided for legislators who receive a consumer issues information newsletter to keep them informed on current consumer problems.

The services of the division are extended to the local level through the Consumers' Affairs Local Assistance Officer Program. This innovative program, initiated in 1971, utilizes both volunteer and paid personnel to aid consumers in every county and many municipalities in New Jersey. Citizens are also aided by the regulatory functions of the division.

The Bureau of Securities

To prevent fraud in the sale of securities, all persons selling securities within or from the state must be registered with the Bureau of Securities. This bureau investigates complaints and, after hearings, may impose penalties. If necessary, the attorney general can seek sanctions from the court. To improve its efficiency in checking the legitimacy of securities, the bureau belongs to the Central Registration Depository operated by the National Association of Securities Dealers in New York. The bureau is also responsible for analyzing corporate takeover proposals.

The Office of Weights and Measures

That the weights and measures in use throughout the state are uniform and in accordance with standards set by the National Bureau of Standards is the responsibility of the Office of Weights and Measures. The office is also charged with making sure that the method of selling and labeling commodities is uniform.

Besides periodic testing of all weighing and measuring devices, the Office of Weights and Measures conducts random checks at the retail level. Indeed, an estimated 50 percent of the staff's time is spent reweighing, remeasuring, and counting the contents of packaged goods prior to sale.

The work of the office requires cooperation, not only with other state departments, but also with the federal government and other states as well. For example, the office is responsible for enforcing federal laws and regulations resulting from the 1966 federal Fair Packaging and Labeling Act. In addition, the office works to reconcile various state requirements to facilitate the interstate shipment of goods.

Occupational Licensing

Many professions and trades are regulated by the state government through boards composed wholly or mainly of members of the particular profession or trade. The purpose of the boards is to protect the public in such matters as health, sanitation, malpractice, fraud, and negligence. But because they also tend to protect those already in the occupation, a 1971 law empowered the governor to appoint one public member and one state official from a closely related department to most of the boards not already having public members. Members of professional boards are compensated at rates of fifty dollars for full-day meetings and twenty-five dollars for partial-day meetings. The Division of Consumer Affairs provides the boards with administrative aid; their operations, however, are financially self-sustaining with the surplus fees (mostly from the Board of Beauty Culture Control) going into the state treasury.

Under the supervision of the division, the professional boards have reviewed or are in the process of reviewing their regulations to eliminate unfair restrictions. A number of the boards have also adopted national examinations for their members. In addition, the boards of Medical Examiners, Nursing, and Dentistry have all established programs to address the problem of drug abuse in their respective professions. These programs focus on both professional discipline and rehabilitation.

The professions regulated by boards supervised by the Division of Consumer Affairs range from midwives to medical examiners, from pharmacists to professional planners. (See figure 14.5.)

Other occupations are regulated by boards located elsewhere in the government. Because the constitution gives the New Jersey Supreme Court sole jurisdiction over admission to the state bar and the disciplining of lawyers, a board of bar examiners appointed by the supreme court licenses lawyers. Real estate brokers and salesmen are licensed by the Real Estate Commission in the Department of Insurance; public school teachers and administrators by a state board of examiners in the Department of Education, and the pilots who guide ships through the channels of New York Bay by the Board of New Jersey Pilot Commissioners in the Department of Environmental Protection.

The powers and duties of these boards depend on their statutory authority and the nature of the occupation. But generally they make rules and regulations, set and admin-

State Professional Boards within the Division of Consumer Affairs

Figure 14.5

Acupuncture Practitioners (non-physicians)

Architects

Barbers Examiners

Beauty Culture Control

Certified Public Accountants

Dental Hygienists

Dentistry

Examiners of Electrical Contractors

Examiners of Master Plumbers

Examiners of Ophthalmic Dispensers and Ophthalmic Technicians

Marriage Counselor Examiners

Medical Examiners (including osteopaths, chiropractors, podiatrists, midwives)

Morturary Science

Nursing

Optometrists

Pharmacy

Physical Therapy

Professional Engineers and Land Surveyors

Professional Planners

Psychological Examiners

Public Movers and Warehousemen

Shorthand Reporting

Veterinary Medical Examiners

ister examinations, issue licenses, issue permits for and inspect premises, collect fees, receive complaints, process violations, and otherwise administer and enforce the law.
Board members usually receive expenses and a per diem
payment while on the business of the board and, in some
cases, a fee for administering examinations. The members
of several boards receive small salaries.

There are numerous other occupations for which a person must have a license or certificate issued by an administrative agency other than a board. Private detectives, for example, who are licensed by the State Police, fall into
this category.

Other Activities

Additional duties assigned to the Department of Consumer
Affairs include the regulation of private agencies and the
staffing of the Legalized Games of Chance Control Commission, which supervises the administration of the licensing laws for bingo and raffles. In addition, the division staffs
the Office of the State Athletic Commission which controls
and supervises all boxing, wrestling, and sparring exhibitions and performances.

Both the Department of Law and Public Safety and the
State Commission of Investigation (SCI) were outgrowths of
extensive research and public hearings conducted in 1968
by the Joint Legislative Committee to Study Crime and the
System of Criminal Justice in New Jersey. The Joint Legislative Committee found that a crisis in crime control did exist in New Jersey, and it attributed the expanding activities
of organized crime to "failure to some considerable degree
in the system itself, official corruption, or both" and recommended creation of the Department of Law and Public
Safety and an independent State Commission of Investigation as its two highest priorities. The committee envisioned
these two agencies as complementary units: the Department
of Law and Public Safety would be a large organization with
extensive manpower and authority to coordinate and conduct criminal investigations and prosecutions throughout
the state, and the State Commission of Investigation would

THE STATE COMMISSION OF INVESTIGATION

be a relatively small but expert body which would conduct fact-finding investigations, bring information to the public's attention, and make recommendations to the governor and the legislature for improvements in laws and the operations of government.

The SCI was structured as a commission of the legislature with the responsibility to expose wrongdoing by fact-finding investigations and by recommending new laws and other remedies to protect the integrity of the political process. To eliminate any appearance of political influence in the commission's operations, no more than two of the four commissioners may be of the same political party. Two commissioners are appointed by the governor and one each by the president of the senate and the speaker of the assembly.

The commission is charged to conduct investigations in connection with:

- the faithful execution and effective enforcement of the laws of the state, with particular reference but not limited to organized crime and racketeering;
- the conduct of public officers and public employees, and of officers and employees of public corporations and authorities;
- any matter concerning the public peace, public safety and public justice.

During the first decade of operation the SCI issued reports containing recommendations on such diverse subjects as the nursing home industry, workers' compensation, dental insurance programs, the New Jersey Housing Finance Agency, the garbage industry, the Medicaid program, and municipal utilities authorities.

Originally constituted in 1968, the agency's existence was reviewed and extended for five-year periods in 1973, 1979, and 1984. To date the committees reviewing the SCI have chosen to maintain the temporary nature of the commission to assure periodic review of its activities and of the statutes under which it operates.

THE UNITED STATES ATTORNEY

At the same time that the New Jersey Legislature was addressing the problems of crime control by establishing the Department of Law and Public Safety and the State Commission of Investigation, the Office of the United States Attorney for New Jersey became very active under the courageous leadership of three successive United States Attorneys: Frederick B. Lacey (1969–1971), Herbert J. Stern (1971–1974), and Jonathan L. Goldstein (1974–1977). These three and their successors established the Office of the United States Attorney as an important partner in the fight against organized crime and corruption in New Jersey.

The Office of the United States Attorney for New Jersey is one of ninety-four federal judicial districts established by the United States Department of Justice to enforce and administer federal law. The United States Attorney for each district is appointed for a four-year term by the president with the consent of the United States Senate and, within a given district, is the principal federal law enforcement officer. The New Jersey office is located in Newark.

The Office of the United States Attorney has many functions, including the representation of federal agencies such as the FBI in legal proceedings and the collection of fines imposed in criminal cases, bail bond forfeitures, and civil liabilities. Yet it is their investigative and prosecutorial activities that bring them into the public eye. The office may be called upon by the FBI, the IRS, the Secret Service, Customs, or the Bureau of Alcohol, Tobacco, and Firearms; the office also may initiate investigations on its own. Evidence of unlawful conduct uncovered by these investigations is presented to a federal grand jury.

The Organized Crime Act of 1970, formally known as the Racketeer Influence and Corrupt Organization Act (the RICO statute), has been the basis for the Office of the United States Attorney to seek both criminal punishment and civil relief (usually in the form of fines) against both racketeering and white-collar criminals. Under the provisions of the RICO statute, triple damages can be assessed in some civil actions involving fraud.

An example of teamwork between the Office of the United States Attorney and New Jersey law enforcement officials is the joint arson-for-hire task force developed in Essex County. The Office of the United States Attorney will be called in on all arsons in the county and will follow up on those that appear to have a financial motive or where there was injury or loss of life.

DEFENSE

Militia units originally banded together for short periods of time to protect lives and property; they were formed independently in each American colony before the Revolutionary War. With the establishment of the new nation, control over the militia was divided between the states and the federal government. Under Article 1 of the United States Constitution Congress was given the power "to provide for calling forth the Militia to execute the Laws of the Union, suppress Insurrections and repel Invasions." Congress also received the authority to organize, arm, and discipline the militia while the states retained the authority to appoint the officers and to train the militia in accordance with congressional regulations. The governor of the state was, and remains, the commander-in-chief of the militia except when the militia is on federal service.

Over the years the state militia (renamed the National Guard by the end of the nineteenth century) changed from state-controlled organizations of local volunteers to a reserve component of the national armed forces. As such, National Guard units are included in the ready reserves and are liable at the call of the president for active duty in times of national emergency or war. They also serve the state; as the organized militia each state's National Guard may be called upon by the governor to protect life and property and to preserve peace, order, and public safety within the state.

In New Jersey the National Guard, composed of Army and Air National Guard units, comes under the command and control of the state's Department of Defense. The department is headed by a chief of staff, appointed by the governor with the consent of the senate. The chief of staff serves under the direction and at the pleasure of the governor on a full-time basis. The primary duty of the department is to direct the recruitment and training of the New Jersey National Guard so that it can meet federal and state readiness requirements.

Composition and Training

The New Jersey Army National Guard is composed of the Fifteenth Armored Division, headquartered in Somerset, and a number of "nondivisional" specialized units. The New Jersey Air National Guard includes tactical fighter air defense and air refueling units.

In 1983 there were about 15,000 officers and enlisted men and women in the National Guard, which also includes 1500 federal employees and 325 state employees providing support services and training.

When the National Guard was called out during the 1967 riots in Newark and other cities, the public realized that few guardsmen were blacks. Believing that a guard more representative of the total population would help control future disorders, the United States Department of Defense chose New Jersey for a test effort to increase the number of black guardsmen. The New Jersey National Guard was allowed to increase its maximum strength by 5 percent and, in a vigorous recruitment drive, found qualified blacks to fill most of the extra positions. By 1983 20 percent of the Guard, including 13 percent of the officers, consisted of minority personnel. In recent years women have also been actively recruited.

The Program for Increased Education (PIE) is an important factor in the Guard's efforts for recruitment and retention. A variety of education plans, the two-year college plan, the four-year college plan, and the high school completion plan, enables applicants to combine education and skills training under Guard aegis.

Upon enlistment, men and women of the guard are first trained for about six months by the regular Army or Air Force. During the remainder of their six-year period of duty they drill (generally one weekend a month) at forty-two state-owned armories or at air bases in New Jersey. In addition, they take fifteen days of field training each year. After serving the six-year period of duty, re-enlistment for another period of duty is possible.

The New Jersey Department of Defense maintains the New Jersey Military Academy at Sea Girt where both commissioned and non-commissioned officers are trained. The facility is also the training headquarters for the New Jersey State Police; the New Jersey State Safety Council conducts training courses there for municipal fire fighters.

As long as the National Guard meets federal standards for strength, training, equipment maintenance, and operational readiness, the federal government pays the training expenses and the salaries of guardsmen and provides all equipment. Administrative costs and the cost of constructing armories are shared by the federal and state governments. For every dollar that New Jersey pays for the New Jersey Department of Defense, the federal government pays more than twelve dollars. However, the state alone pays for any cost incurred when the Guard is called up by the governor.

Community Service

One of the Guard's programs is community service in time of emergency. They have been especially active in responding to water crises: providing potable water to civilians in times of drought, contamination of water systems, or water system breakdowns. They also help in times of floods, blizzards, and other natural disasters.

The National Guard armories are used for community service as well as for providing space for other state agencies. The General Services Administration is looking at additional ways to enhance dual use of armories with other state agencies. It is expected the overall cost of accommodating these state agencies in armory space will be less than is presently expended for leasing space in private sector buildings.

Sources For
Further Information

The sources mentioned in this section were among those consulted in the preparation of this book. In addition, information was obtained through personal interviews and telephone conversations with officials and outside authorities. However, this section is not intended to provide footnotes and specific references, but rather to offer a description of sources that may be particularly useful to the interested reader.

Your local library has publications that offer the interested citizen a wealth of information on New Jersey government to supplement this text.

Fitzgerald's Legislative Manual of New Jersey 19–
(Edward J. Mullin, Editor and Publisher, P.O. Box 2150, Trenton, N.J. 08607–2150) Revised annually early in the calendar year, this book contains the text of the federal and state constitutions, information on departments, budgets, elections, taxes, government institutions and facilities, and much more. Browse through the table of contents and check the index—there is an abundance of up-to-date information here.

Legislator's Handbook
Ask for the edition prepared for the current legislative session. This handbook is prepared by the Office of Legislative

Services under the direction of the Legislative Services Commission for use by the new and returning legislators. However, it is an invaluable aid for students of New Jersey government who seek the most current information on the operations of the legislature.

Official Directory State of New Jersey
19– to 19–

Semi-annual publication of the Department of State, State House, Trenton. This directory not only lists the addresses and telephone numbers of state officials by department and agency, it also lists key members of policy-making boards and commissions (including term expiration dates), judges, legislators, members of congress, and key county officials. Brief descriptions of the charge of various commissions and boards are given along with the method of selecting members. The publication is available without charge as long as supplies last.

State of New Jersey Budget for Fiscal
19– to 19–

This is the governor's budget proposal, presented to the legislature in January or February of each year. The budget contains not only details about revenues and expenditures but also concise descriptions of the objectives and programs of the departments and their evaluation data. Both the specific program information and the general information on trends in the state budget (increases and decreases, the role of federal funds, the contributions from gaming revenues, and so forth) can contribute to the laypersons's understanding of our government.

Annual Reports of Government
Departments and Agencies

These reports are published by each department and by a number of agencies in the spring of the year for the past fiscal year—thus, the material is usually about nine months old by publication. The time lag before these reports reach the designated depository libraries may be a year or more; however, copies may be requested directly from the Office of Public Information of the agency being studied. There is no charge, but supplies are limited. These reports generally assume some foreknowledge by the reader of the general responsibilities and duties and only describe what the agency has accomplished in the past year. However, used in conjunction with a general text such as this book, they can be quite useful.

Reports of Study Commissions

Study reports by official study commissions or, on occasion, by state executive departments are probably least known among fruitful sources of information. Many include detailed well-reasoned analyses of the issues under study. Watch your favorite newspaper for headlines announcing reports from these commissions, then call the agency listed for your copy.

Laws and Court Decisions
of the State of New Jersey

Besides the state constitution the laws themselves are the single most important source of information. In many cases they contain specific details on the intent of the act, whom the act will affect, how it will be applied, and the powers of the administering agency (if any). All area libraries and many county libraries have bound volumes of the statutes. Ask the reference librarian for help. Decisions of the New Jersey Supreme Court are also available at these libraries. The text of the Mount Laurel II decision, for example, is certainly worth reading.

Eagleton Institute of Politics
at Rutgers University

The politics of the American states is the focus of study by this group of scholars. *The Political State of New Jersey* (New Brunswick: Rutgers University Press, forthcoming) is a collection of well-researched essays on political issues in our state. *The Political Life of the American States* (New York: Praeger, 1984) edited by Alan Rosenthal and Maureen Moakley, is a collection of essays from the Eagleton Institute on a number of states. It includes a thoughtful chapter "On Analyzing States" by Alan Rosenthal and a chapter on New Jersey by Maureen Moakley that captures a sense of the political climate of our state in the mid-1980s.

The Center for Analysis of Public Issues, Princeton, New Jersey

The center is an independent, non-partisan, non-profit research organization charged with fostering public awareness and understanding of public affairs in New Jersey. The center publishes the highly readable monthly magazine *New Jersey Reporter*, and special studies are published from time to time (more than twenty within the last ten years). One of the first, *The American Way of Graft*, is a fascinating study of graft and corruption in New Jersey, Maryland, and Illinois in the mid-1970s.

The Council on New Jersey Affairs, Princeton University

The council is a citizens' group composed of former governors, business, labor, and civic leaders working with the Woodrow Wilson School of Public and International Affairs. Their studies (called working papers) are short, well written, timely, and available without cost. Watch your newspaper for announcement of new studies. Call or write for a listing of currently available studies.

Publications by Organizations

Periodicals and other publications by professional, governmental, academic, and citizens' organizations are valuable sources of information. Most of these organizations are listed in the telephone directory. Among these groups are the following:

    League of Women Voters of New Jersey
    New Jersey Taxpayers Association
    New Jersey League of Municipalities
    The Regional Plan Association, New Jersey Committee
    American Lung Association of New Jersey
    Eagleton Institute of Politics
    Rutgers University Center for Urban Policy Research
    The Sierra Club
    The Audobon Society
    The Association of New Jersey Environmental Councils (ANJEC)

There are other organizations that also produce excellent materials; limitations of space prevent a more comprehensive listing. (Note: The New Jersey League of Municipalities and the New Jersey State Builders Association funded a study by the Center for Urban Policy Research at Rutgers University, *Mount Laurel II: Challenge and Delivery of Low-Cost Housing,* by Robert W. Burchell. This 1983 volume is a must for serious students of the low-cost housing issue.)

Periodicals Published in and about New Jersey.

Access to the wealth of information contained in these magazines is now available through *New Jersey Index*, ed. Laird Klingler (Bridgewater, New Jersey: ProWord Systems). All larger libraries and many smaller ones now have this valuable cumulative index (starting with 1982–1983) for finding information on numerous topics of interest to New Jersey citizens.

Newspapers

In a state dominated by New York City and Philadelphia media the *Newark Star Ledger* is the closest thing to a statewide newspaper, although strong regional newspapers exist. The *Star Ledger* publishes an "Action in Trenton" section when the legislature is in session, covers statewide and county politics, and influences the political agenda by their investigative reporting.

Bill Watching

Keeping abreast of proposed legislation is a challenge in light of the thousands of bills and resolutions introduced each year. The major newspapers provide some information both of action in floor and committee debate and what is on the calendar for consideration in committee. The *Newark Star Ledger*, for example, devotes a section to "Action in Trenton" the day after the legislature meets. Two private publications, the *Legislative Index* and the *Legislative News*, are printed after each meeting of either house and distributed to legislators and other interested parties. Ask for them at your library.

Official copies of bills may be obtained in person, by mail, or by telephone from the Legislative Bill Room operated by the Office of Legislative Services. The Bill Room is located in Room 14 (in the basement) of the State House Annex and is open five days a week from 8:30 A.M. to 5:00 P.M. Call (609) 292–6395 or 6240, and be sure to have the specific bill number when making a request.

Library Collections on New Jersey

Excellent collections of New Jersey materials are available at the New Jersey State Library, the New Jersey Historical Society, the Newark Public Library, the Alexander Library at Rutgers University in New Brunswick, and at a number of public libraries, such as the Morris County Free Library which has both an extensive collection and a full-time New Jersey librarian.

Index

Cahill, William T. (governor 1970–1974), 6, 61
Camden and Amboy Railroad, 170–171
Campaign Contributions and Reporting Act, 104, 105–106
Campaign financing, 70, 99, 103–106
Candidates, selection of, 102, 107. *See also* Political parties, selection of candidates by
CAP. *See* County Assistance Program (CAP)
Capital Budgeting and Planning, Commission on, 128–129
Capital punishment, 84, 86, 256, 293
"Caps," school budget, 152–153
Case management system. *See* Courts, administration of
Casino Control Act, 31, 334
Casino gambling. *See* Gambling and gaming
Casino Reinvestment Development Authority, 203
Casino Revenue Fund, 122
Caucuses, 49, 56. *See also* Political parties
Certified Public Manager Program, 33–34
CETA. *See* Comprehensive Employment and Training Act (CETA)
Chancery Division. *See* Superior Court, Chancery Division
Chief Justice. *See* Courts, administration of
Child Placement Advisory Council, 89
Child Study Teams, 157

Child support, 95
Children: lost, 331; services for, 317–318. *See also* Aid to Families with Dependent Children (AFDC); Corrections, Department of, juvenile services; Youth and Family Services, Division of
Citizen initiative. *See* Constitution (N.J.), amendment of
Citizen participation: at the polls, 115; in education, 148, 162; on institutional boards, 307; in judicial appointments, 87; on juries, 80; in local government, 277; on proposed rules, 29–30
Civil Court. *See* Superior Court, Law Division
Civil rights, 10–11, 279, 343–346. *See also* Affirmative action
Civil service, 25, 28, 32–37, 211
Clean Air Act, 232
Clean Air Council, 231
Clean Water Act, 229–230
Coalition of Northeast Governors (CONEG), 233–234
Coastal Area Facilities Review Act (CAFRA), 273
Code of Criminal Justice, xix, 77, 82, 84, 290, 293
Colleges and universities, 158–167
Commerce and Economic Development, Department of, xv–xvi, 125–127, 187, 199–200
Community Affairs, Department of, xvi, 205, 227, 258, 265, 268, 274, 277–285; housing and development, 279–280, 281–283; local

government services, 278–279; social services, 280, 284–285
Community development grants, 279
Community Mental Health Services Act, 316–317
Comprehensive Employment and Training Act (CETA), 187
CONEG. *See* Coalition of Northeast Governors (CONEG)
Conflict of interest. *See* Ethical standards
Conrail, 171
Constitution (N.J.), 3–15; amendment of, 14–15, 40, 57–58; and apportionment, 5–9, 40–42, 98, 100; Bill of Rights, 9–10, 80; and the budget, 118, 121, 130; and civil rights, 343; and the courts, 76; and education, 144; Equal Rights Amendment, 4, 10; and the governor, 20–21, 65; history of, 3, 5, 7–14, 61, 64; and impeachment, 19; and labor practices, 6, 10, 36; and legalized gambling, 126, 334; and the legislature, 40–41, 54–55; and zoning, 4–5, 261
Consumer protection, 211–215, 346–351. *See also* Public Advocate, Department of the
Cooperman, Saul, 146, 150, 154
Corrections, Department of, xix, 27, 90, 157, 285–296; alternatives to imprisonment, 288, 289, 295–296; juvenile services, 287–288,

New Jersey Real Estate Commission, 218
New Jersey Register, 29–30
New Jersey Sports and Exposition Authority, 133
New Jersey State Apportionment Commission, 41–42
New Jersey State Board of Examiners, 146
New Jersey State Board of Mediation, 192
New Jersey State Library, 157–158
New Jersey Supreme Court. *See* Supreme Court (N.J.)
New Jersey Transit Corp., xvii, 171, 176–180
New Jersey Turnpike Authority, 24, 170, 174
New Jersey Water Supply Management Act, 224–226
NJ Transit. *See* New Jersey Transit Corp.
NJDOE. *See* Energy, Department of (DOE)
NJEA. *See* New Jersey Education Association (NJEA)
NJIT. *See* New Jersey Institute of Technology
No-fault automobile insurance. *See* Insurance, motor vehicle
Nomination for public office. *See* Candidates, selection of
NRC. *See* Nuclear Regulatory Commission (NRC)
Nuclear reactors, 252
Nuclear Regulatory Commission (NRC), 214

OAL. *See* Administrative Law, Office of (OAL)
Occupational Safety and Health Act (OSHA), 189–190, 191, 192, 254
Official Directory, 37
Ombudsman, Office of the, 256, 290
Open space preservation. *See* Green Acres Program; Land-use planning; Pinelands
OSHA. *See* Occupational Safety and Health Act (OSHA)

PACs. *See* Political action committees
Parks, 236–239
Parks and Forestry, Division of, 238–239
Parole. *See under* Corrections, Department of, parole
Parole Board, 290–292
Patrolmen's Benevolent Association, 36
Patronage, 102
Pennsylvania Railroad, 171
PERC. *See* Public Employment Relations Commission (PERC)
Personnel. *See* Civil service
Pesticide/Toxic Substance Laboratory, 234
Petit jury. *See* Courts, jury system of the
Philbrook, Mary, 10
Pinelands, 237, 239, 269, 270–272
Pinelands Protection Act, 271
Plea bargaining, 82
Police. *See* State Police
Political action committees, 104, 111
Political contributions. *See* Campaign financing
Political parties: and elections, 41, 108–109, 111, 113; and the legislature, 48–51; organization of, 97-98, 100–103, 108; selection of candidates by, 99
Pollution. *See* Environmental Protection, Department of
Population trends, 98
Port Authority of New York and New Jersey, xvii–xviii, 24, 170, 176, 178, 180, 182–185
Pre-Trial Intervention, 92–93
Prisons, 286–290, 292–295
Private Industry Council, 187
Probate, 78, 79, 81
Probation, 91, 94–95, 295
Project Access, 179
Property Tax Relief Fund, 121, 122, 125
Public Advocate, Department of the, 27, 93, 213–214, 255–264, 290
Public Defender, Office of the, 82, 90, 256
Public Employees Retirement System, 35
Public Employment Relations Commission (PERC), 6, 36–37, 192–193
Public financing of elections. *See* Campaign financing
Public health. *See* Health, Department of
Public Health Council, 296, 291
Public Interest Advocacy, Division of, 258–259
Public School Education Act, 144, 148–153
Public television. *See* New Jersey Network
Public Utility Gross Receipts Tax, 135
Public Welfare, Division of, 311

About the League of
Women Voters

The League of Women Voters of the United States was established in 1920—the year suffrage for women was written into the United States Constitution. It is a nonpartisan organization whose purpose is twofold: to promote political responsibility through the informed and active participation of citizens in government; and to act on selected governmental issues.

The League is organized at the local, state, and national levels. All league members are members of the League of Women Voters of the United States. Basically the League's work is divided into two parts:

1. Voters Service includes distribution of nonpartisan information on candidates and issues; campaigns to encourage registration and voting; candidates forums; seminars in practical politics; "go see" trips to observe how and where government functions.

2. League Program includes governmental issues selected by the members for study, decision, and action at all governmental levels. Political action by the league is limited to those selected issues which are on the program. League positions on these issues are reached through thorough study and consideration by the members. This explains why there are many important public issues

on which the league does not take positions. It can only act with the full understanding and participation of its members.

Although the league encourages all members (except those currently serving on league boards) to be active in the political parties, the league is nonpartisan and never supports or opposes candidates or political parties.

The League of Women Voters of New Jersey has local leagues throughout the state and an office in Trenton with a small professional staff. All other work is carried on by volunteers who undertake research on the program, lobby on league issues, develop the voter service projects, and write the publications. Full voting membership is open to all citizens, men and women, of voting age; associate membership is open to all others.

For information about your nearest league (or how to form one) and on publications and services, call or write:

The League of Women Voters of New Jersey
204 West State Street
Trenton, New Jersey 08608
(609) 394–3303 or (800) 792–VOTE

The Biological Basis of Clinical Observations

Accurate clinical observations are key to good patient care and fundamental to clinical practice. A thorough understanding of the biological science underlying vital observations such as taking the temperature or measuring the pulse enables health professionals to make well-informed clinical decisions quickly and accurately. To be fully competent in these basic skills, there is a need to understand not only how and why procedures are performed, but also how results are affected, for example, by variation in technique or the health status of the patient.

This new edition integrates clear explanations of the techniques involved in these procedures with the biological knowledge which gives them meaning. For each topic, William T. Blows explains the pathological basis for variations in observed results, focusing on relevant anatomy and physiology, genetics and pharmacology and the basic principles of care. This helpful text gives health practitioners at all levels the understanding needed to:

- perform clinical observations accurately;
- make accurate judgements about the patient's condition;
- make accurate decisions concerning patient care.

In addition to all-new chapters on observations of nutrition, fluid balance and hydration, drug side effects and interactions, and skin and pain, the text looks at:

- temperature;
- cardiovascular observations;
- respiratory observations;
- urinary and bowel observations;
- neurological observations.

The Biological Basis of Clinical Observations is a unique text which integrates explanations of essential procedures with the biological knowledge that underpins practice. It is essential reading for all students preparing for clinical practice.

William T. Blows is Lecturer in Applied Biological Sciences at City University, London. He is also the author of *The Biological Basis of Mental Health Nursing* and *The Biological Basis of Nursing: Cancer*.